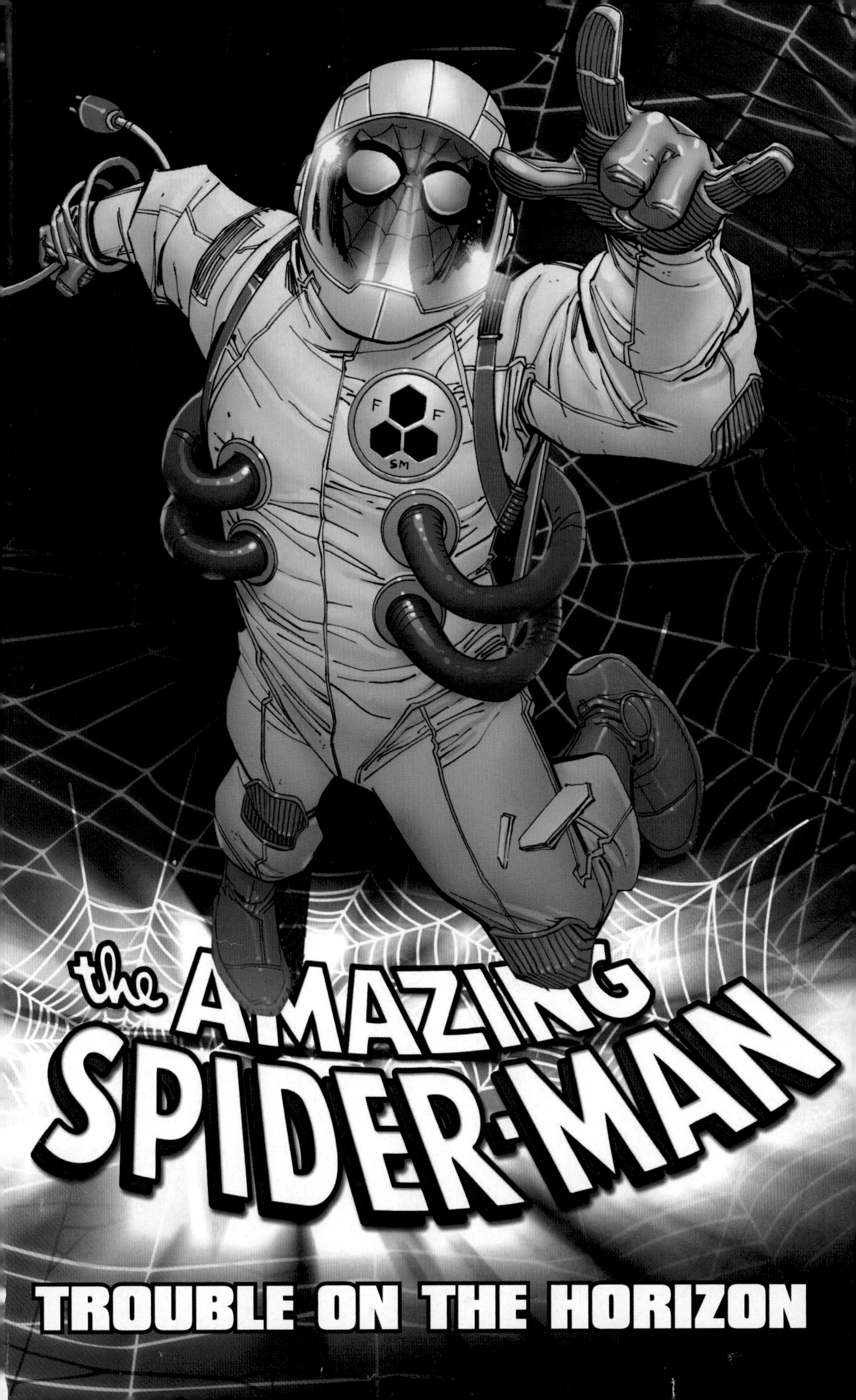
the AMAZING
SPIDER-MAN
TROUBLE ON THE HORIZON

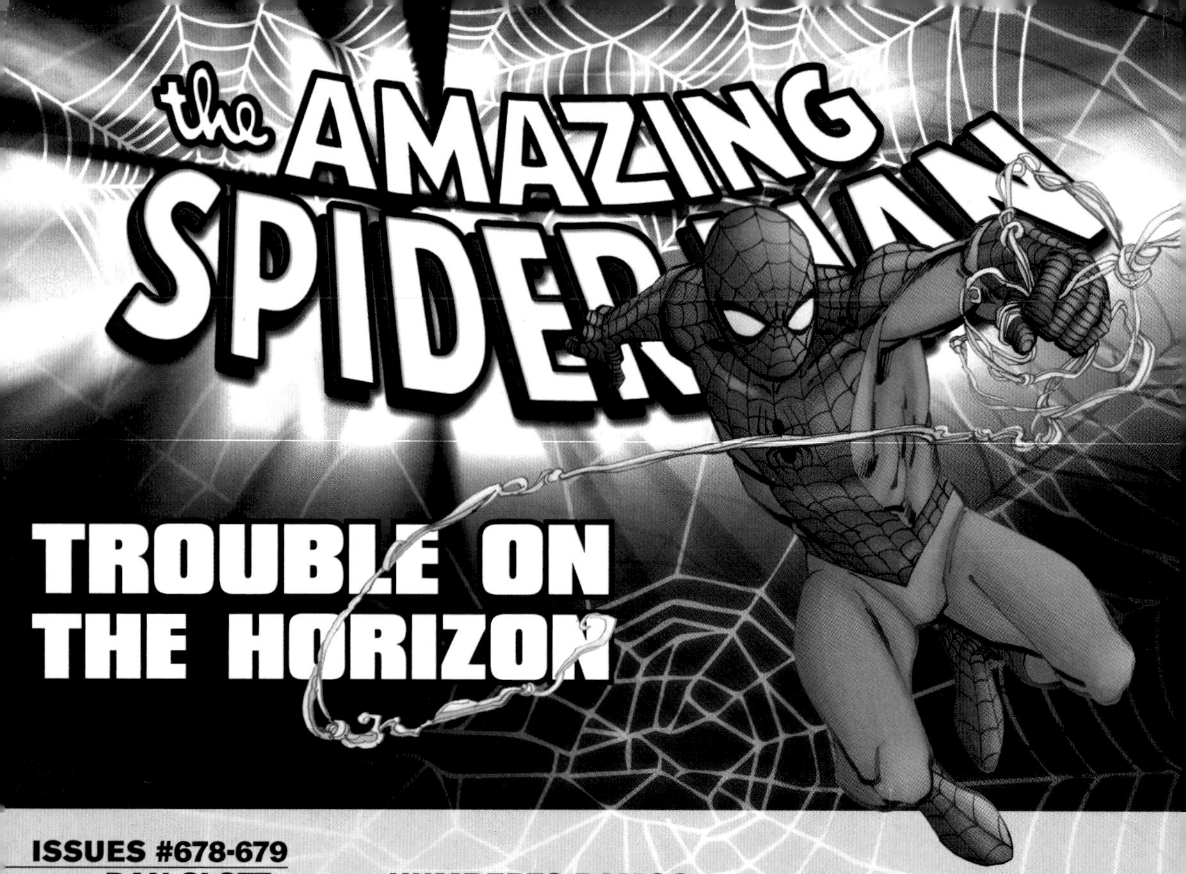
the AMAZING SPIDER-MAN

TROUBLE ON THE HORIZON

ISSUES #678-679

Writer: **DAN SLOTT** • Penciler: **HUMBERTO RAMOS**
Inker: **VICTOR OLAZABA**
Colorist: **EDGAR DELGADO** • Cover Art: **MICHAEL DEL MUNDO**

ISSUE #679.1

Writers: **DAN SLOTT** & **CHRIS YOST** • Penciler: **MATTHEW CLARK**
Inker: **TOM PALMER** • Colorist: **ROB SCHWAGER**
Cover Art: **JOHN TYLER CHRISTOPHER**

ISSUES #680-681

Writers: **DAN SLOTT** & **CHRIS YOST** • Penciler: **GIUSEPPE CAMUNCOLI**
Inker: **KLAUS JANSON** • Colorist: **FRANK D'ARMATA**
Cover Art: **GIUSEPPE CAMUNCOLI, KLAUS JANSON** & **FRANK D'ARMATA**

Letterer: **VC'S JOE CARAMAGNA** • Assistant Editor: **ELLIE PYLE** • Senior Editor: **STEPHEN WACKER**

Collection Editor: **JENNIFER GRÜNWALD** • Assistant Editors: **ALEX STARBUCK** & **NELSON RIBEIRO**
Editor, Special Projects: **MARK D. BEAZLEY** • Senior Editor, Special Projects: **JEFF YOUNGQUIST**
Senior Vice President of Sales: **DAVID GABRIEL** • SVP of Brand Planning & Communications: **MICHAEL PASCIULLO**

Editor in Chief: **AXEL ALONSO** • Chief Creative Officer: **JOE QUESADA** • Publisher: **DAN BUCKLEY** • Executive Producer: **ALAN FINE**

SPIDER-MAN: TROUBLE ON THE HORIZON. Contains material originally published in magazine form as AMAZING SPIDER-MAN #678-681 and #679.1. First printing 2012. Hardcover ISBN# 978-0-7851-6003-8. Softcover ISBN# 978-0-7851-6004-5. Published by MARVEL WORLDWIDE, INC., a subsidiary of MARVEL ENTERTAINMENT, LLC. OFFICE OF PUBLICATION: 135 West 50th Street, New York, NY 10020. Hardcover: $19.99 per copy in the U.S. and $21.99 in Canada (GST #R127032852). Softcover: $16.99 per copy in the U.S. and $18.99 in Canada (GST #R127032852). Canadian Agreement #40668537. **Printed in the U.S.A.** ALAN FINE, EVP - Office of the President, Marvel Worldwide, Inc. and EVP & CMO Marvel Characters B.V.; DAN BUCKLEY, Publisher & President - Print, Animation & Digital Divisions; JOE QUESADA, Chief Creative Officer; TOM BREVOORT, SVP of Publishing; DAVID BOGART, SVP of Operations & Procurement, Publishing; RUWAN JAYATILLEKE, SVP & Associate Publisher, Publishing; C.B. CEBULSKI, SVP of Creator & Content Development; DAVID GABRIEL, SVP of Publishing Sales & Circulation; MICHAEL PASCIULLO, SVP of Brand Planning & Communications; JIM O'KEEFE, VP of Operations & Logistics; DAN CARR, Executive Director of Publishing Technology; SUSAN CRESPI, Editorial Operations Manager; ALEX MORALES, Publishing Operations Manager; STAN LEE, Chairman Emeritus. For information regarding advertising in Marvel Comics or on Marvel.com, please contact John Dokes, SVP Integrated Sales and Marketing, at jdokes@marvel.com. For Marvel subscription inquiries, please call 800-217-9158. **Manufactured between 5/7/2012 and 6/4/2012 (hardcover), and 5/7/2012 and 12/3/2012 (softcover), by R.R. DONNELLEY, INC., SALEM, VA, USA.**

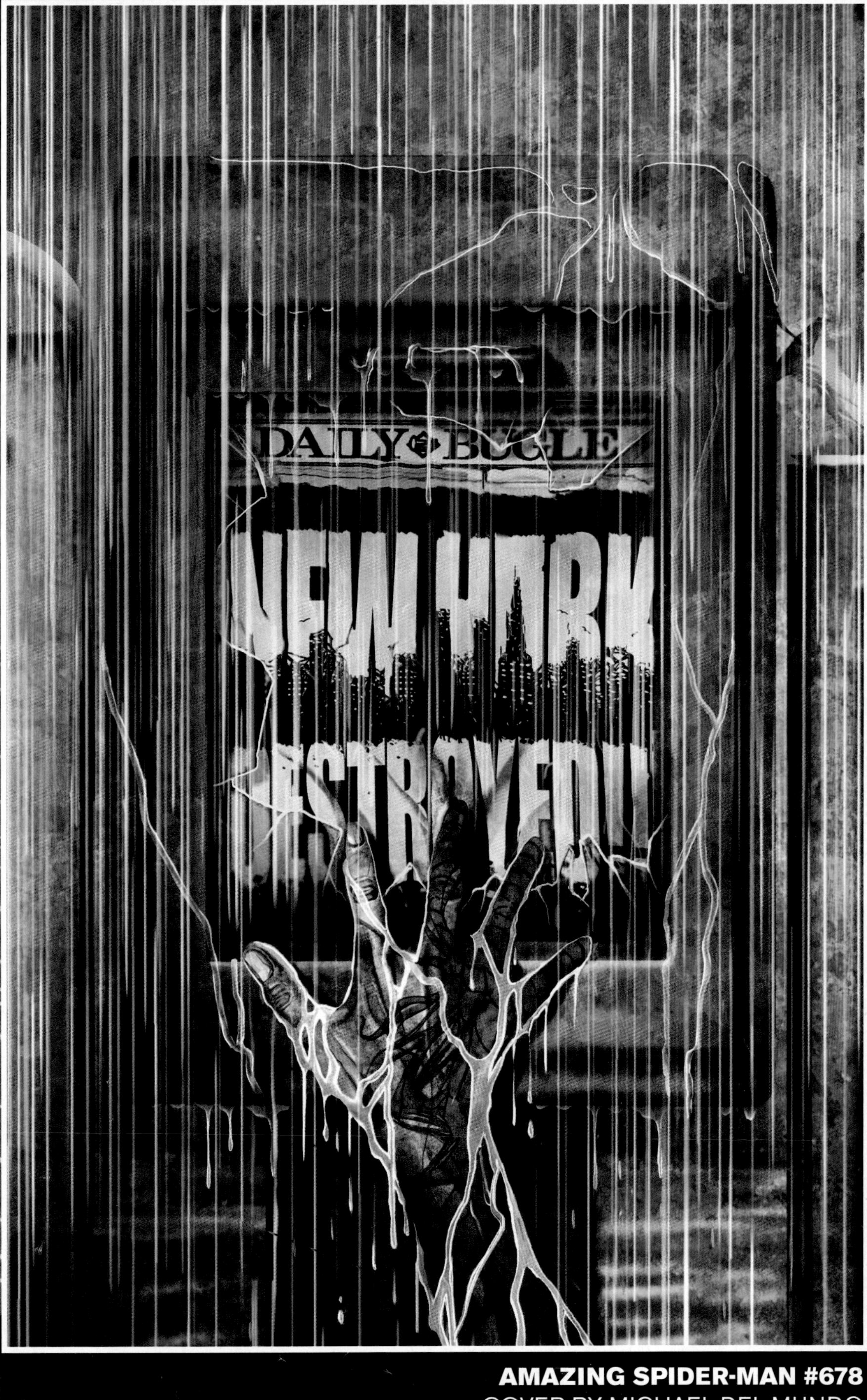
DAILY BUGLE

AMAZING SPIDER-MAN #678
COVER BY MICHAEL DEL MUNDO

FINAL ☆☆☆☆

DAILY BUGLE®

NEW YORK'S FINEST DAILY NEWSPAPER

SINCE 1897 ☆☆☆☆ $1.00 (in NYC) $1.50 (outside city)

INSIDE: GROUNDWATER OR GRAVE ROBBERS? EXCHANGE EXPERIENCES PUNISHING FATALITIES! RUMOR: VENOM IN VEGAS?

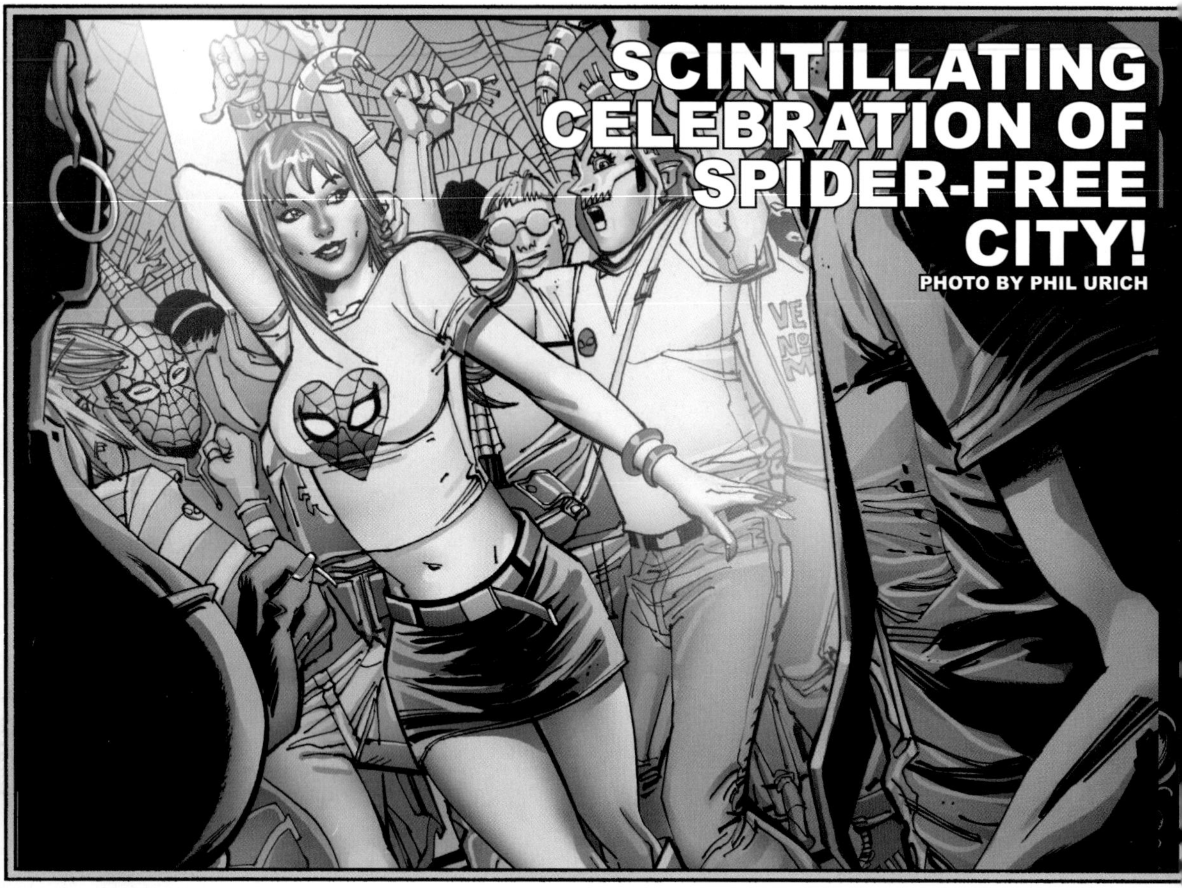

SCINTILLATING CELEBRATION OF SPIDER-FREE CITY!

PHOTO BY PHIL URICH

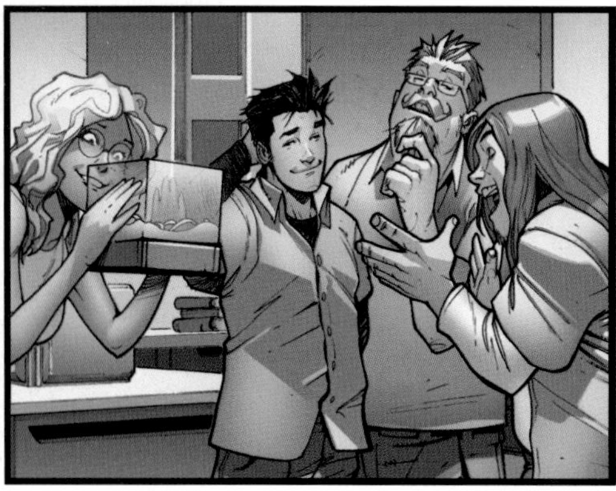

HORIZON LABS: A UNIQUE WORK ENVIRONMENT

THE SUPER-GENUISES AT HORIZON LABS ARE ALL STRIVING TO FIND THE NEXT BIG IDEA. FRESH OFF THE SUCESS OF THEIR CURE FOR THE SPIDER-ISLAND VIRUS, EVERYONE IS WONDERING WHAT INVALUABLE INVENTION THIS BRAIN TRUST WILL THINK OF NEXT.

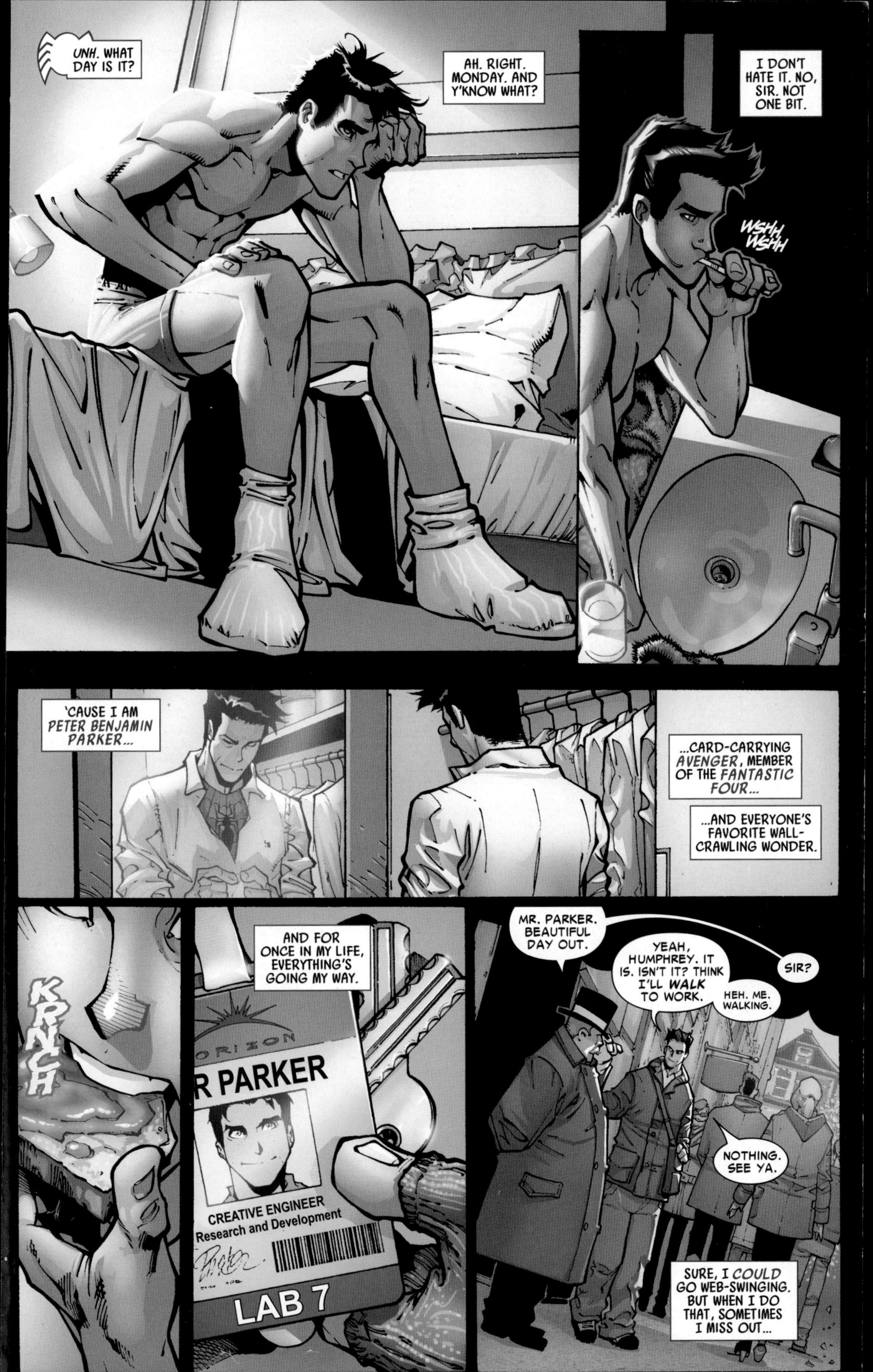
UNH. WHAT DAY IS IT?
AH. RIGHT. MONDAY. AND Y'KNOW WHAT?
I DON'T HATE IT. NO, SIR. NOT ONE BIT.
WSHH WSHH
'CAUSE I AM PETER BENJAMIN PARKER...
...CARD-CARRYING AVENGER, MEMBER OF THE FANTASTIC FOUR...
...AND EVERYONE'S FAVORITE WALL-CRAWLING WONDER.
KRNCH
AND FOR ONCE IN MY LIFE, EVERYTHING'S GOING MY WAY.
ORIZON
R PARKER
CREATIVE ENGINEER
Research and Development
LAB 7
MR. PARKER. BEAUTIFUL DAY OUT.
YEAH, HUMPHREY. IT IS. ISN'T IT? THINK I'LL WALK TO WORK.
HEH. ME. WALKING.
SIR?
NOTHING. SEE YA.
SURE, I COULD GO WEB-SWINGING. BUT WHEN I DO THAT, SOMETIMES I MISS OUT...

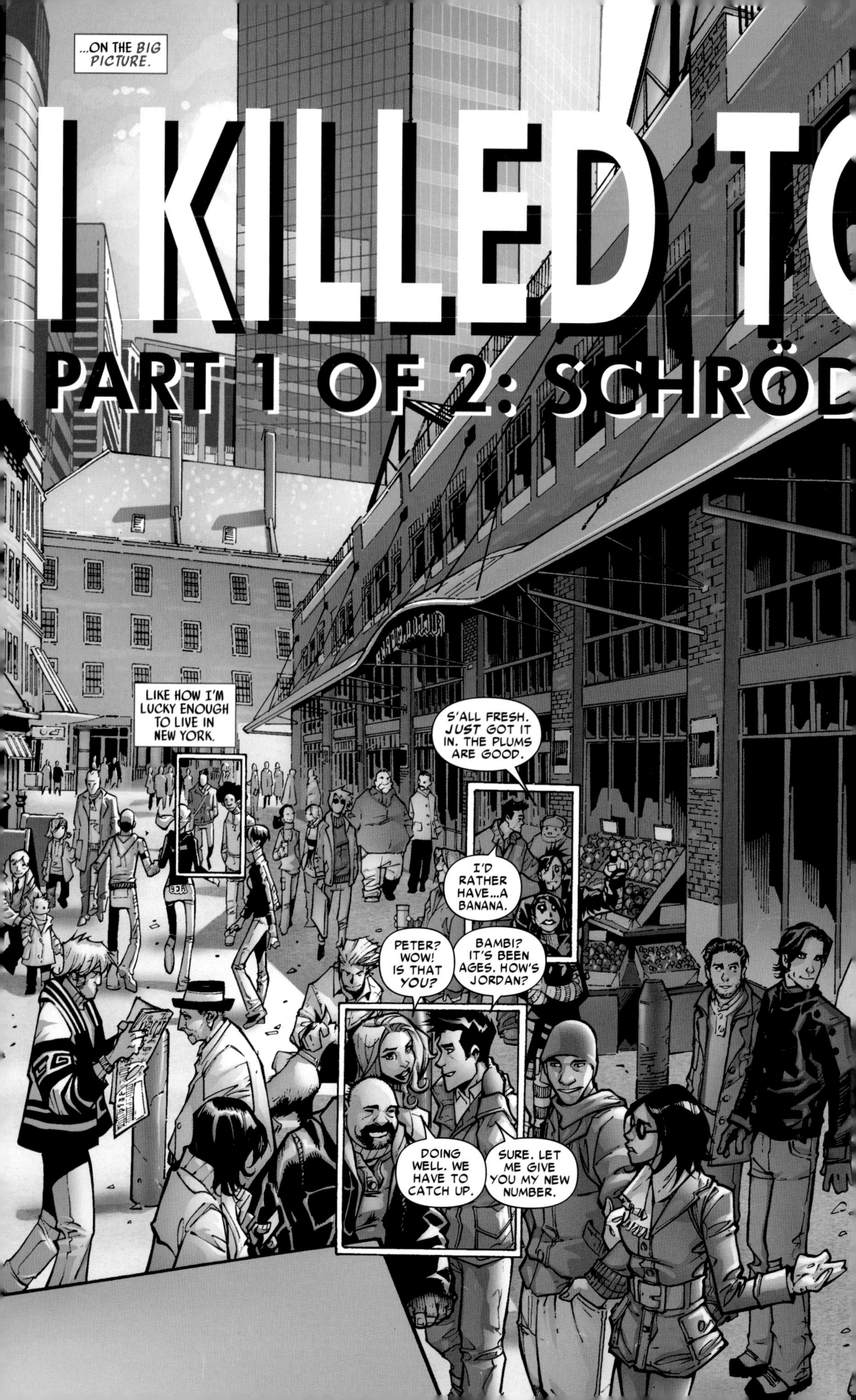

...ON THE BIG PICTURE.
I KILLED TO
PART 1 OF 2: SCHRÖD
LIKE HOW I'M LUCKY ENOUGH TO LIVE IN NEW YORK.
S'ALL FRESH. JUST GOT IT IN. THE PLUMS ARE GOOD.
I'D RATHER HAVE...A BANANA.
PETER? WOW! IS THAT YOU?
BAMBI? IT'S BEEN AGES. HOW'S JORDAN?
DOING WELL. WE HAVE TO CATCH UP.
SURE. LET ME GIVE YOU MY NEW NUMBER.

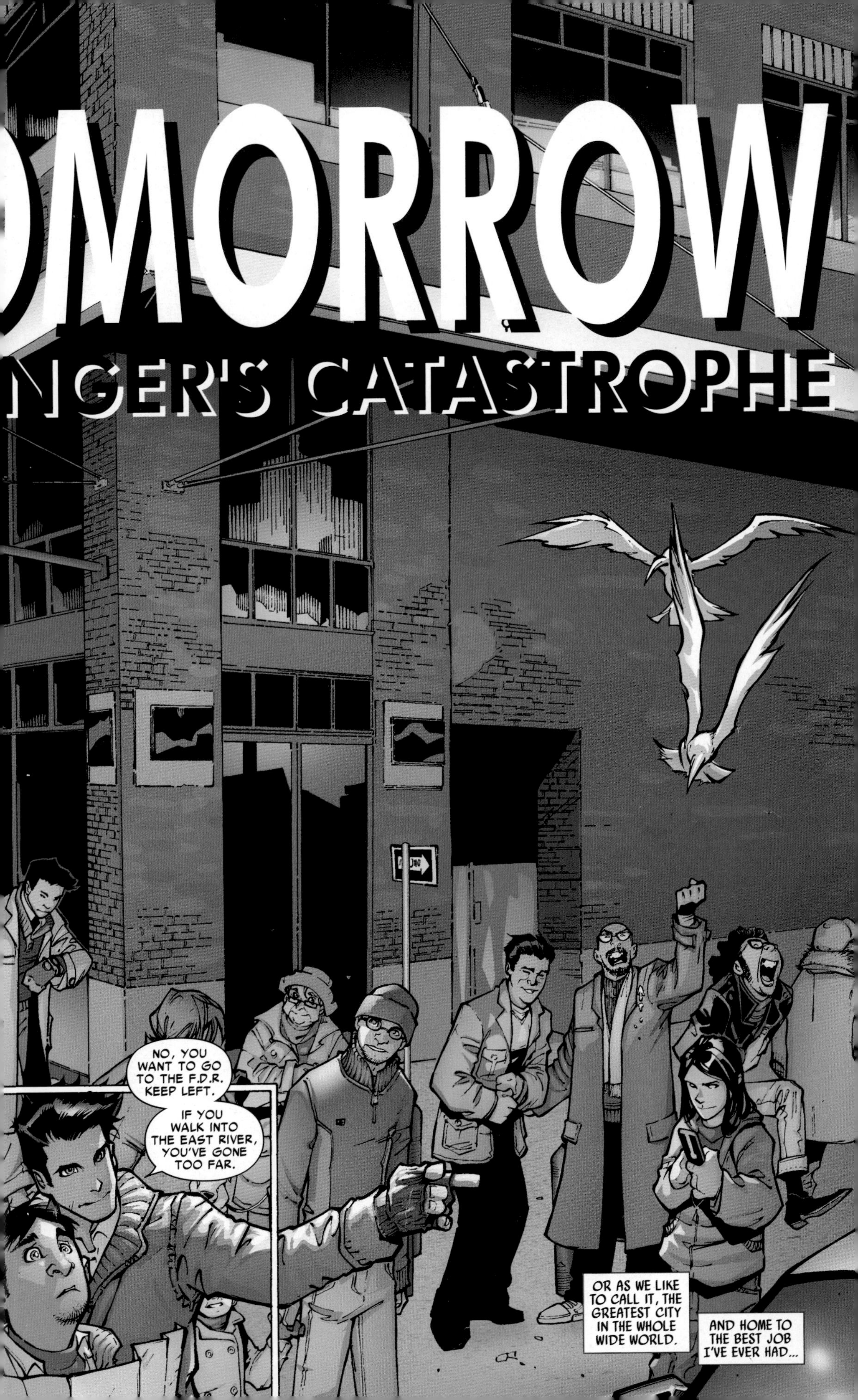
OMORROW
NGER'S CATASTROPHE
NO, YOU WANT TO GO TO THE F.D.R. KEEP LEFT.
IF YOU WALK INTO THE EAST RIVER, YOU'VE GONE TOO FAR.
OR AS WE LIKE TO CALL IT, THE GREATEST CITY IN THE WHOLE WIDE WORLD.
AND HOME TO THE BEST JOB I'VE EVER HAD...

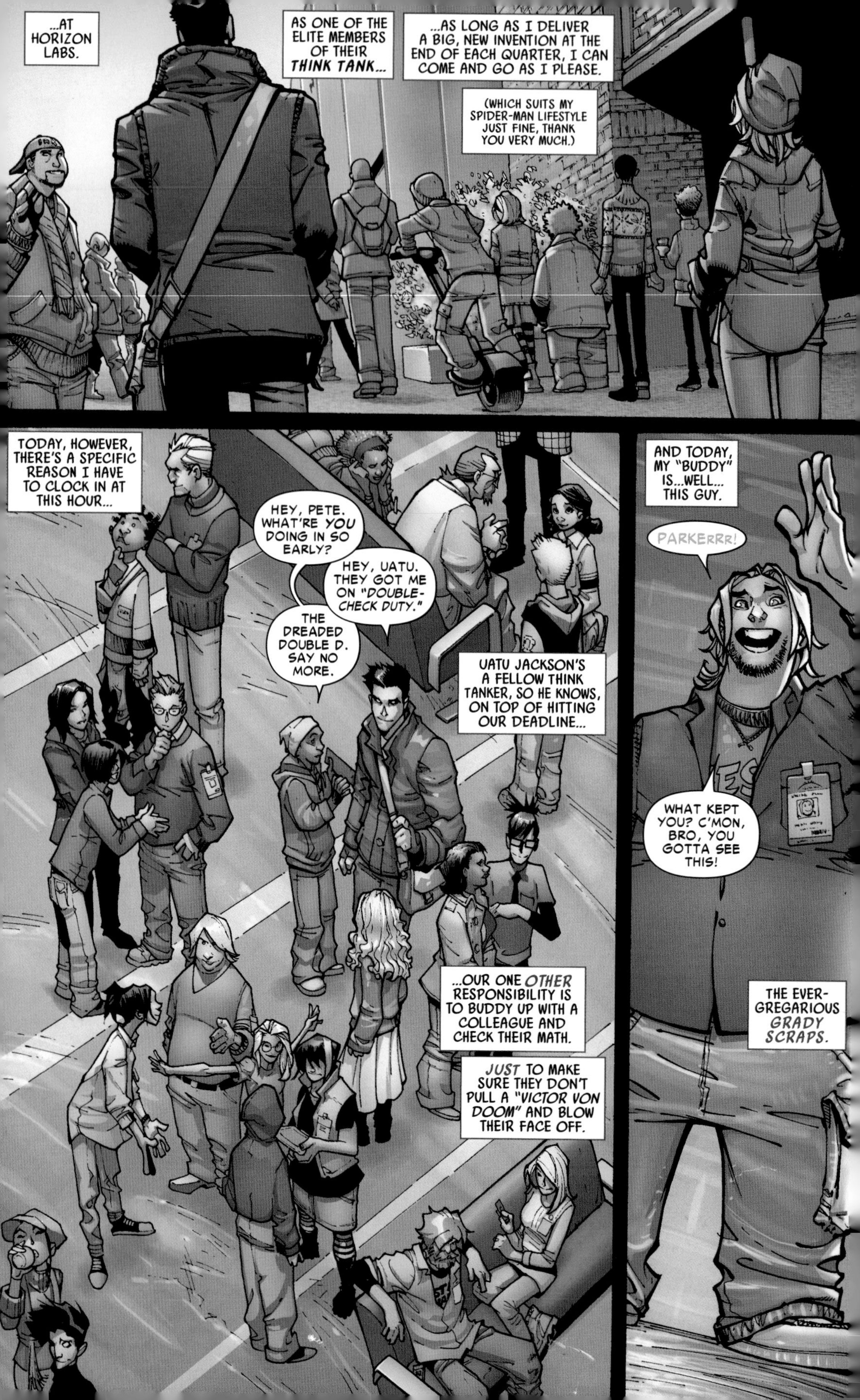
...AT HORIZON LABS.
AS ONE OF THE ELITE MEMBERS OF THEIR *THINK TANK*...
...AS LONG AS I DELIVER A BIG, NEW INVENTION AT THE END OF EACH QUARTER, I CAN COME AND GO AS I PLEASE.
(WHICH SUITS MY SPIDER-MAN LIFESTYLE JUST FINE, THANK YOU VERY MUCH.)
TODAY, HOWEVER, THERE'S A SPECIFIC REASON I HAVE TO CLOCK IN AT THIS HOUR...
HEY, PETE. WHAT'RE *YOU* DOING IN SO EARLY?
HEY, UATU. THEY GOT ME ON "*DOUBLE-CHECK DUTY*."
THE DREADED DOUBLE D. SAY NO MORE.
UATU JACKSON'S A FELLOW THINK TANKER, SO HE KNOWS, ON TOP OF HITTING OUR DEADLINE...
...OUR ONE *OTHER* RESPONSIBILITY IS TO BUDDY UP WITH A COLLEAGUE AND CHECK THEIR MATH.
JUST TO MAKE SURE THEY DON'T PULL A "*VICTOR VON DOOM*" AND BLOW THEIR FACE OFF.
AND TODAY, MY "BUDDY" IS...WELL... THIS GUY.
PARKERrRr!
WHAT KEPT YOU? C'MON, BRO, YOU GOTTA SEE THIS!
THE EVER-GREGARIOUS *GRADY SCRAPS*.

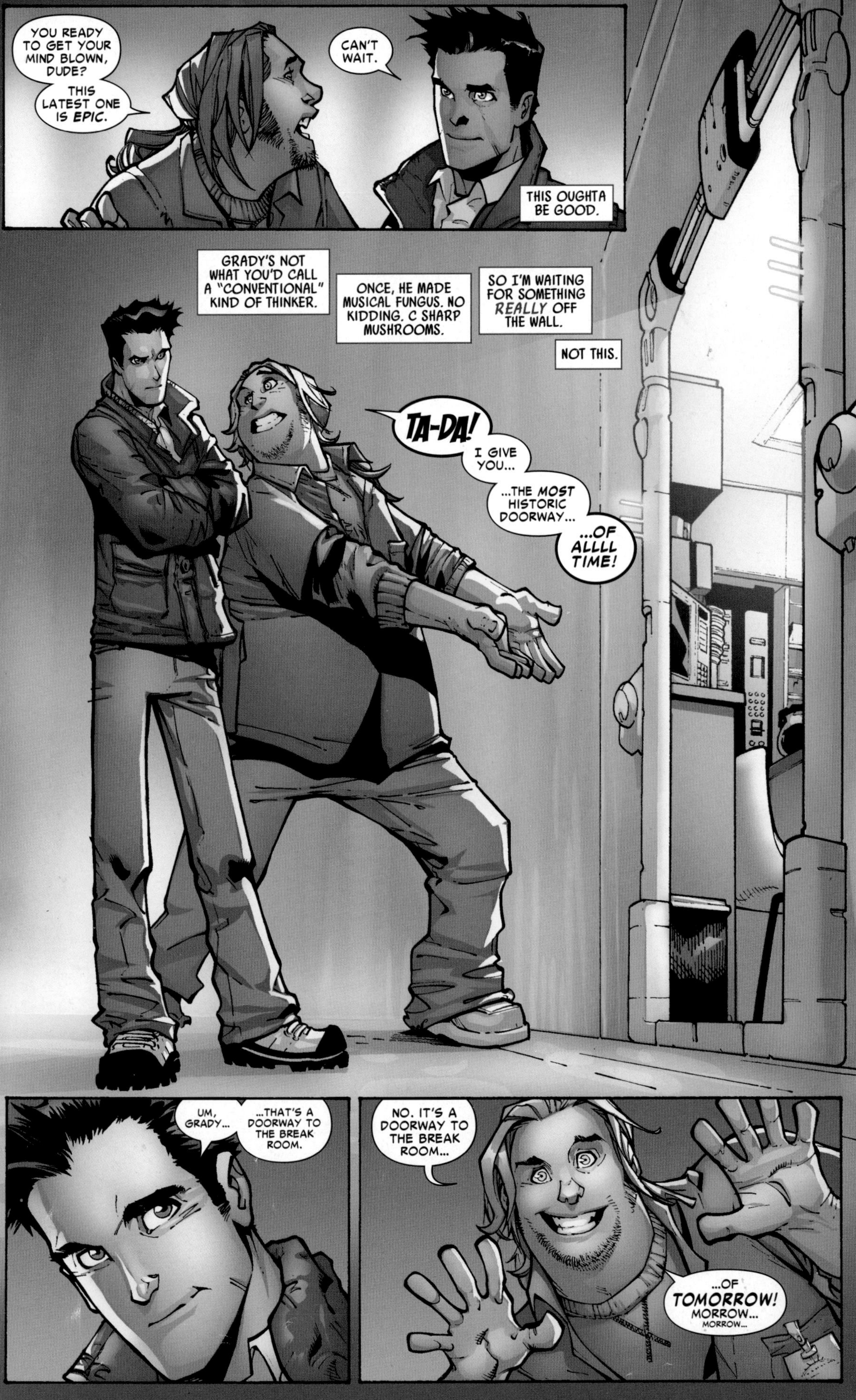
YOU READY TO GET YOUR MIND BLOWN, DUDE?
THIS LATEST ONE IS EPIC.
CAN'T WAIT.
THIS OUGHTA BE GOOD.
GRADY'S NOT WHAT YOU'D CALL A "CONVENTIONAL" KIND OF THINKER.
ONCE, HE MADE MUSICAL FUNGUS. NO KIDDING. C SHARP MUSHROOMS.
SO I'M WAITING FOR SOMETHING REALLY OFF THE WALL.
NOT THIS.
TA-DA!
I GIVE YOU...
...THE MOST HISTORIC DOORWAY...
...OF ALLLL TIME!
UM, GRADY...
...THAT'S A DOORWAY TO THE BREAK ROOM.
NO. IT'S A DOORWAY TO THE BREAK ROOM...
...OF TOMORROW! MORROW... MORROW...

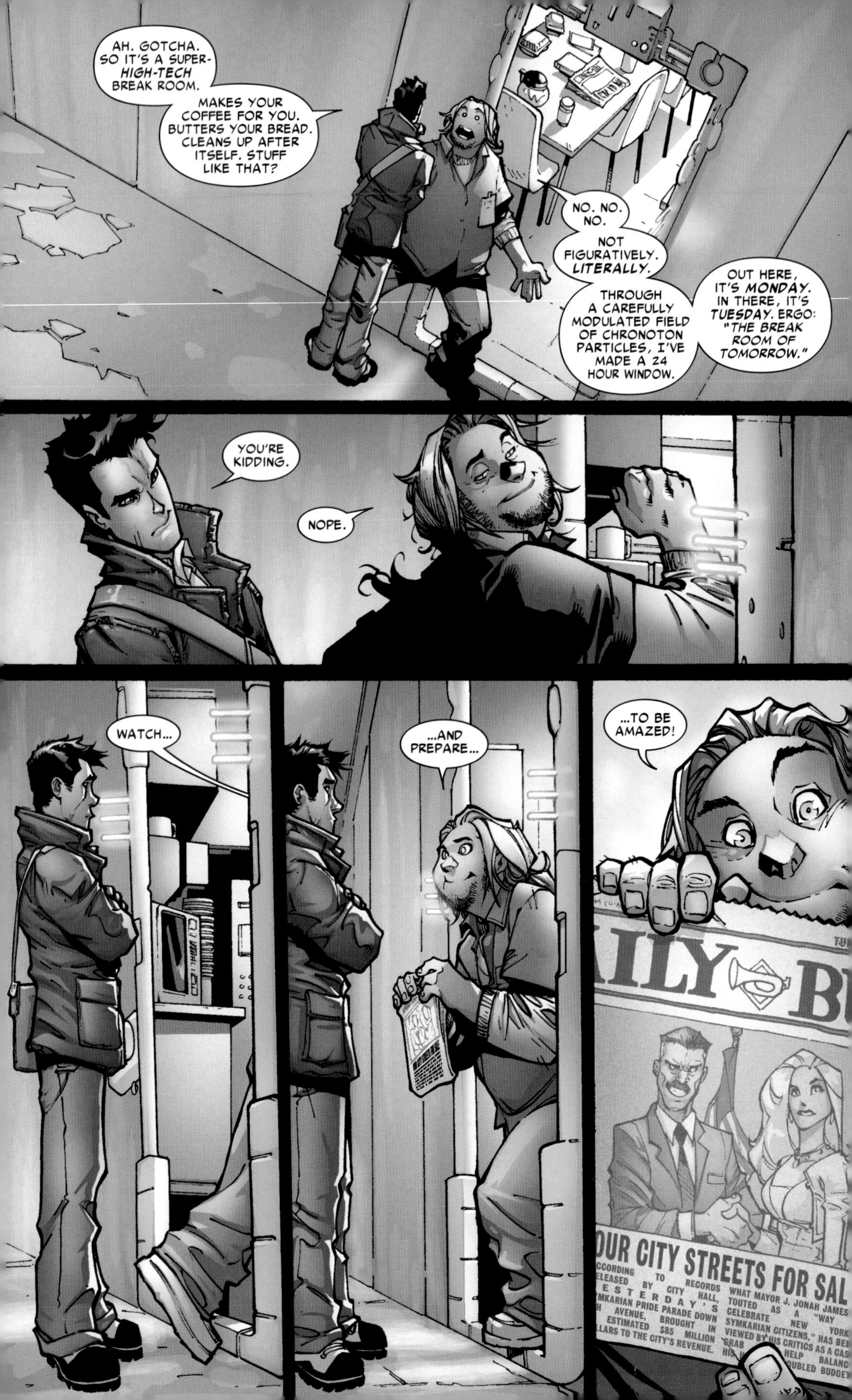
AH. GOTCHA. SO IT'S A SUPER-*HIGH-TECH* BREAK ROOM.
MAKES YOUR COFFEE FOR YOU. BUTTERS YOUR BREAD. CLEANS UP AFTER ITSELF. STUFF LIKE THAT?
NO. NO. NO.
NOT FIGURATIVELY. ***LITERALLY.***
THROUGH A CAREFULLY MODULATED FIELD OF CHRONOTON PARTICLES, I'VE MADE A 24 HOUR WINDOW.
OUT HERE, IT'S *MONDAY*. IN THERE, IT'S *TUESDAY*. ERGO: *"THE BREAK ROOM OF TOMORROW."*
YOU'RE KIDDING.
NOPE.
WATCH...
...AND PREPARE...
...TO BE AMAZED!
OUR CITY STREETS FOR SAL

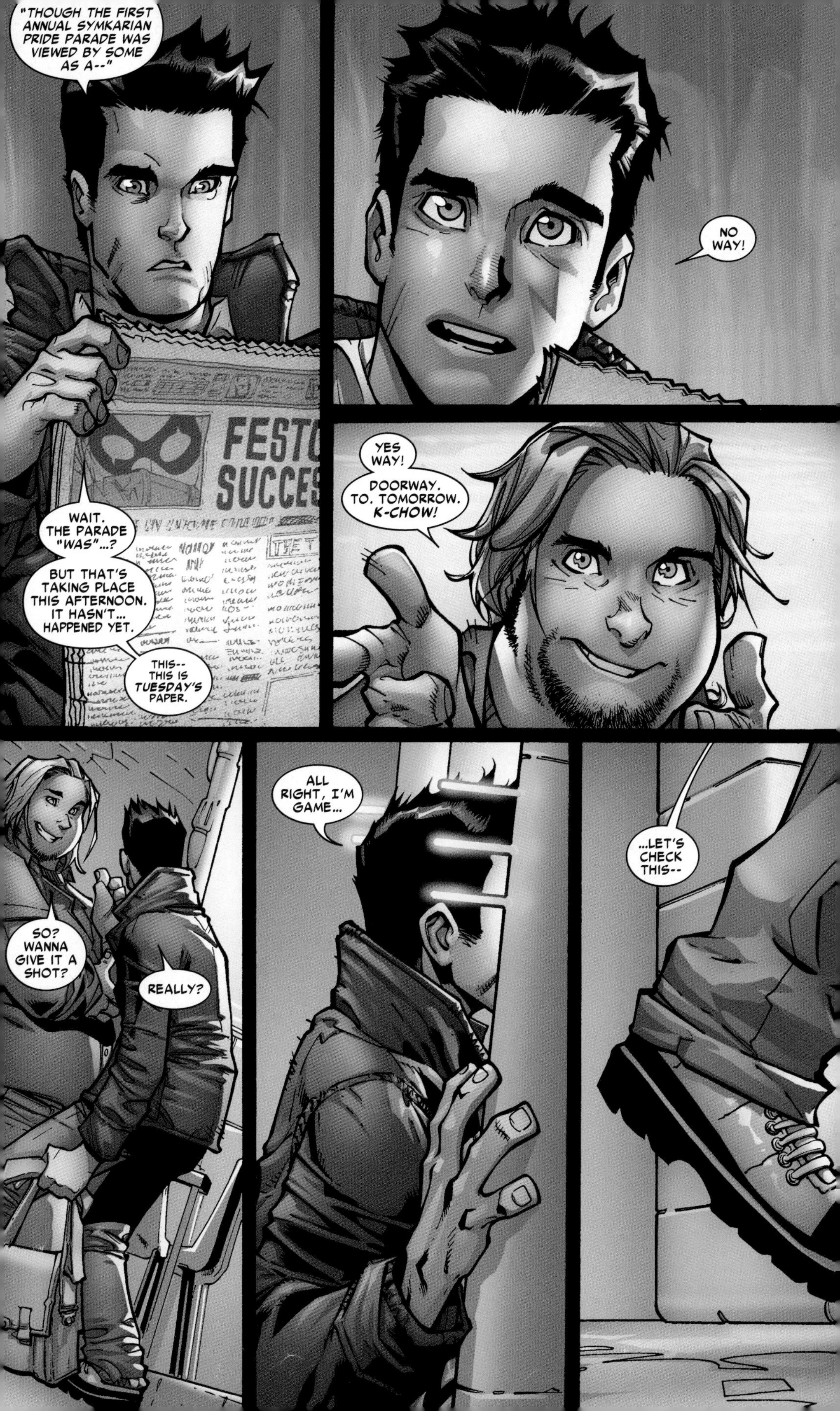
"THOUGH THE FIRST ANNUAL SYMKARIAN PRIDE PARADE WAS VIEWED BY SOME AS A--"
NO WAY!
FESTO SUCCES
WAIT. THE PARADE "WAS"...?
BUT THAT'S TAKING PLACE THIS AFTERNOON. IT HASN'T... HAPPENED YET.
THIS-- THIS IS TUESDAY'S PAPER.
YES WAY!
DOORWAY. TO. TOMORROW. K-CHOW!
SO? WANNA GIVE IT A SHOT?
REALLY?
ALL RIGHT, I'M GAME...
...LET'S CHECK THIS--

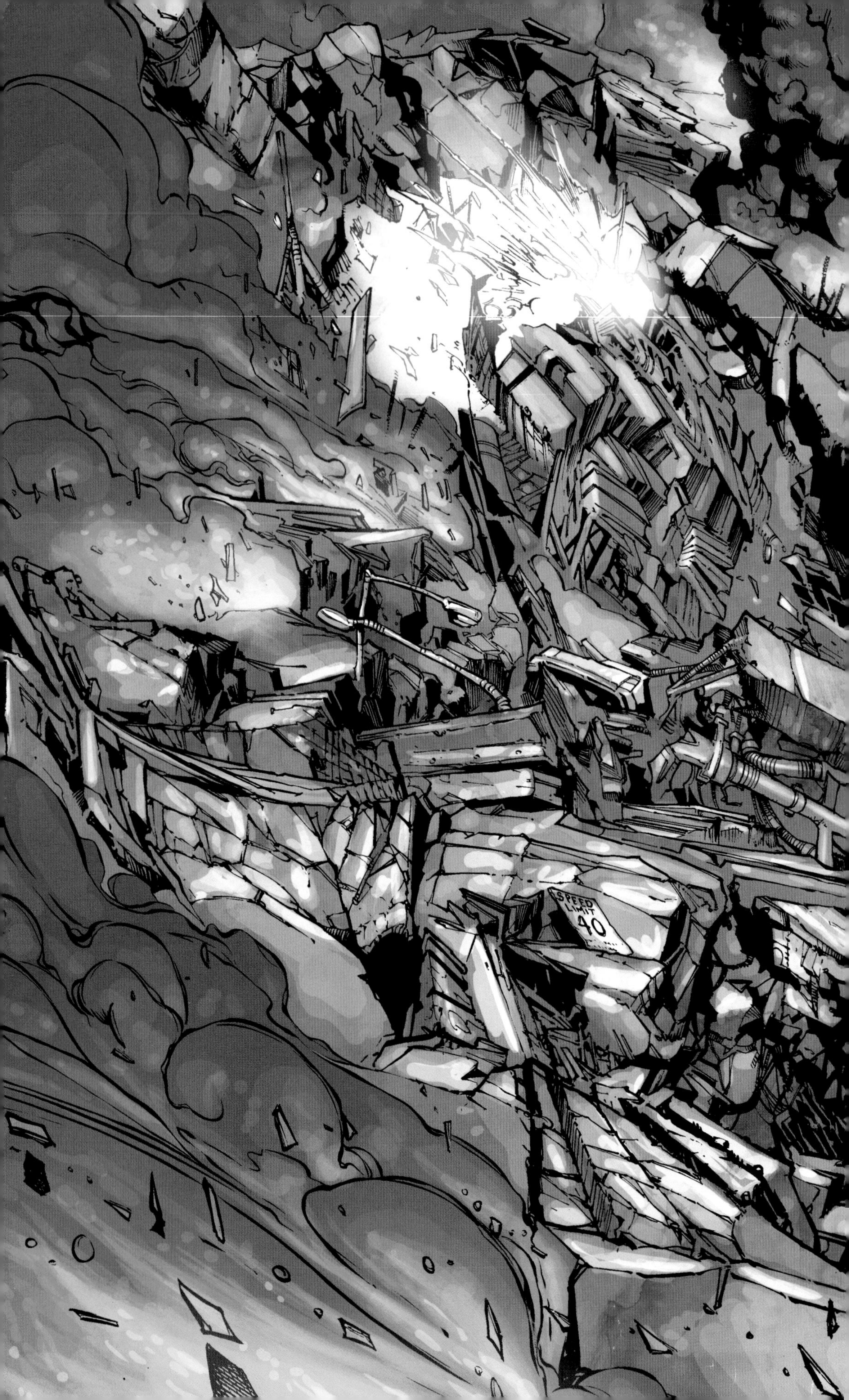
SPEED LIMIT 40

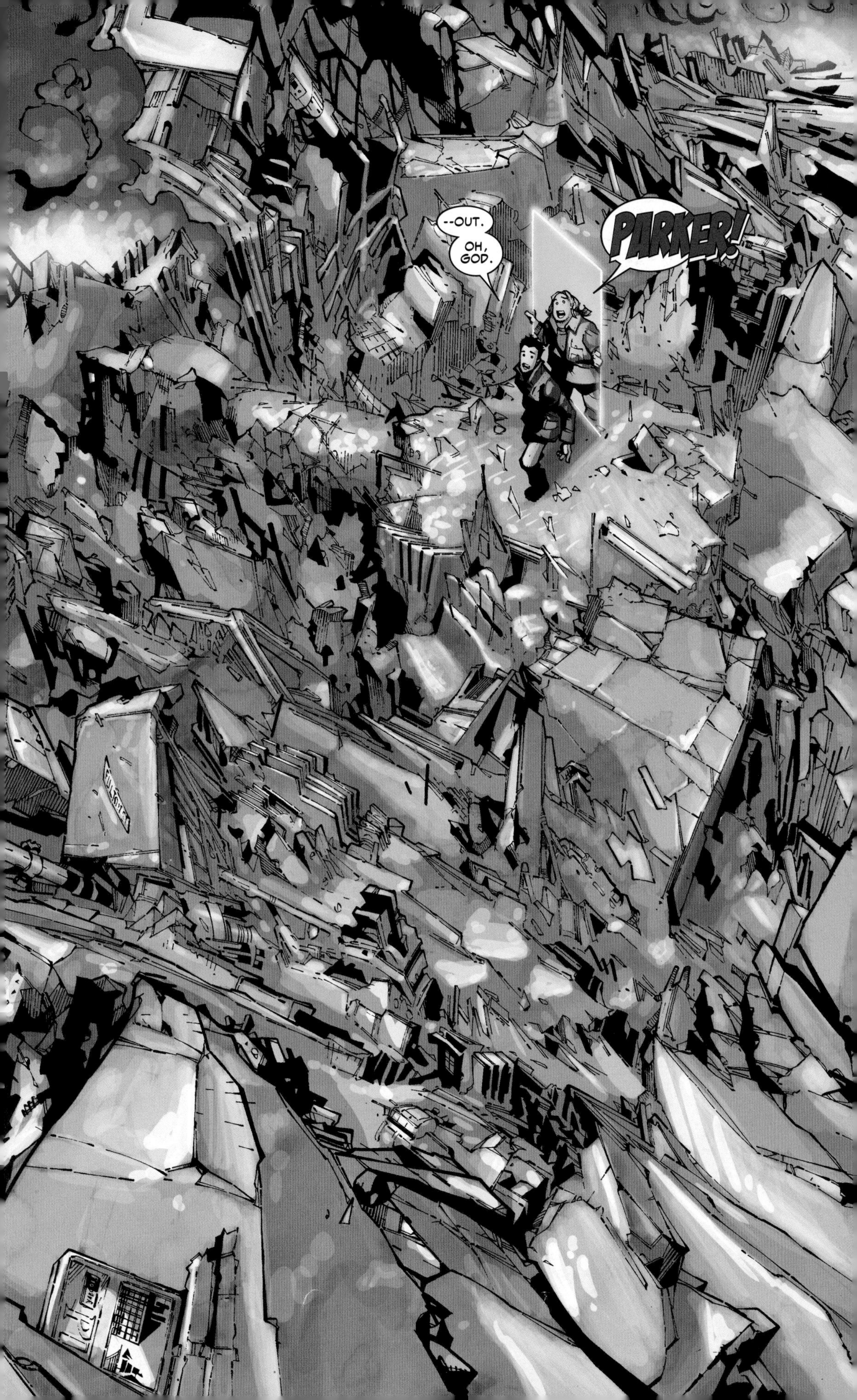

--OUT.
OH, GOD.
PARKER!

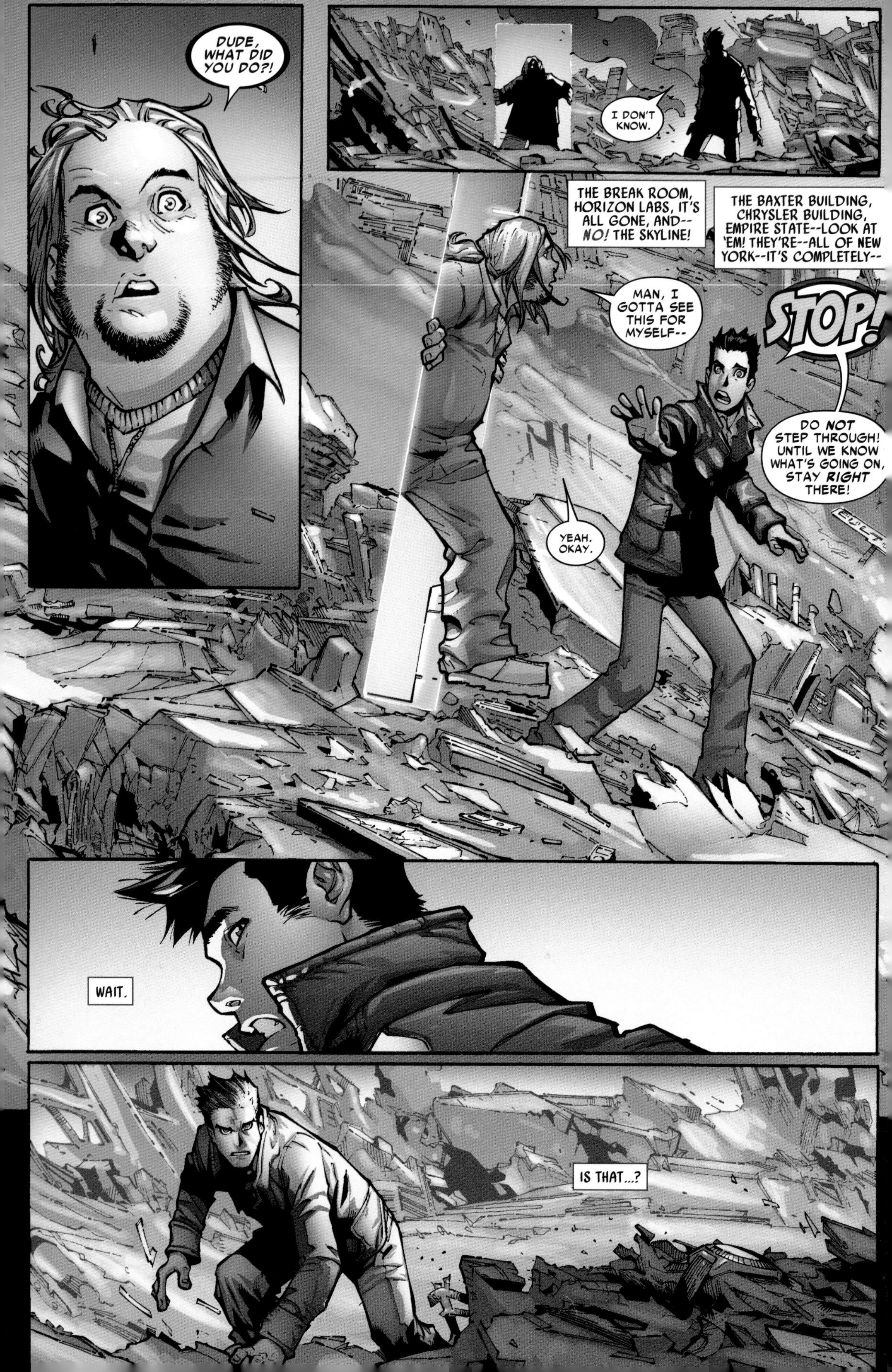
DUDE, WHAT DID YOU DO?!
I DON'T KNOW.
THE BREAK ROOM, HORIZON LABS, IT'S ALL GONE, AND-- NO! THE SKYLINE!
THE BAXTER BUILDING, CHRYSLER BUILDING, EMPIRE STATE--LOOK AT 'EM! THEY'RE--ALL OF NEW YORK--IT'S COMPLETELY--
MAN, I GOTTA SEE THIS FOR MYSELF--
STOP!
DO NOT STEP THROUGH! UNTIL WE KNOW WHAT'S GOING ON, STAY RIGHT THERE!
YEAH. OKAY.
WAIT.
IS THAT...?

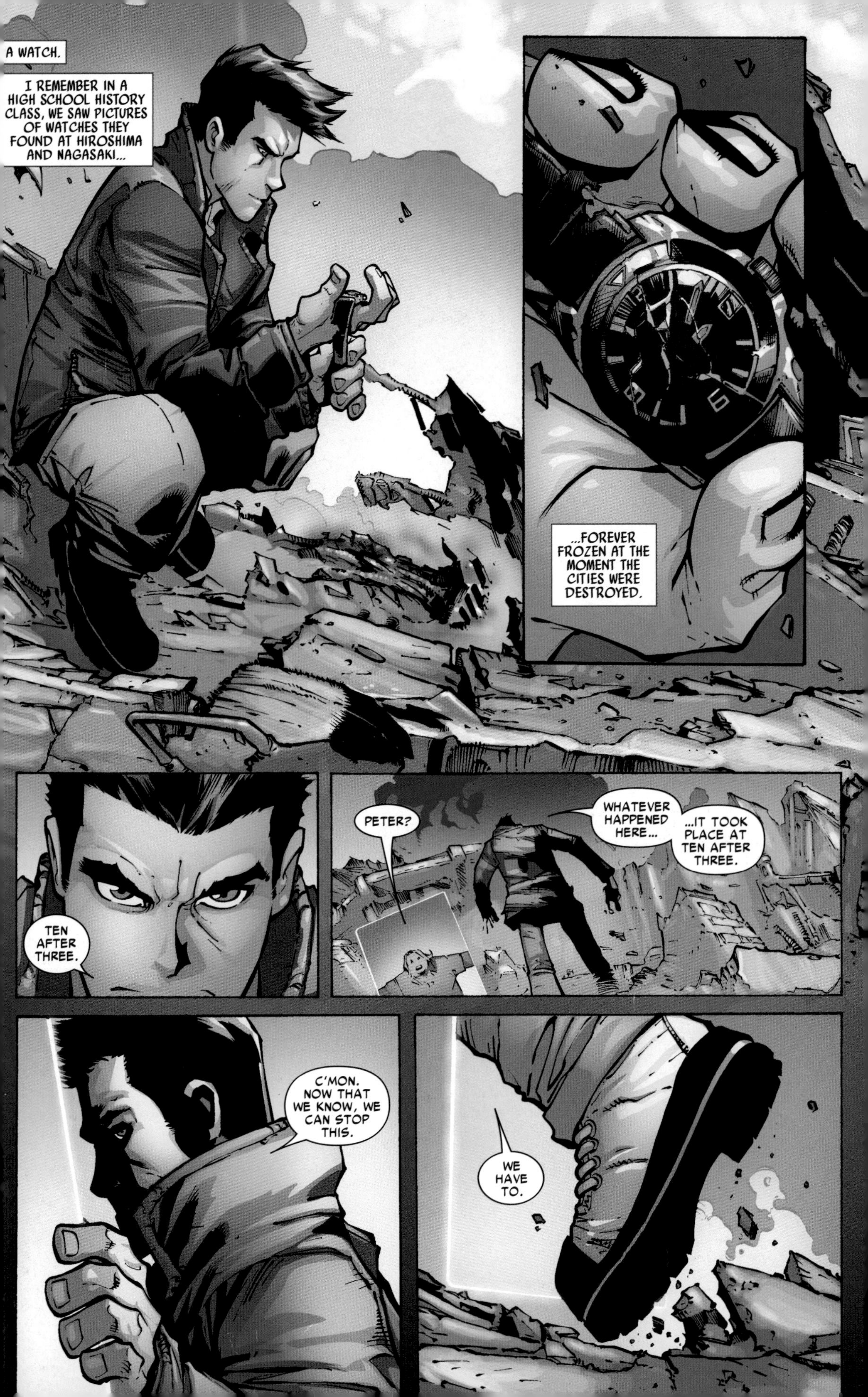
A WATCH.
I REMEMBER IN A HIGH SCHOOL HISTORY CLASS, WE SAW PICTURES OF WATCHES THEY FOUND AT HIROSHIMA AND NAGASAKI...
...FOREVER FROZEN AT THE MOMENT THE CITIES WERE DESTROYED.
TEN AFTER THREE.
PETER?
WHATEVER HAPPENED HERE...
...IT TOOK PLACE AT TEN AFTER THREE.
C'MON. NOW THAT WE KNOW, WE CAN STOP THIS.
WE HAVE TO.

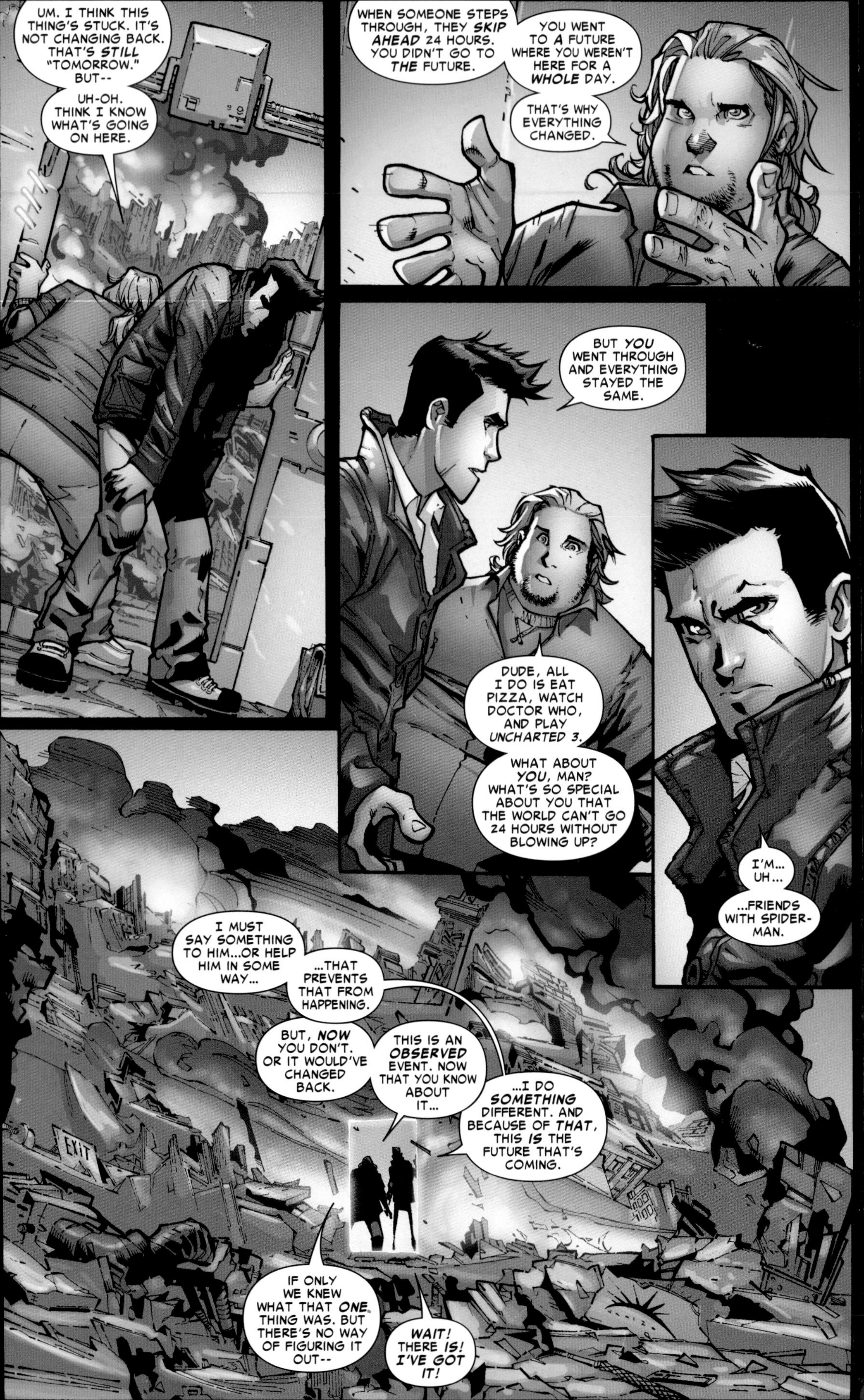
UM. I THINK THIS THING'S STUCK. IT'S NOT CHANGING BACK. THAT'S STILL "TOMORROW." BUT--
UH-OH. THINK I KNOW WHAT'S GOING ON HERE.
WHEN SOMEONE STEPS THROUGH, THEY SKIP AHEAD 24 HOURS. YOU DIDN'T GO TO THE FUTURE.
YOU WENT TO A FUTURE WHERE YOU WEREN'T HERE FOR A WHOLE DAY.
THAT'S WHY EVERYTHING CHANGED.
BUT YOU WENT THROUGH AND EVERYTHING STAYED THE SAME.
DUDE, ALL I DO IS EAT PIZZA, WATCH DOCTOR WHO, AND PLAY UNCHARTED 3.
WHAT ABOUT YOU, MAN? WHAT'S SO SPECIAL ABOUT YOU THAT THE WORLD CAN'T GO 24 HOURS WITHOUT BLOWING UP?
I'M... UH...
...FRIENDS WITH SPIDER-MAN.
I MUST SAY SOMETHING TO HIM...OR HELP HIM IN SOME WAY...
...THAT PREVENTS THAT FROM HAPPENING.
BUT, NOW YOU DON'T. OR IT WOULD'VE CHANGED BACK.
THIS IS AN OBSERVED EVENT. NOW THAT YOU KNOW ABOUT IT...
...I DO SOMETHING DIFFERENT. AND BECAUSE OF THAT, THIS IS THE FUTURE THAT'S COMING.
EXIT
IF ONLY WE KNEW WHAT THAT ONE THING WAS. BUT THERE'S NO WAY OF FIGURING IT OUT--
WAIT! THERE IS! I'VE GOT IT!

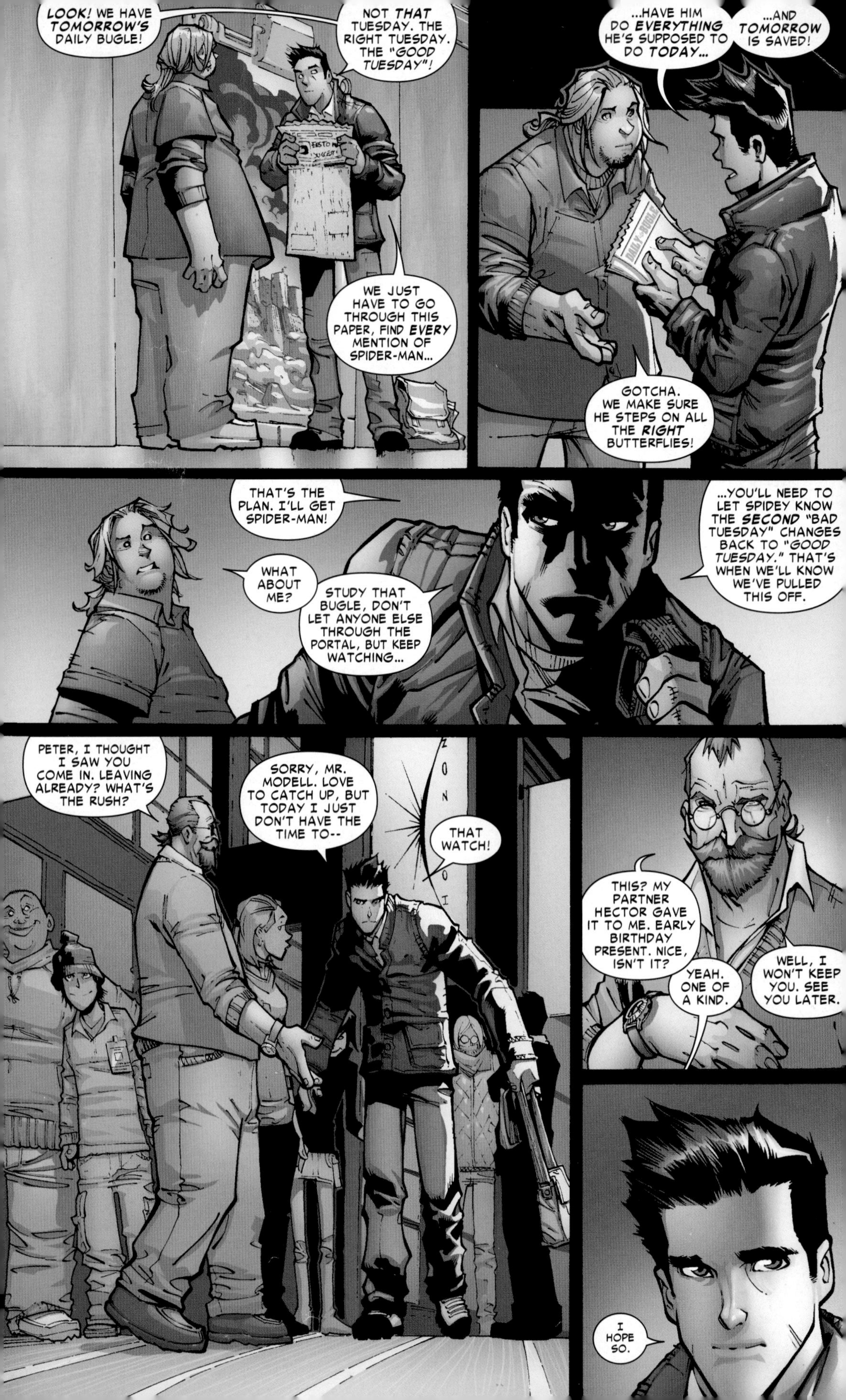
LOOK! WE HAVE TOMORROW'S DAILY BUGLE!
NOT THAT TUESDAY. THE RIGHT TUESDAY. THE "GOOD TUESDAY"!
WE JUST HAVE TO GO THROUGH THIS PAPER, FIND EVERY MENTION OF SPIDER-MAN...
...HAVE HIM DO EVERYTHING HE'S SUPPOSED TO DO TODAY...
...AND TOMORROW IS SAVED!
DAILY BUGLE
GOTCHA. WE MAKE SURE HE STEPS ON ALL THE RIGHT BUTTERFLIES!
THAT'S THE PLAN. I'LL GET SPIDER-MAN!
WHAT ABOUT ME?
STUDY THAT BUGLE, DON'T LET ANYONE ELSE THROUGH THE PORTAL, BUT KEEP WATCHING...
...YOU'LL NEED TO LET SPIDEY KNOW THE SECOND "BAD TUESDAY" CHANGES BACK TO "GOOD TUESDAY." THAT'S WHEN WE'LL KNOW WE'VE PULLED THIS OFF.
PETER, I THOUGHT I SAW YOU COME IN. LEAVING ALREADY? WHAT'S THE RUSH?
SORRY, MR. MODELL. LOVE TO CATCH UP, BUT TODAY I JUST DON'T HAVE THE TIME TO--
THAT WATCH!
THIS? MY PARTNER HECTOR GAVE IT TO ME. EARLY BIRTHDAY PRESENT. NICE, ISN'T IT?
YEAH. ONE OF A KIND.
WELL, I WON'T KEEP YOU. SEE YOU LATER.
I HOPE SO.

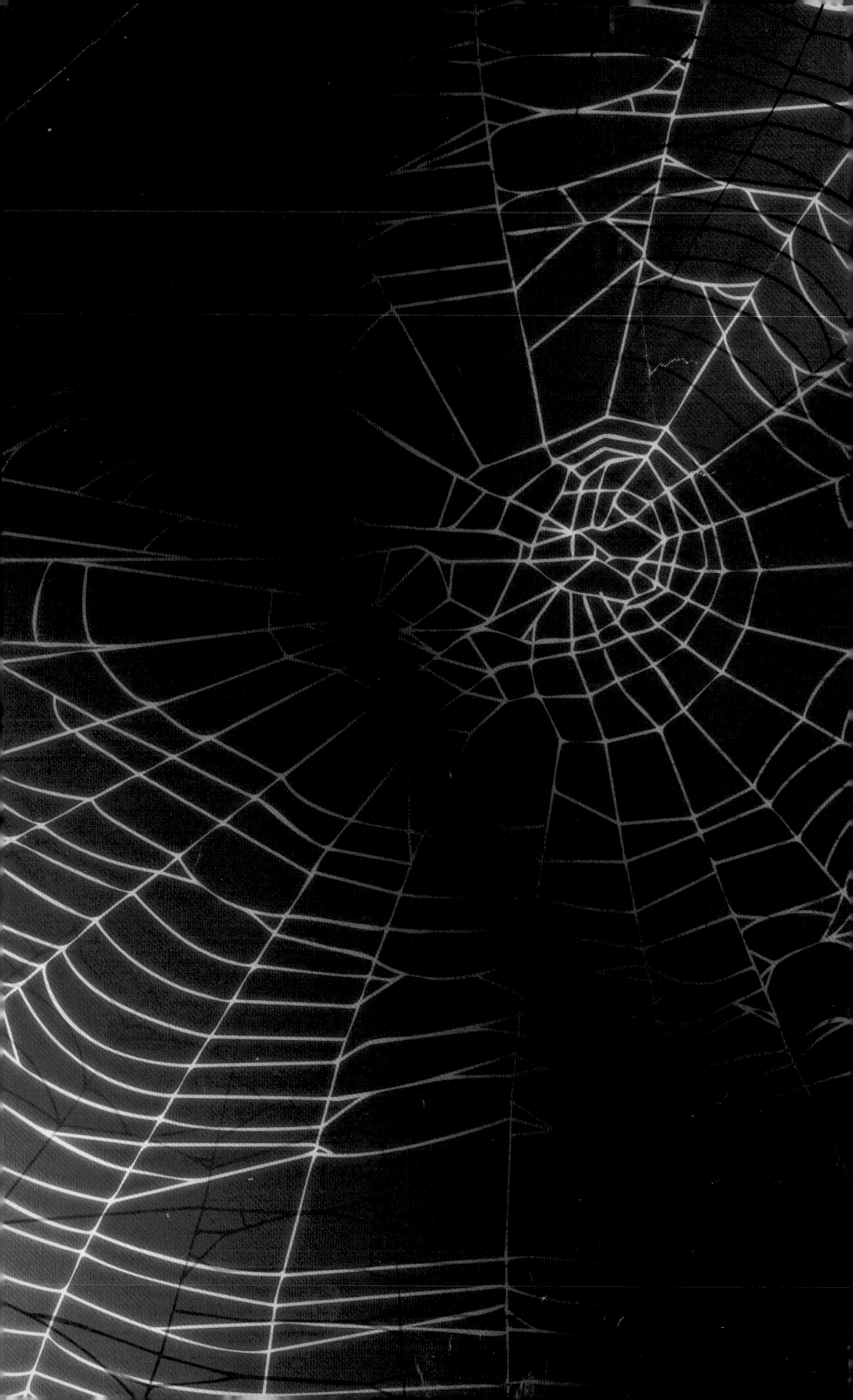

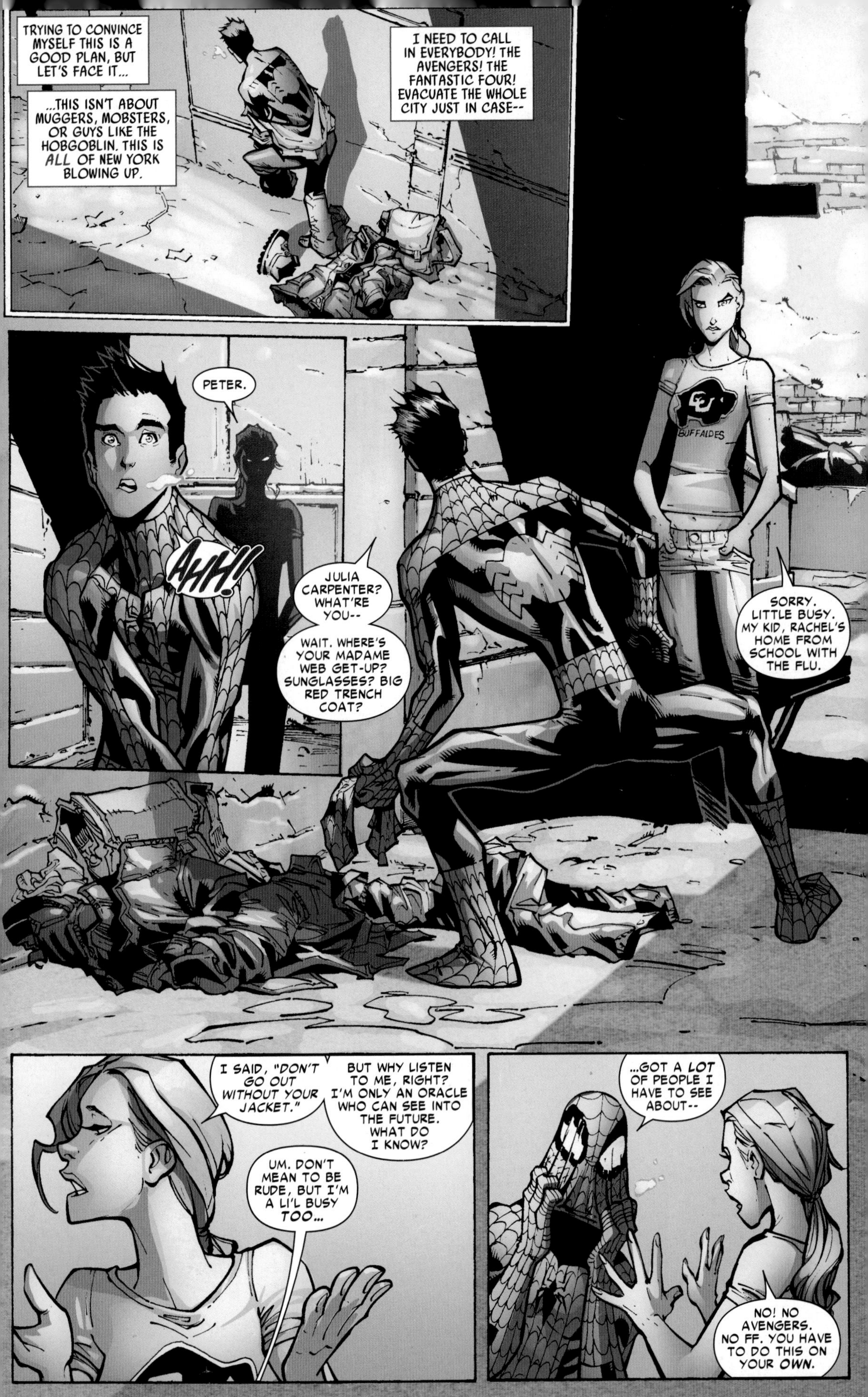
TRYING TO CONVINCE MYSELF THIS IS A GOOD PLAN, BUT LET'S FACE IT...
...THIS ISN'T ABOUT MUGGERS, MOBSTERS, OR GUYS LIKE THE HOBGOBLIN. THIS IS ALL OF NEW YORK BLOWING UP.
I NEED TO CALL IN EVERYBODY! THE AVENGERS! THE FANTASTIC FOUR! EVACUATE THE WHOLE CITY JUST IN CASE--
PETER.
AHH!
JULIA CARPENTER? WHAT'RE YOU--
WAIT. WHERE'S YOUR MADAME WEB GET-UP? SUNGLASSES? BIG RED TRENCH COAT?
SORRY. LITTLE BUSY. MY KID, RACHEL'S HOME FROM SCHOOL WITH THE FLU.
I SAID, "DON'T GO OUT WITHOUT YOUR JACKET."
BUT WHY LISTEN TO ME, RIGHT? I'M ONLY AN ORACLE WHO CAN SEE INTO THE FUTURE. WHAT DO I KNOW?
UM. DON'T MEAN TO BE RUDE, BUT I'M A LI'L BUSY TOO...
...GOT A LOT OF PEOPLE I HAVE TO SEE ABOUT--
NO! NO AVENGERS. NO FF. YOU HAVE TO DO THIS ON YOUR OWN.

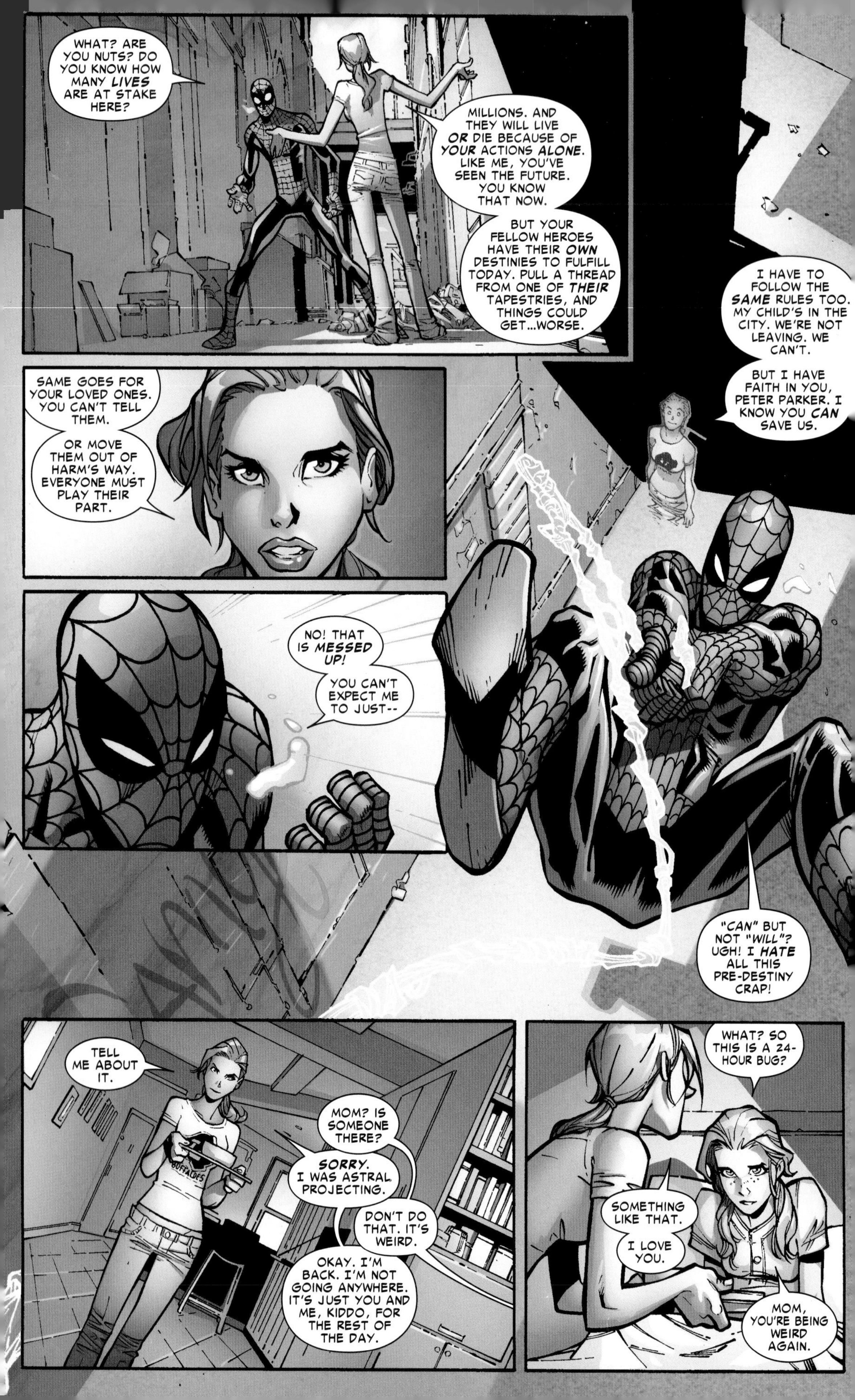
WHAT? ARE YOU NUTS? DO YOU KNOW HOW MANY LIVES ARE AT STAKE HERE?
MILLIONS. AND THEY WILL LIVE OR DIE BECAUSE OF YOUR ACTIONS ALONE. LIKE ME, YOU'VE SEEN THE FUTURE. YOU KNOW THAT NOW.
BUT YOUR FELLOW HEROES HAVE THEIR OWN DESTINIES TO FULFILL TODAY. PULL A THREAD FROM ONE OF THEIR TAPESTRIES, AND THINGS COULD GET...WORSE.
SAME GOES FOR YOUR LOVED ONES. YOU CAN'T TELL THEM.
OR MOVE THEM OUT OF HARM'S WAY. EVERYONE MUST PLAY THEIR PART.
NO! THAT IS MESSED UP!
YOU CAN'T EXPECT ME TO JUST--
I HAVE TO FOLLOW THE SAME RULES TOO. MY CHILD'S IN THE CITY. WE'RE NOT LEAVING. WE CAN'T.
BUT I HAVE FAITH IN YOU, PETER PARKER. I KNOW YOU CAN SAVE US.
"CAN" BUT NOT "WILL"? UGH! I HATE ALL THIS PRE-DESTINY CRAP!
TELL ME ABOUT IT.
MOM? IS SOMEONE THERE?
SORRY. I WAS ASTRAL PROJECTING.
DON'T DO THAT. IT'S WEIRD.
OKAY. I'M BACK. I'M NOT GOING ANYWHERE. IT'S JUST YOU AND ME, KIDDO, FOR THE REST OF THE DAY.
WHAT? SO THIS IS A 24-HOUR BUG?
SOMETHING LIKE THAT.
I LOVE YOU.
MOM, YOU'RE BEING WEIRD AGAIN.

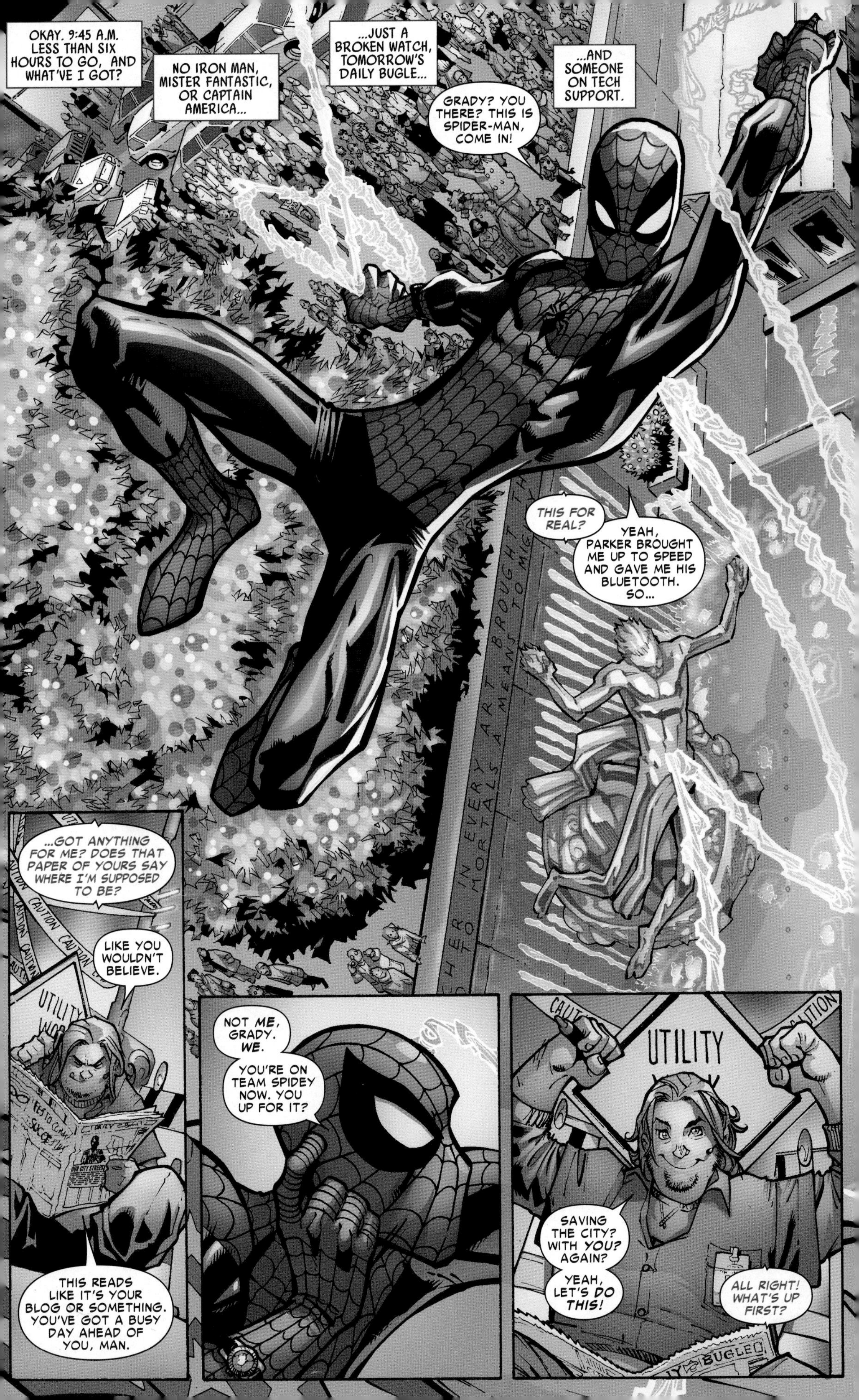
OKAY. 9:45 A.M. LESS THAN SIX HOURS TO GO, AND WHAT'VE I GOT?
NO IRON MAN, MISTER FANTASTIC, OR CAPTAIN AMERICA...
...JUST A BROKEN WATCH, TOMORROW'S DAILY BUGLE...
GRADY? YOU THERE? THIS IS SPIDER-MAN, COME IN!
...AND SOMEONE ON TECH SUPPORT.
THIS FOR REAL?
YEAH, PARKER BROUGHT ME UP TO SPEED AND GAVE ME HIS BLUETOOTH. SO...
...GOT ANYTHING FOR ME? DOES THAT PAPER OF YOURS SAY WHERE I'M SUPPOSED TO BE?
LIKE YOU WOULDN'T BELIEVE.
THIS READS LIKE IT'S YOUR BLOG OR SOMETHING. YOU'VE GOT A BUSY DAY AHEAD OF YOU, MAN.
NOT ME, GRADY. WE.
YOU'RE ON TEAM SPIDEY NOW. YOU UP FOR IT?
UTILITY
SAVING THE CITY? WITH YOU? AGAIN?
YEAH, LET'S DO THIS!
ALL RIGHT! WHAT'S UP FIRST?

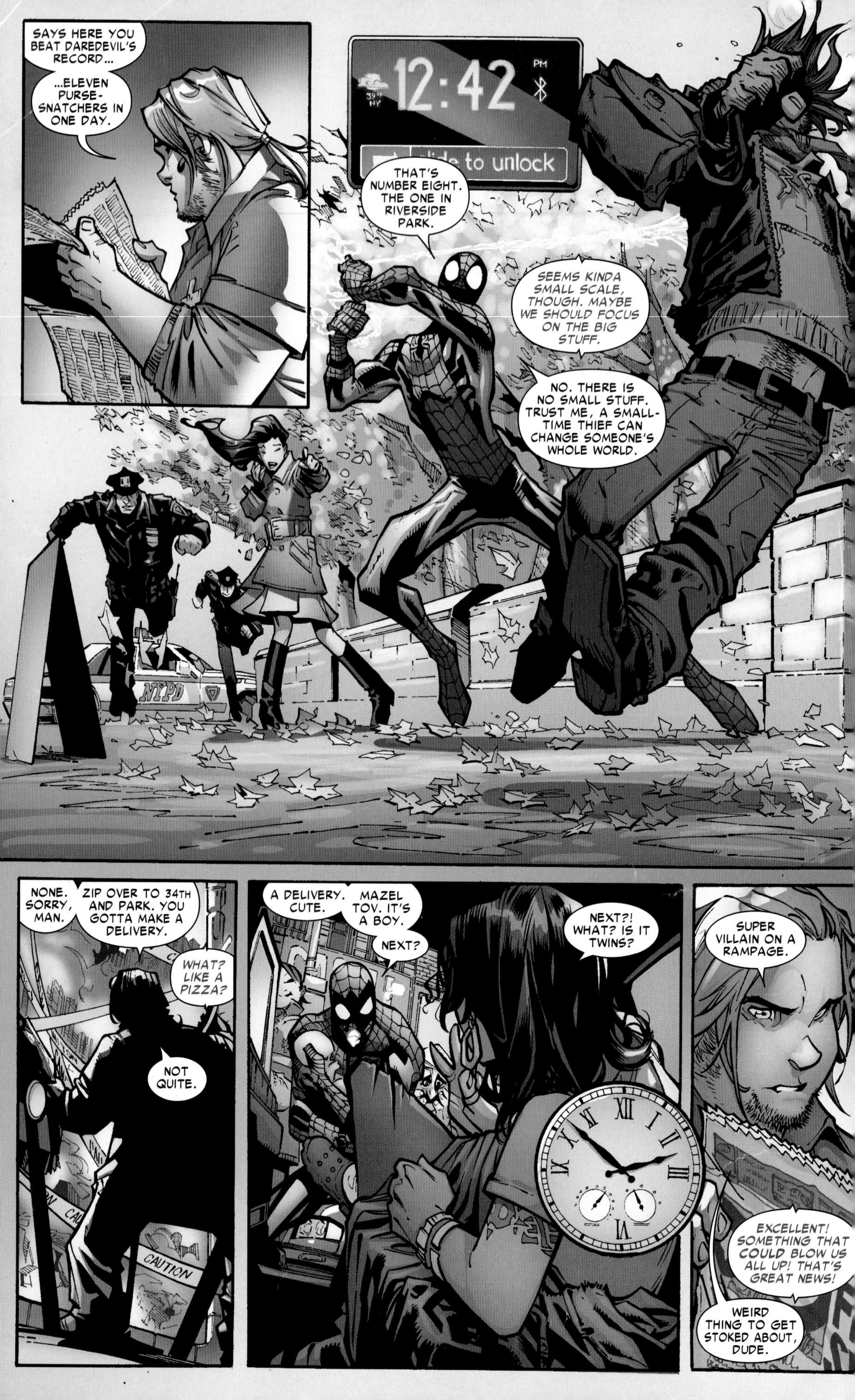
SAYS HERE YOU BEAT DAREDEVIL'S RECORD...
...ELEVEN PURSE-SNATCHERS IN ONE DAY.
12:42
PM
39° NY
slide to unlock
THAT'S NUMBER EIGHT. THE ONE IN RIVERSIDE PARK.
SEEMS KINDA SMALL SCALE, THOUGH. MAYBE WE SHOULD FOCUS ON THE BIG STUFF.
NO. THERE IS NO SMALL STUFF. TRUST ME, A SMALL-TIME THIEF CAN CHANGE SOMEONE'S WHOLE WORLD.
NYPD
NONE. SORRY, MAN.
ZIP OVER TO 34TH AND PARK. YOU GOTTA MAKE A DELIVERY.
WHAT? LIKE A PIZZA?
NOT QUITE.
CAUTION
A DELIVERY. CUTE.
MAZEL TOV. IT'S A BOY.
NEXT?
NEXT?! WHAT? IS IT TWINS?
SUPER VILLAIN ON A RAMPAGE.
EXCELLENT! SOMETHING THAT COULD BLOW US ALL UP! THAT'S GREAT NEWS!
WEIRD THING TO GET STOKED ABOUT, DUDE.

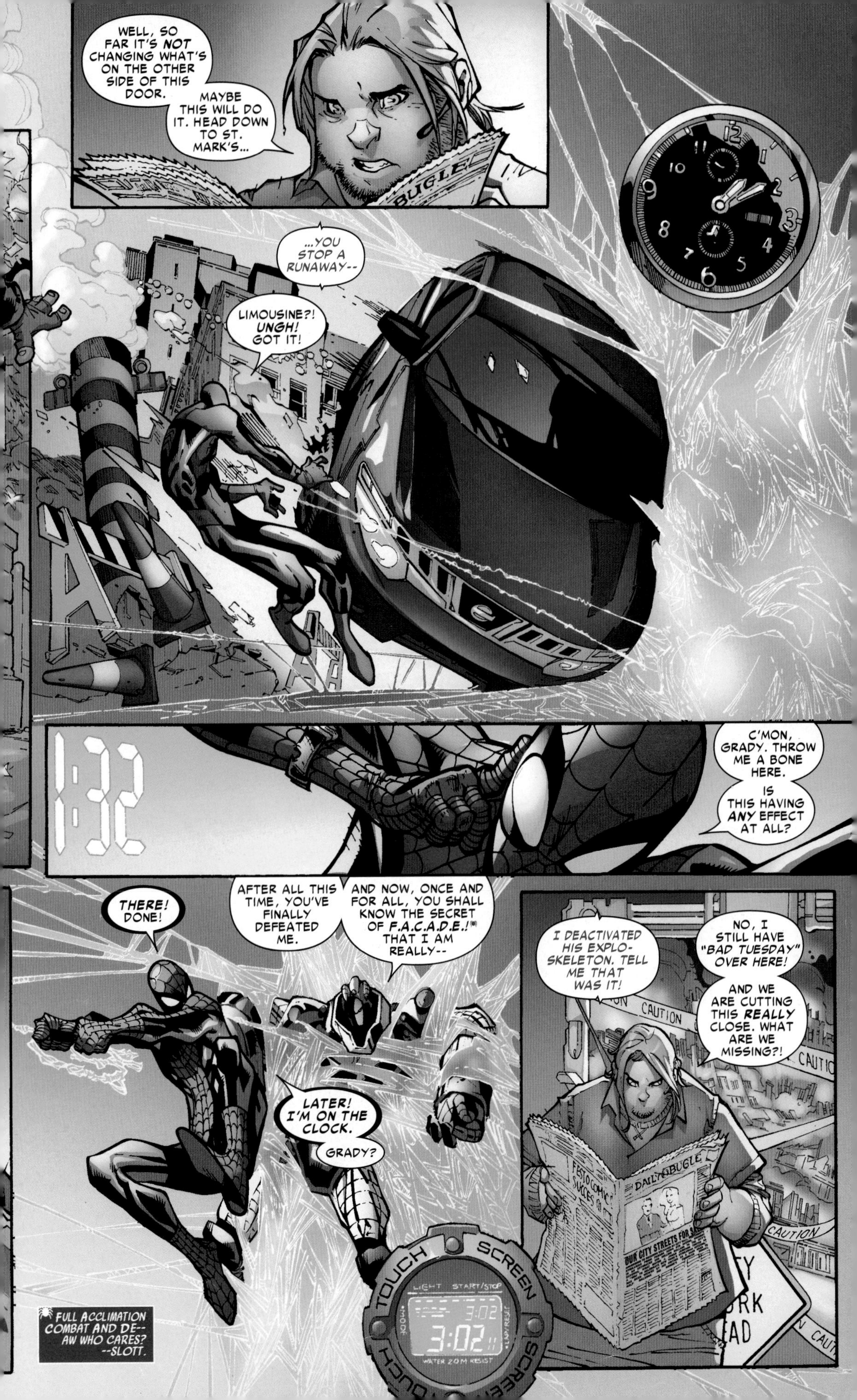

WELL, SO FAR IT'S NOT CHANGING WHAT'S ON THE OTHER SIDE OF THIS DOOR.
MAYBE THIS WILL DO IT. HEAD DOWN TO ST. MARK'S...
BUGLE
...YOU STOP A RUNAWAY--
LIMOUSINE?! UNGH! GOT IT!
1:32
C'MON, GRADY. THROW ME A BONE HERE.
IS THIS HAVING ANY EFFECT AT ALL?
THERE! DONE!
AFTER ALL THIS TIME, YOU'VE FINALLY DEFEATED ME.
AND NOW, ONCE AND FOR ALL, YOU SHALL KNOW THE SECRET OF F.A.C.A.D.E.!* THAT I AM REALLY--
LATER! I'M ON THE CLOCK.
GRADY?
I DEACTIVATED HIS EXPLO-SKELETON. TELL ME THAT WAS IT!
NO, I STILL HAVE "BAD TUESDAY" OVER HERE!
AND WE ARE CUTTING THIS REALLY CLOSE. WHAT ARE WE MISSING?!
CAUTION
DAILY BUGLE
OUR CITY STREETS FOR SALE
TOUCH SCREEN
LIGHT START/STOP
3:02
WATER 20M RESIST
*FULL ACCLIMATION COMBAT AND DE-- AW WHO CARES? --SLOTT.

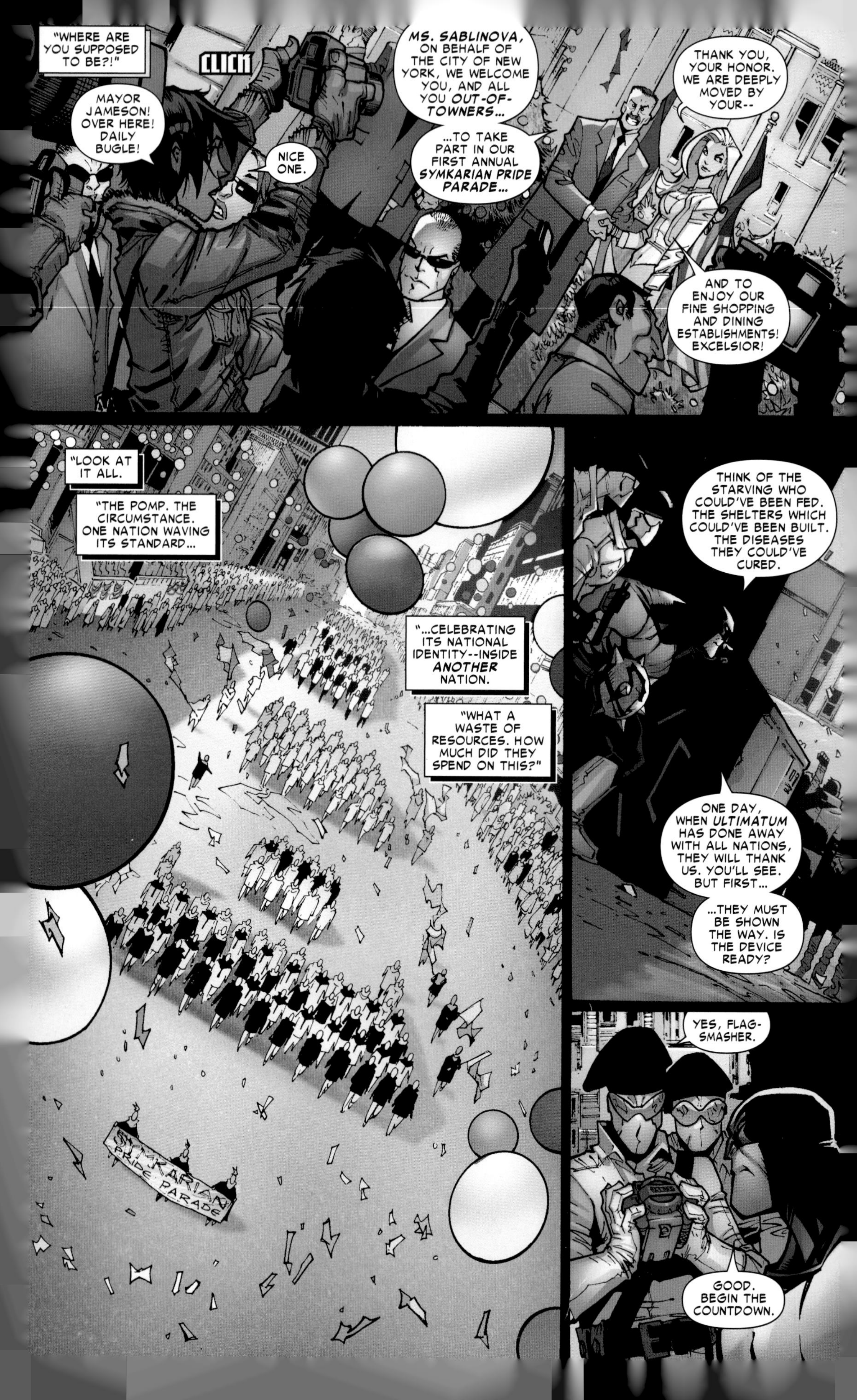
"WHERE ARE YOU SUPPOSED TO BE?!"
CLICK
MAYOR JAMESON! OVER HERE! DAILY BUGLE!
NICE ONE.
MS. SABLINOVA, ON BEHALF OF THE CITY OF NEW YORK, WE WELCOME YOU, AND ALL YOU OUT-OF-TOWNERS...
...TO TAKE PART IN OUR FIRST ANNUAL SYMKARIAN PRIDE PARADE...
THANK YOU, YOUR HONOR. WE ARE DEEPLY MOVED BY YOUR--
AND TO ENJOY OUR FINE SHOPPING AND DINING ESTABLISHMENTS! EXCELSIOR!
"LOOK AT IT ALL.
"THE POMP. THE CIRCUMSTANCE. ONE NATION WAVING ITS STANDARD...
"...CELEBRATING ITS NATIONAL IDENTITY--INSIDE ANOTHER NATION.
"WHAT A WASTE OF RESOURCES. HOW MUCH DID THEY SPEND ON THIS?"
SYMKARIAN PRIDE PARADE
THINK OF THE STARVING WHO COULD'VE BEEN FED. THE SHELTERS WHICH COULD'VE BEEN BUILT. THE DISEASES THEY COULD'VE CURED.
ONE DAY, WHEN ULTIMATUM HAS DONE AWAY WITH ALL NATIONS, THEY WILL THANK US. YOU'LL SEE. BUT FIRST...
...THEY MUST BE SHOWN THE WAY. IS THE DEVICE READY?
YES, FLAG-SMASHER.
GOOD. BEGIN THE COUNTDOWN.

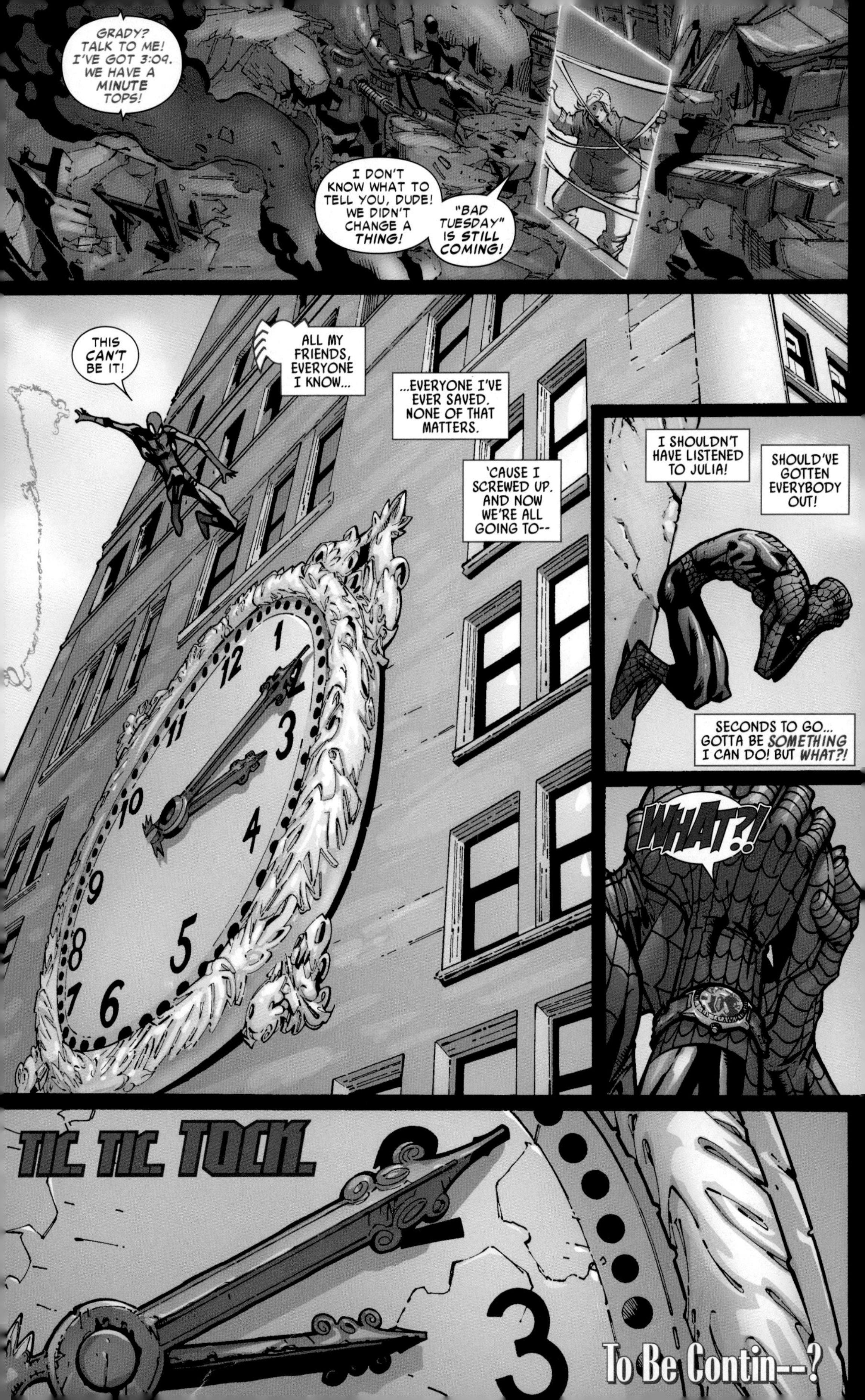
GRADY? TALK TO ME! I'VE GOT 3:09. WE HAVE A MINUTE TOPS!
I DON'T KNOW WHAT TO TELL YOU, DUDE! WE DIDN'T CHANGE A THING!
"BAD TUESDAY" IS STILL COMING!
THIS CAN'T BE IT!
ALL MY FRIENDS, EVERYONE I KNOW...
...EVERYONE I'VE EVER SAVED. NONE OF THAT MATTERS.
'CAUSE I SCREWED UP. AND NOW WE'RE ALL GOING TO--
I SHOULDN'T HAVE LISTENED TO JULIA!
SHOULD'VE GOTTEN EVERYBODY OUT!
SECONDS TO GO... GOTTA BE SOMETHING I CAN DO! BUT WHAT?!
WHAT?!
TIC. TIC. TOCK.
To Be Contin--?

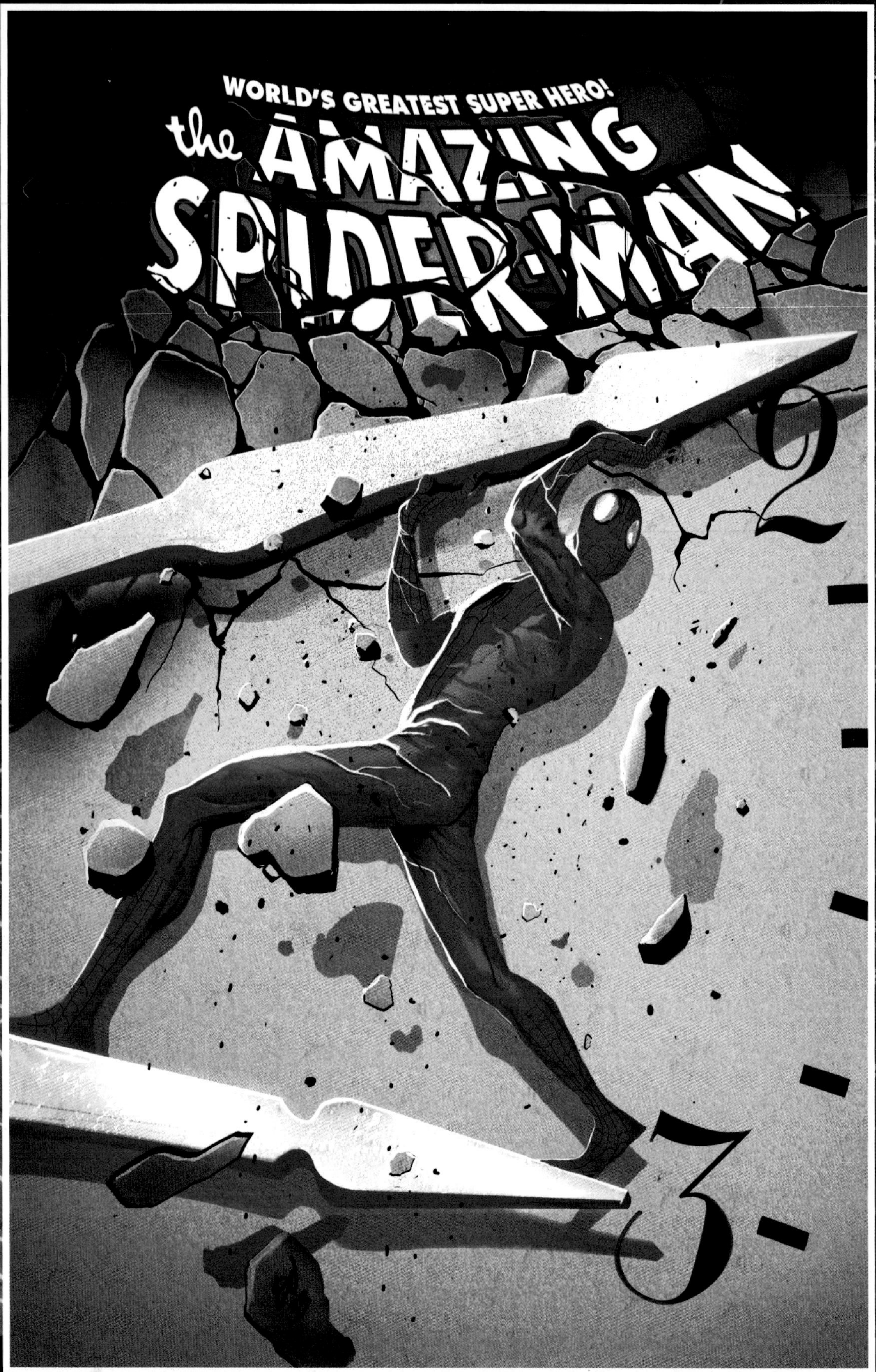
WORLD'S GREATEST SUPER HERO!
the AMAZING SPIDER-MAN

AMAZING SPIDER-MAN #679
COVER BY MICHAEL DEL MUNDO

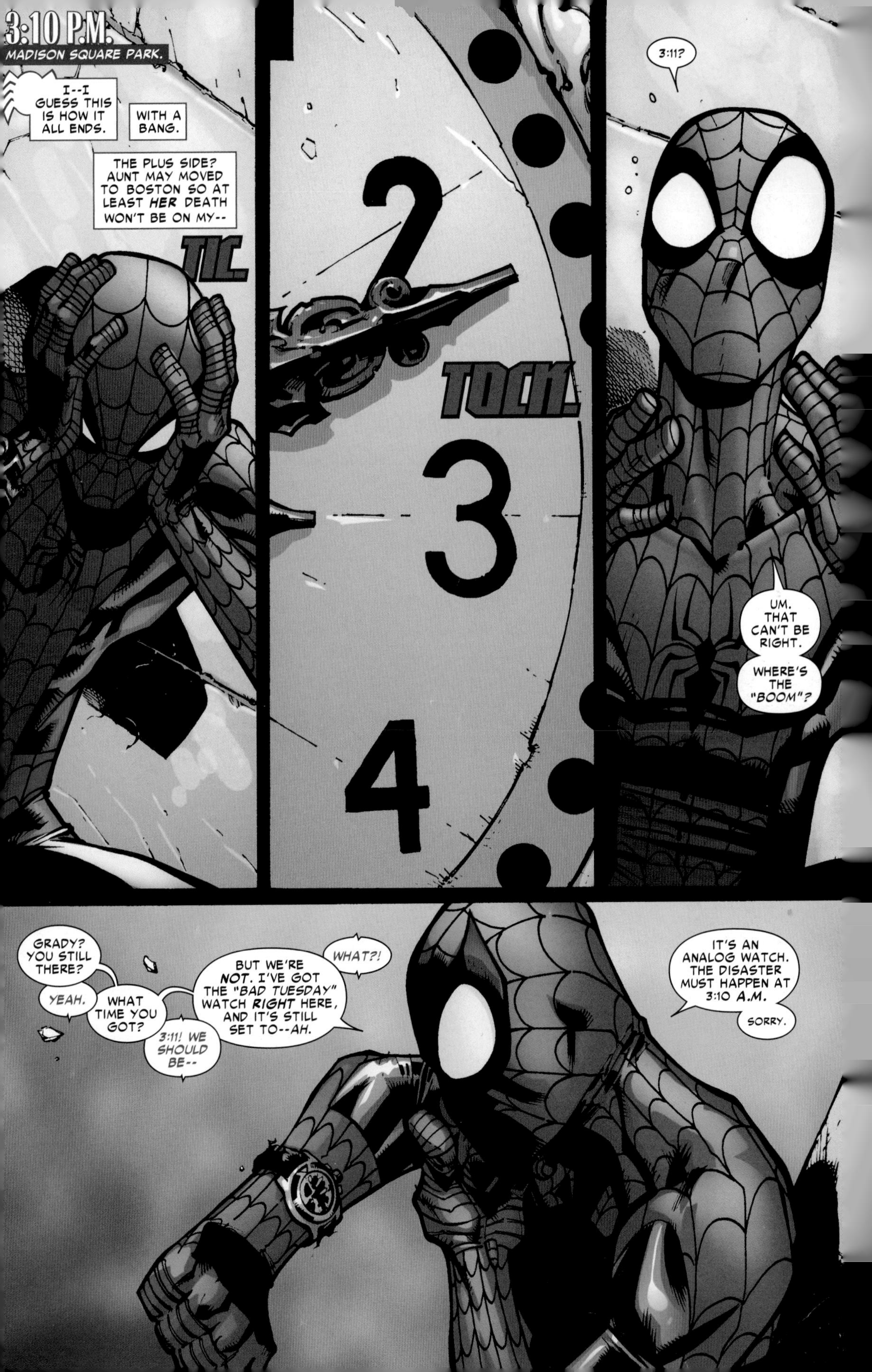
3:10 P.M.
MADISON SQUARE PARK.
I--I GUESS THIS IS HOW IT ALL ENDS.
WITH A BANG.
THE PLUS SIDE? AUNT MAY MOVED TO BOSTON SO AT LEAST HER DEATH WON'T BE ON MY--
TIC.
TOCK.
3:11?
UM. THAT CAN'T BE RIGHT.
WHERE'S THE "BOOM"?
GRADY? YOU STILL THERE?
YEAH.
WHAT TIME YOU GOT?
3:11! WE SHOULD BE--
BUT WE'RE NOT. I'VE GOT THE "BAD TUESDAY" WATCH RIGHT HERE, AND IT'S STILL SET TO--AH.
WHAT?!
IT'S AN ANALOG WATCH. THE DISASTER MUST HAPPEN AT 3:10 A.M.
SORRY.

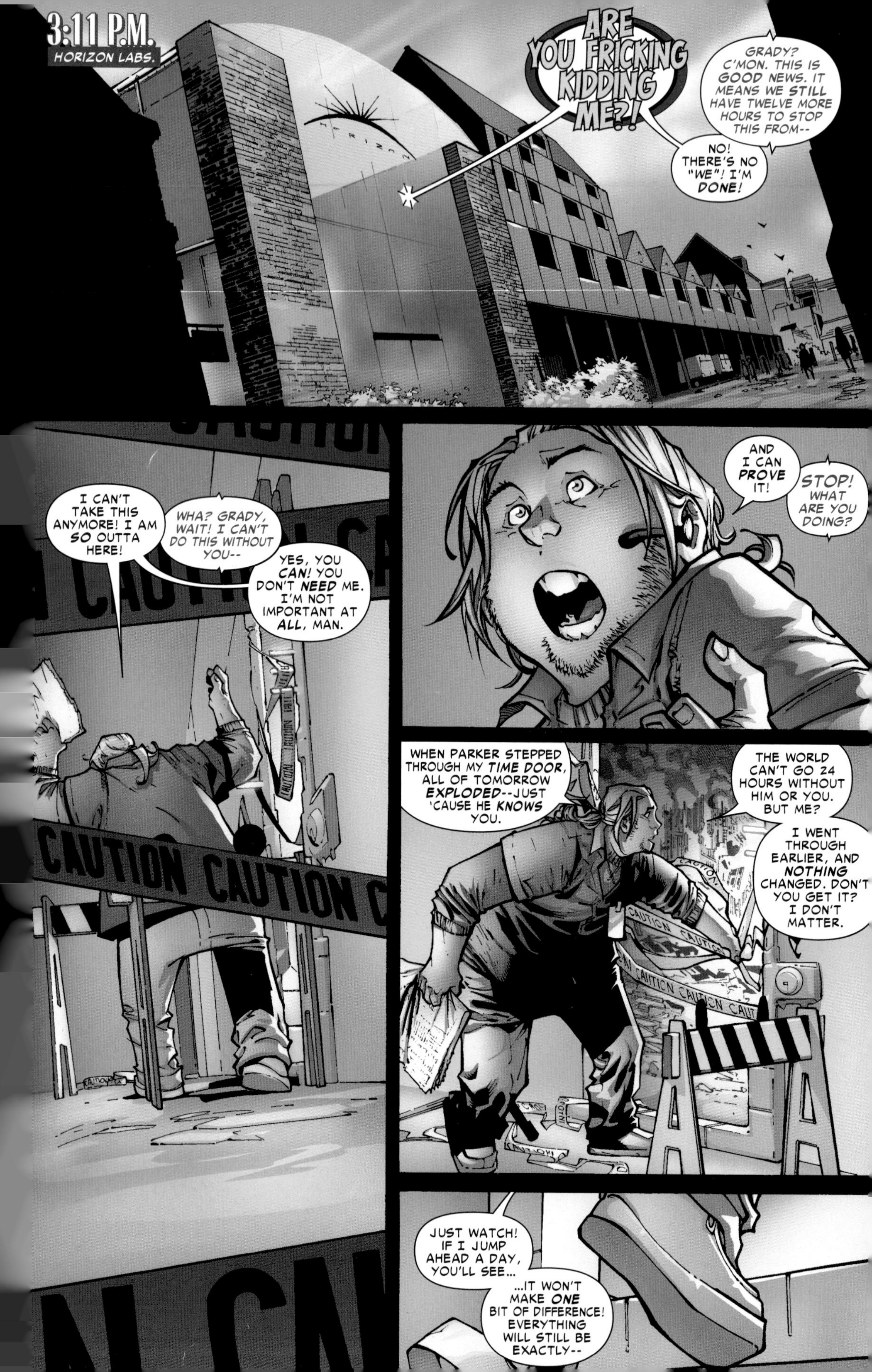
3:11 P.M.
HORIZON LABS.
HORIZON
ARE YOU FRICKING KIDDING ME?!
GRADY? C'MON. THIS IS GOOD NEWS. IT MEANS WE STILL HAVE TWELVE MORE HOURS TO STOP THIS FROM--
NO! THERE'S NO "WE"! I'M DONE!
I CAN'T TAKE THIS ANYMORE! I AM SO OUTTA HERE!
WHA? GRADY, WAIT! I CAN'T DO THIS WITHOUT YOU--
YES, YOU CAN! YOU DON'T NEED ME. I'M NOT IMPORTANT AT ALL, MAN.
CAUTION CAUTION
AND I CAN PROVE IT!
STOP! WHAT ARE YOU DOING?
WHEN PARKER STEPPED THROUGH MY TIME DOOR, ALL OF TOMORROW EXPLODED--JUST 'CAUSE HE KNOWS YOU.
THE WORLD CAN'T GO 24 HOURS WITHOUT HIM OR YOU. BUT ME?
I WENT THROUGH EARLIER, AND NOTHING CHANGED. DON'T YOU GET IT? I DON'T MATTER.
JUST WATCH! IF I JUMP AHEAD A DAY, YOU'LL SEE...
...IT WON'T MAKE ONE BIT OF DIFFERENCE! EVERYTHING WILL STILL BE EXACTLY--

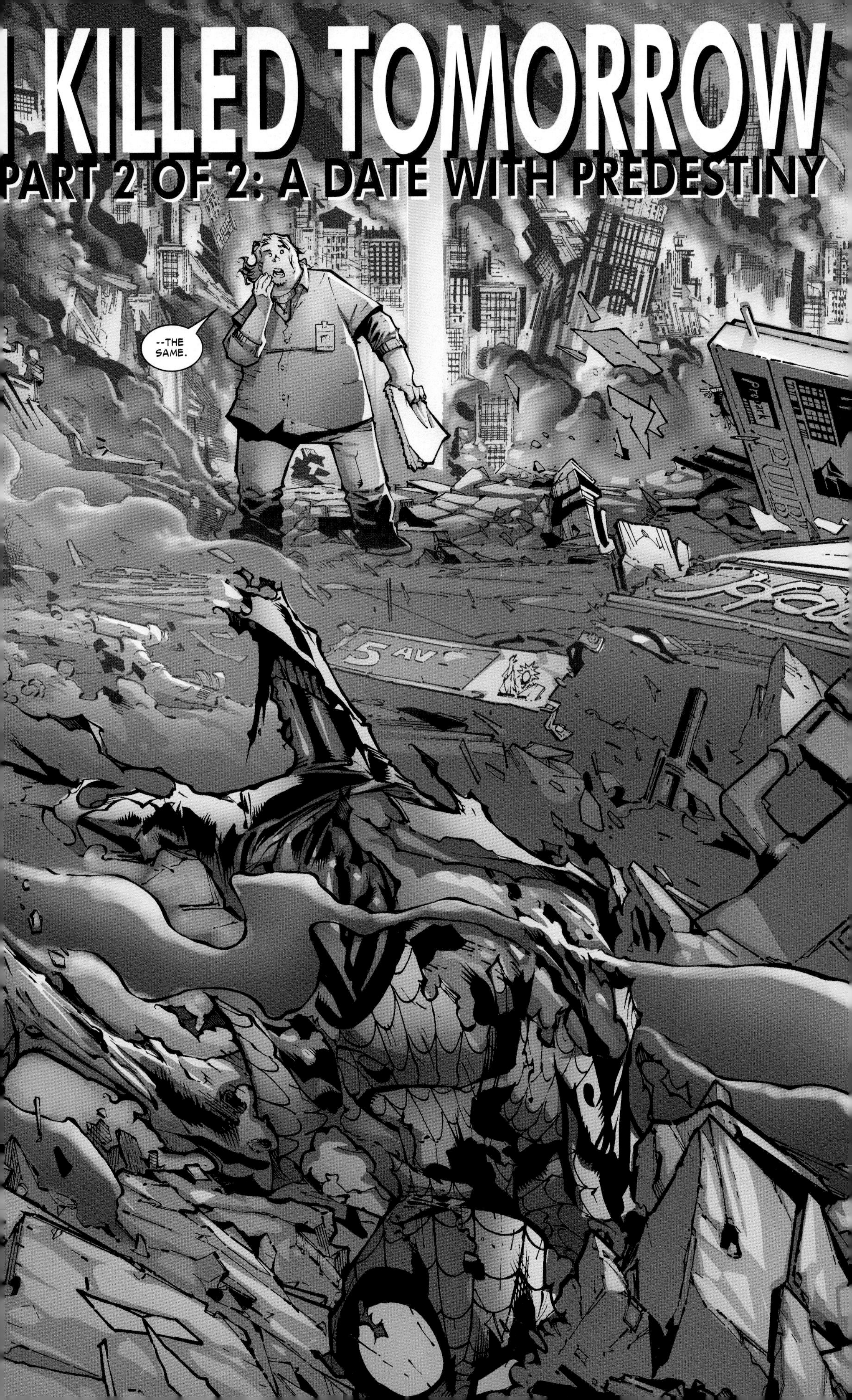
I KILLED TOMORROW
PART 2 OF 2: A DATE WITH PREDESTINY
--THE SAME.
5 AV

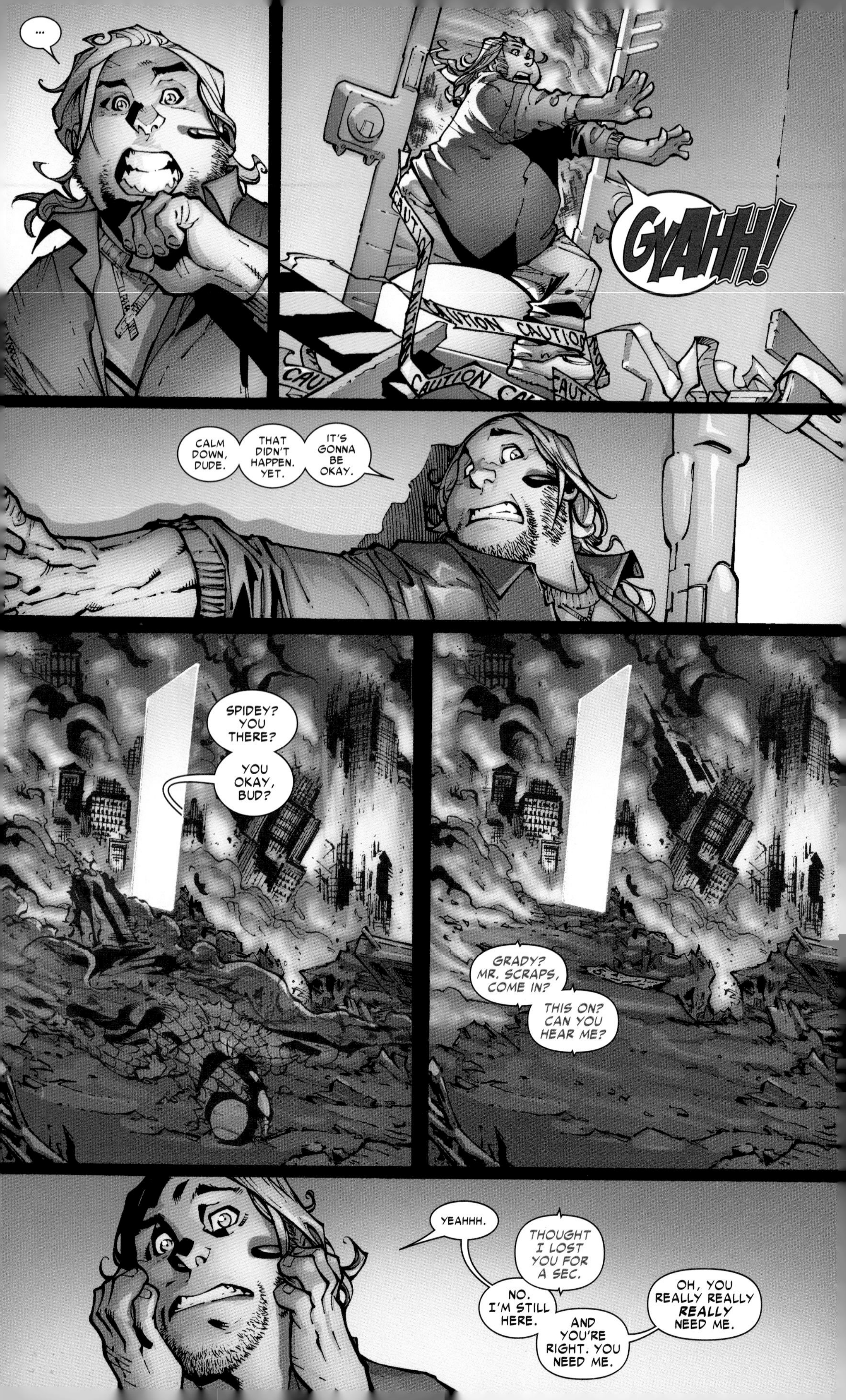
...
GYAHH!
CAUTION
CALM DOWN, DUDE.
THAT DIDN'T HAPPEN. YET.
IT'S GONNA BE OKAY.
SPIDEY? YOU THERE?
YOU OKAY, BUD?
GRADY? MR. SCRAPS, COME IN?
THIS ON? CAN YOU HEAR ME?
YEAHHH.
THOUGHT I LOST YOU FOR A SEC.
NO. I'M STILL HERE.
AND YOU'RE RIGHT. YOU NEED ME.
OH, YOU REALLY REALLY REALLY NEED ME.

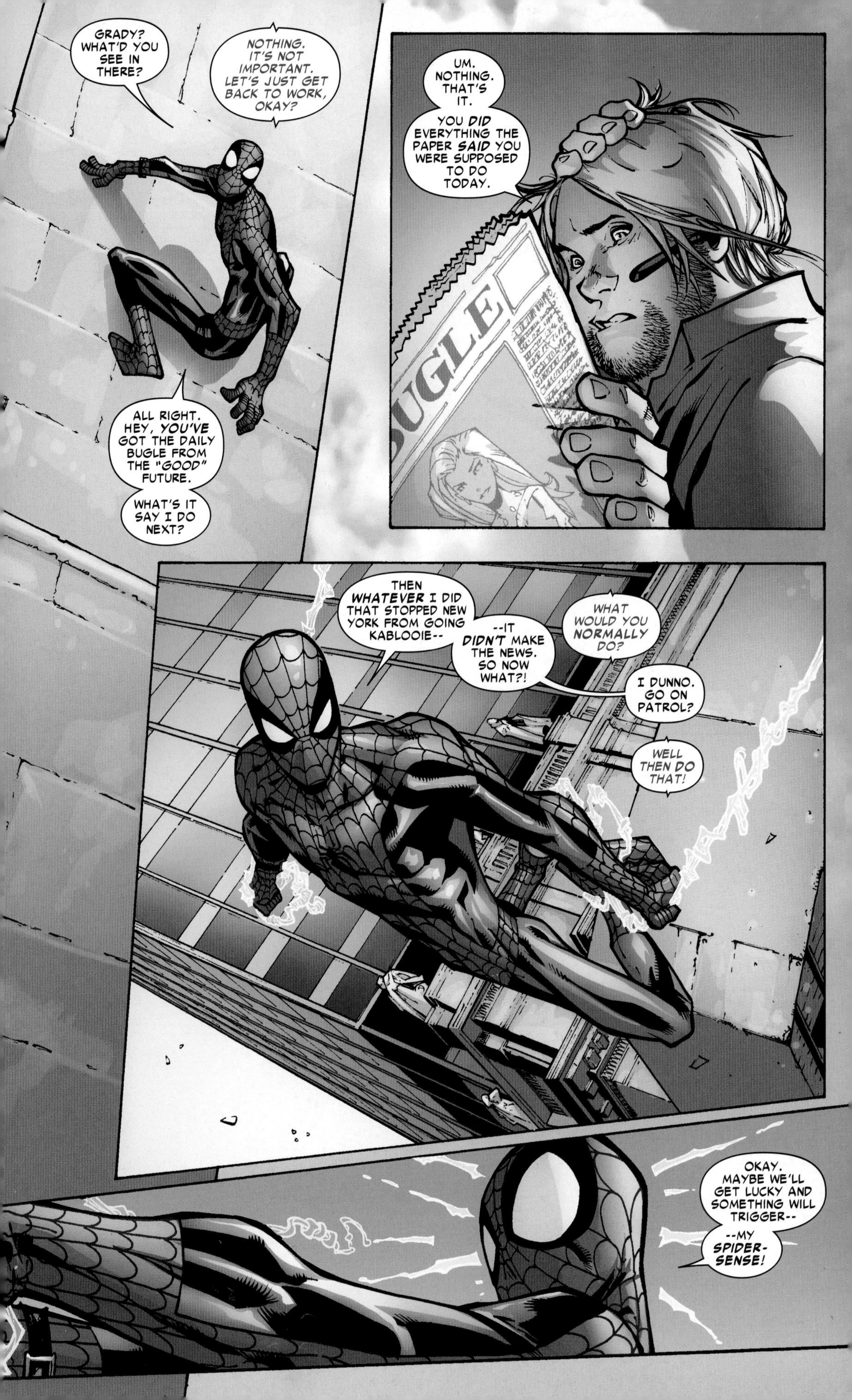
GRADY? WHAT'D YOU SEE IN THERE?
NOTHING. IT'S NOT IMPORTANT. LET'S JUST GET BACK TO WORK, OKAY?
ALL RIGHT. HEY, YOU'VE GOT THE DAILY BUGLE FROM THE "GOOD" FUTURE.
WHAT'S IT SAY I DO NEXT?
UM. NOTHING. THAT'S IT.
YOU DID EVERYTHING THE PAPER SAID YOU WERE SUPPOSED TO DO TODAY.
BUGLE
THEN WHATEVER I DID THAT STOPPED NEW YORK FROM GOING KABLOOIE--
--IT DIDN'T MAKE THE NEWS. SO NOW WHAT?!
WHAT WOULD YOU NORMALLY DO?
I DUNNO. GO ON PATROL?
WELL THEN DO THAT!
OKAY. MAYBE WE'LL GET LUCKY AND SOMETHING WILL TRIGGER--
--MY SPIDER-SENSE!

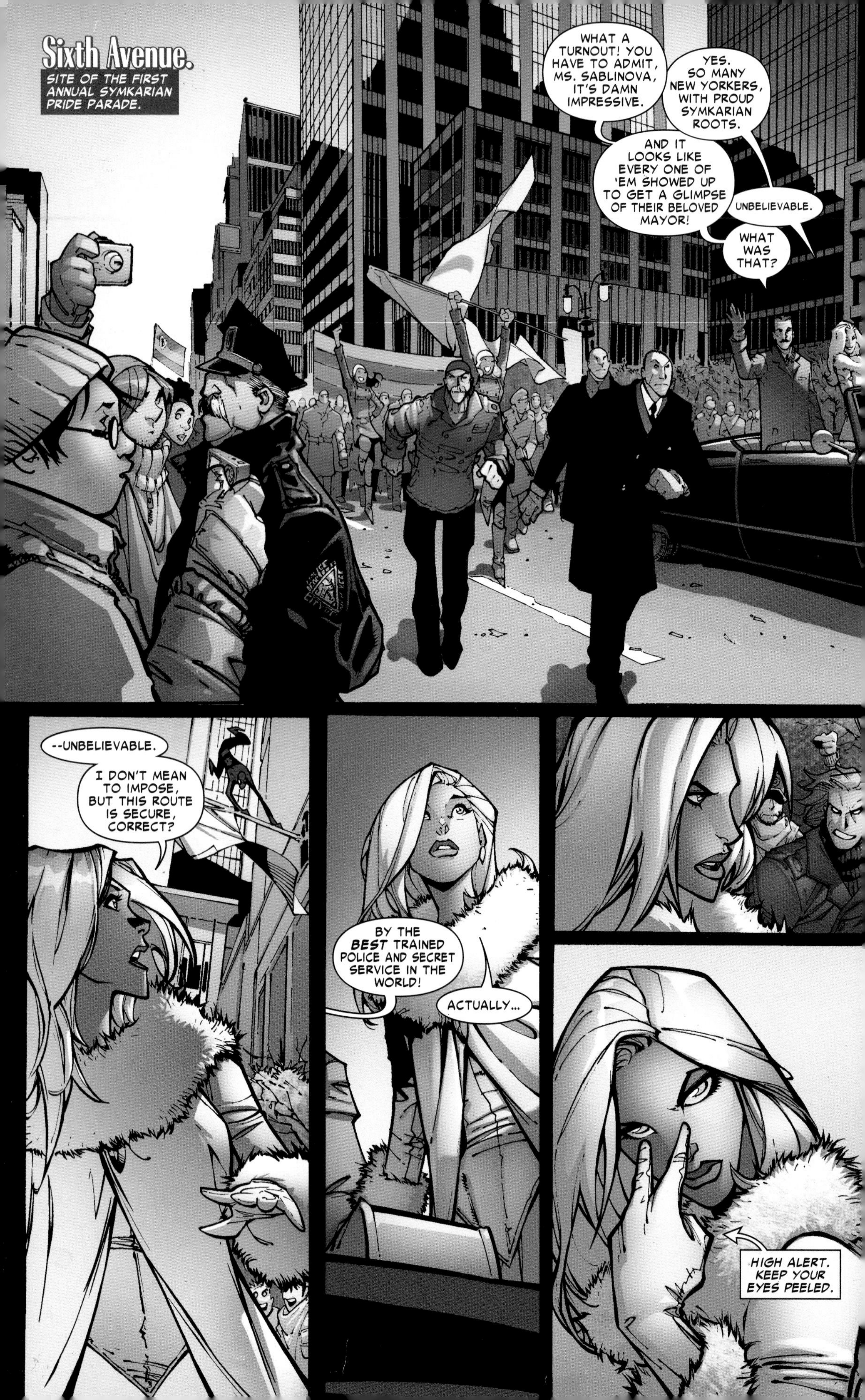
Sixth Avenue.
SITE OF THE FIRST ANNUAL SYMKARIAN PRIDE PARADE.
WHAT A TURNOUT! YOU HAVE TO ADMIT, MS. SABLINOVA, IT'S DAMN IMPRESSIVE.
YES. SO MANY NEW YORKERS, WITH PROUD SYMKARIAN ROOTS.
AND IT LOOKS LIKE EVERY ONE OF 'EM SHOWED UP TO GET A GLIMPSE OF THEIR BELOVED MAYOR!
UNBELIEVABLE.
WHAT WAS THAT?
--UNBELIEVABLE.
I DON'T MEAN TO IMPOSE, BUT THIS ROUTE IS SECURE, CORRECT?
BY THE BEST TRAINED POLICE AND SECRET SERVICE IN THE WORLD!
ACTUALLY...
HIGH ALERT. KEEP YOUR EYES PEELED.

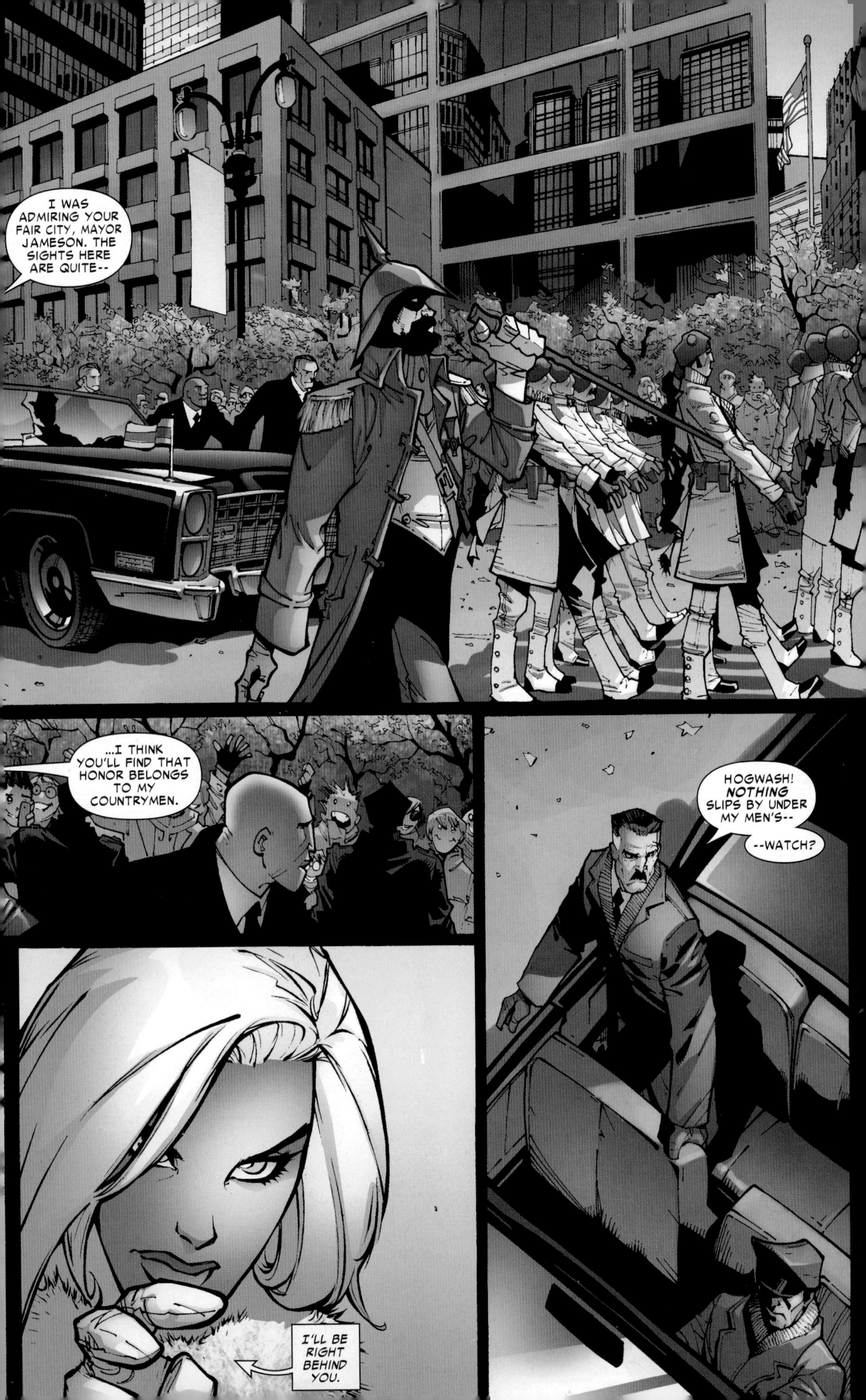
I WAS ADMIRING YOUR FAIR CITY, MAYOR JAMESON. THE SIGHTS HERE ARE QUITE--
...I THINK YOU'LL FIND THAT HONOR BELONGS TO MY COUNTRYMEN.
HOGWASH! NOTHING SLIPS BY UNDER MY MEN'S--
--WATCH?
I'LL BE RIGHT BEHIND YOU.

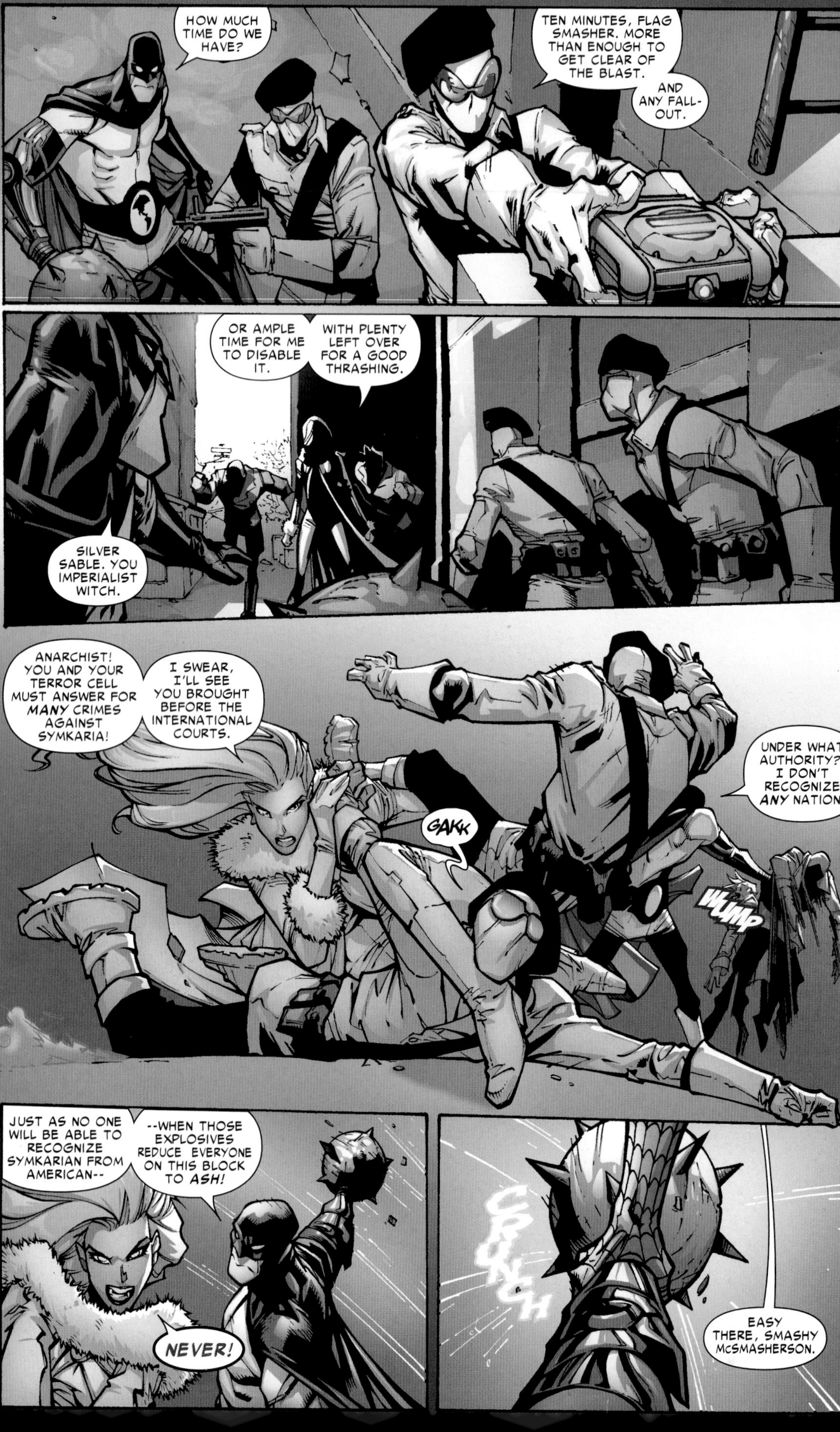

HOW MUCH TIME DO WE HAVE?
TEN MINUTES, FLAG SMASHER. MORE THAN ENOUGH TO GET CLEAR OF THE BLAST.
AND ANY FALL-OUT.
OR AMPLE TIME FOR ME TO DISABLE IT.
WITH PLENTY LEFT OVER FOR A GOOD THRASHING.
SILVER SABLE. YOU IMPERIALIST WITCH.
ANARCHIST! YOU AND YOUR TERROR CELL MUST ANSWER FOR *MANY* CRIMES AGAINST SYMKARIA!
I SWEAR, I'LL SEE YOU BROUGHT BEFORE THE INTERNATIONAL COURTS.
UNDER WHAT AUTHORITY?! I DON'T RECOGNIZE *ANY* NATION!
GAKK
WUMP
JUST AS NO ONE WILL BE ABLE TO RECOGNIZE SYMKARIAN FROM AMERICAN--
--WHEN THOSE EXPLOSIVES REDUCE EVERYONE ON THIS BLOCK TO *ASH!*
NEVER!
CRUNCH
EASY THERE, SMASHY McSMASHERSON.

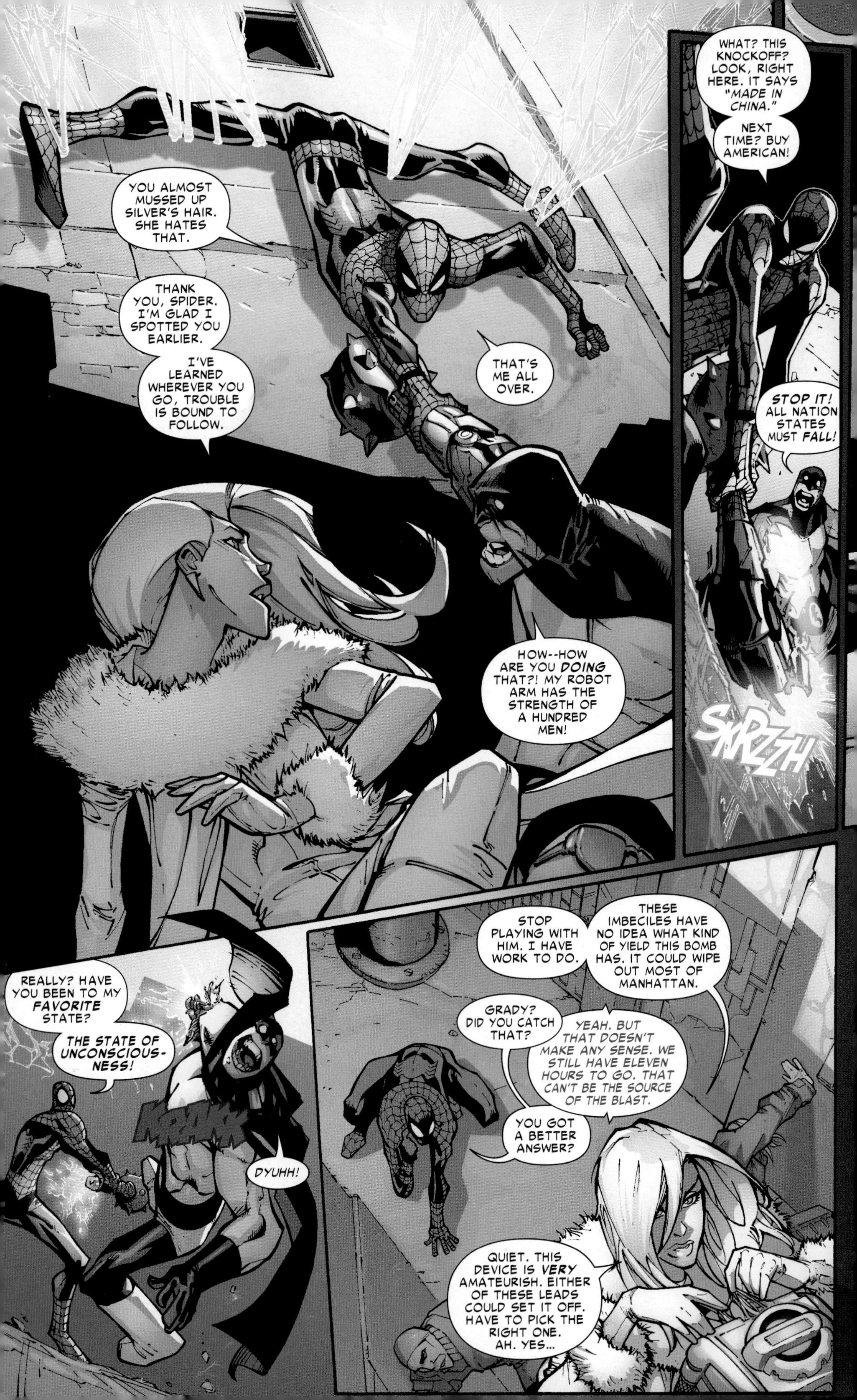
YOU ALMOST MUSSED UP SILVER'S HAIR. SHE HATES THAT.
THANK YOU, SPIDER. I'M GLAD I SPOTTED YOU EARLIER.
I'VE LEARNED WHEREVER YOU GO, TROUBLE IS BOUND TO FOLLOW.
THAT'S ME ALL OVER.
HOW--HOW ARE YOU DOING THAT?! MY ROBOT ARM HAS THE STRENGTH OF A HUNDRED MEN!
WHAT? THIS KNOCKOFF? LOOK, RIGHT HERE. IT SAYS "MADE IN CHINA."
NEXT TIME? BUY AMERICAN!
STOP IT! ALL NATION STATES MUST FALL!
SKRZZH
REALLY? HAVE YOU BEEN TO MY FAVORITE STATE?
THE STATE OF UNCONSCIOUS-NESS!
DYUHH!
STOP PLAYING WITH HIM. I HAVE WORK TO DO.
THESE IMBECILES HAVE NO IDEA WHAT KIND OF YIELD THIS BOMB HAS. IT COULD WIPE OUT MOST OF MANHATTAN.
GRADY? DID YOU CATCH THAT?
YEAH. BUT THAT DOESN'T MAKE ANY SENSE. WE STILL HAVE ELEVEN HOURS TO GO. THAT CAN'T BE THE SOURCE OF THE BLAST.
YOU GOT A BETTER ANSWER?
QUIET. THIS DEVICE IS VERY AMATEURISH. EITHER OF THESE LEADS COULD SET IT OFF. HAVE TO PICK THE RIGHT ONE. AH. YES...

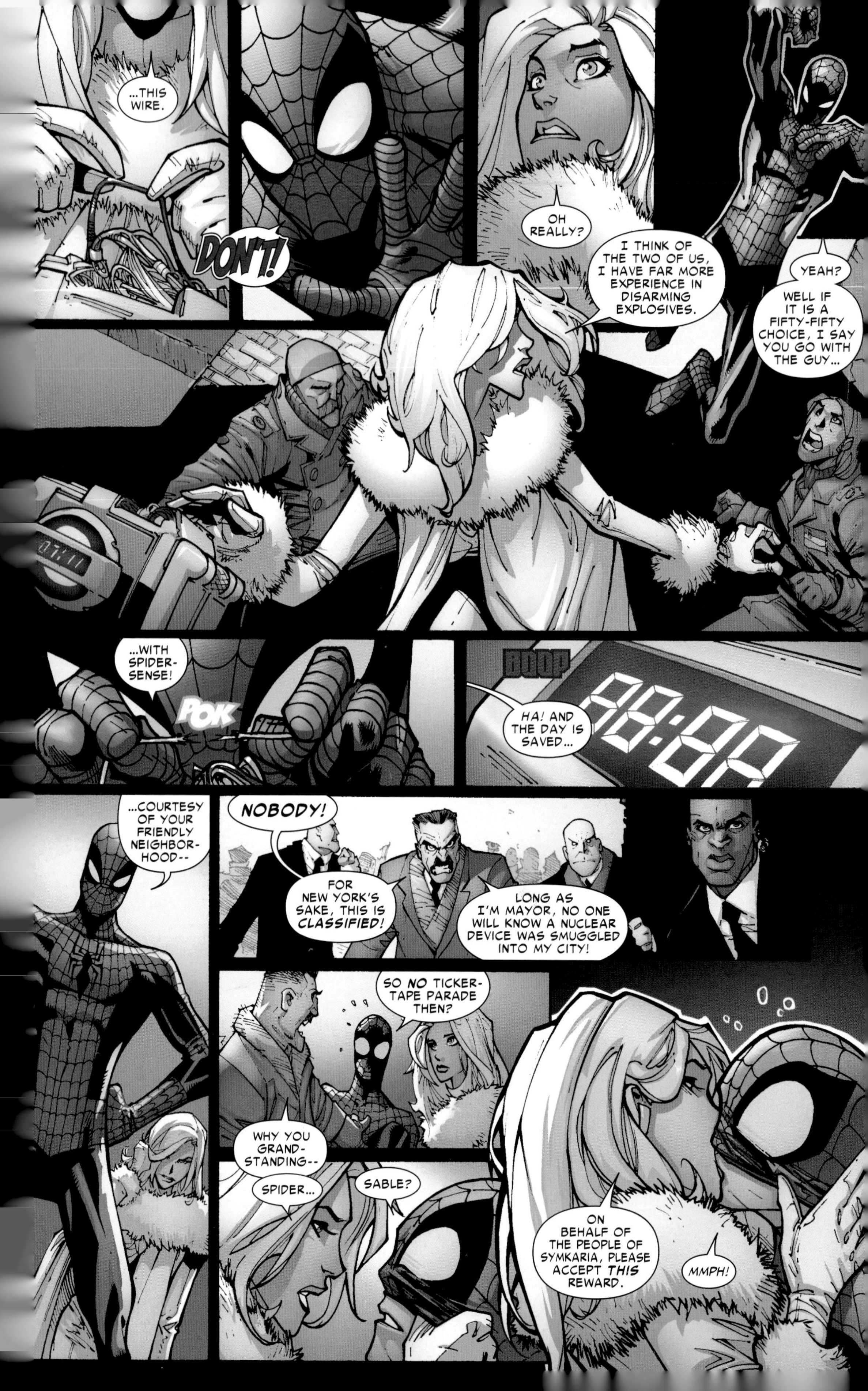
...THIS WIRE.
DON'T!
OH REALLY?
I THINK OF THE TWO OF US, I HAVE FAR MORE EXPERIENCE IN DISARMING EXPLOSIVES.
YEAH?
WELL IF IT IS A FIFTY-FIFTY CHOICE, I SAY YOU GO WITH THE GUY...
...WITH SPIDER-SENSE!
POK
BOOP
HA! AND THE DAY IS SAVED...
...COURTESY OF YOUR FRIENDLY NEIGHBOR-HOOD--
NOBODY!
FOR NEW YORK'S SAKE, THIS IS CLASSIFIED!
LONG AS I'M MAYOR, NO ONE WILL KNOW A NUCLEAR DEVICE WAS SMUGGLED INTO MY CITY!
SO NO TICKER-TAPE PARADE THEN?
WHY YOU GRAND-STANDING--
SPIDER...
SABLE?
ON BEHALF OF THE PEOPLE OF SYMKARIA, PLEASE ACCEPT THIS REWARD.
MMPH!

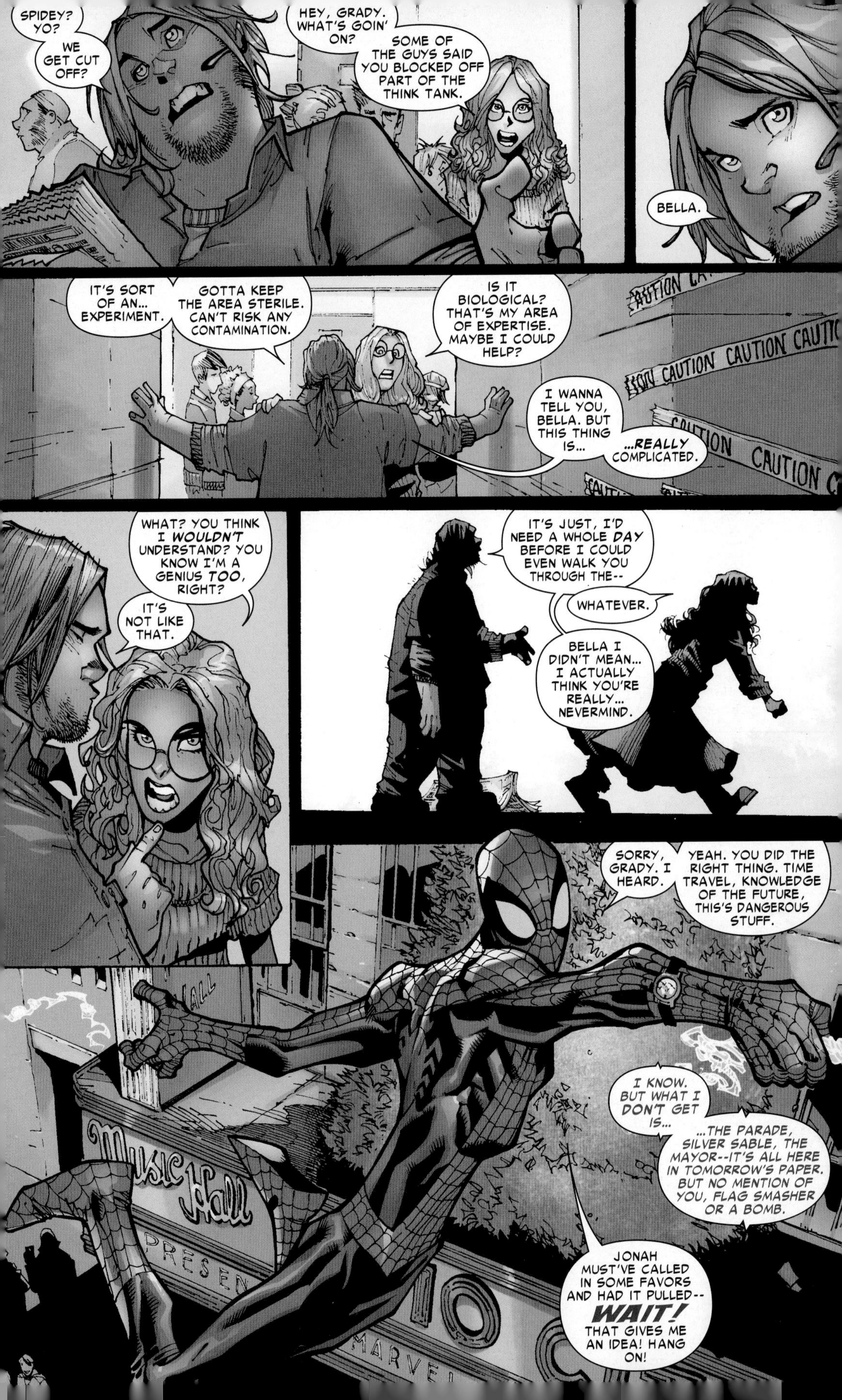

SPIDEY? YO?
WE GET CUT OFF?
HEY, GRADY. WHAT'S GOIN' ON?
SOME OF THE GUYS SAID YOU BLOCKED OFF PART OF THE THINK TANK.
BELLA.
IT'S SORT OF AN... EXPERIMENT.
GOTTA KEEP THE AREA STERILE. CAN'T RISK ANY CONTAMINATION.
IS IT BIOLOGICAL? THAT'S MY AREA OF EXPERTISE. MAYBE I COULD HELP?
CAUTION CAUTION CAUTION
I WANNA TELL YOU, BELLA. BUT THIS THING IS...
...REALLY COMPLICATED.
WHAT? YOU THINK I WOULDN'T UNDERSTAND? YOU KNOW I'M A GENIUS TOO, RIGHT?
IT'S NOT LIKE THAT.
IT'S JUST, I'D NEED A WHOLE DAY BEFORE I COULD EVEN WALK YOU THROUGH THE--
WHATEVER.
BELLA I DIDN'T MEAN... I ACTUALLY THINK YOU'RE REALLY... NEVERMIND.
SORRY, GRADY. I HEARD.
YEAH. YOU DID THE RIGHT THING. TIME TRAVEL, KNOWLEDGE OF THE FUTURE, THIS'S DANGEROUS STUFF.
I KNOW. BUT WHAT I DON'T GET IS...
...THE PARADE, SILVER SABLE, THE MAYOR--IT'S ALL HERE IN TOMORROW'S PAPER. BUT NO MENTION OF YOU, FLAG SMASHER OR A BOMB.
JONAH MUST'VE CALLED IN SOME FAVORS AND HAD IT PULLED-- WAIT! THAT GIVES ME AN IDEA! HANG ON!
Music Hall

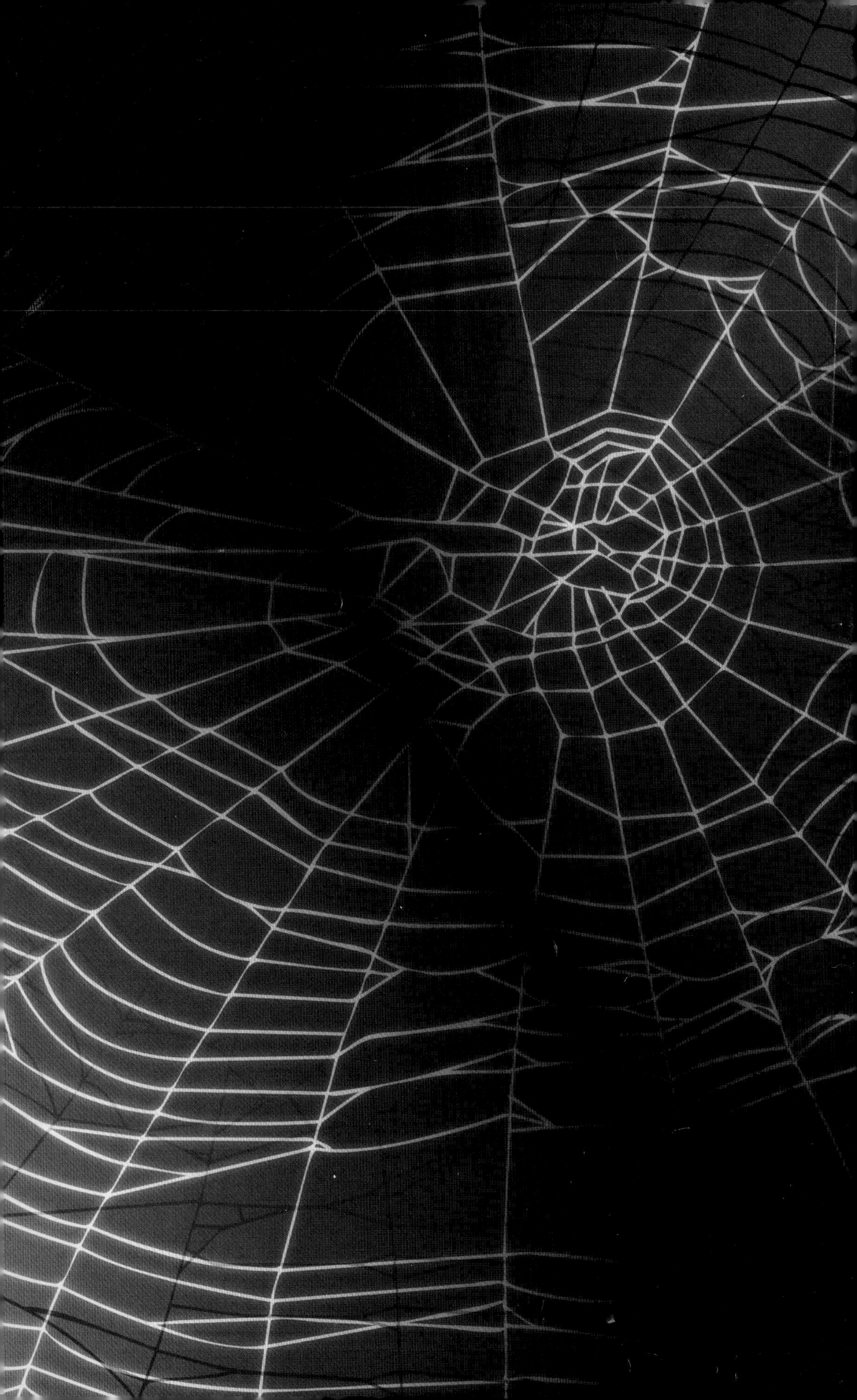

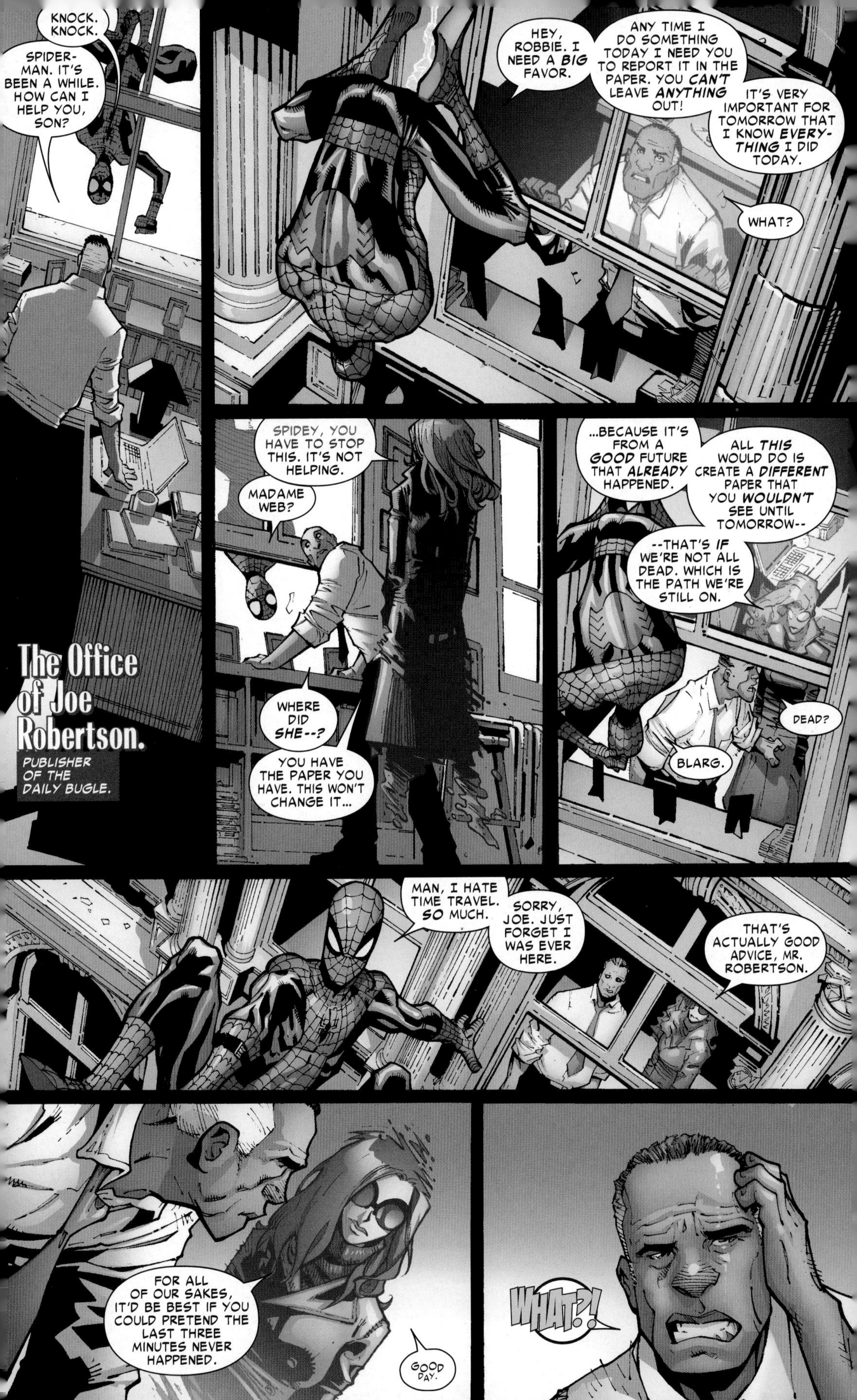

KNOCK. KNOCK.
SPIDER-MAN. IT'S BEEN A WHILE. HOW CAN I HELP YOU, SON?
HEY, ROBBIE. I NEED A BIG FAVOR.
ANY TIME I DO SOMETHING TODAY I NEED YOU TO REPORT IT IN THE PAPER. YOU CAN'T LEAVE ANYTHING OUT!
IT'S VERY IMPORTANT FOR TOMORROW THAT I KNOW EVERY-THING I DID TODAY.
WHAT?
The Office of Joe Robertson.
PUBLISHER OF THE DAILY BUGLE.
SPIDEY, YOU HAVE TO STOP THIS. IT'S NOT HELPING.
MADAME WEB?
WHERE DID SHE--?
YOU HAVE THE PAPER YOU HAVE. THIS WON'T CHANGE IT...
...BECAUSE IT'S FROM A GOOD FUTURE THAT ALREADY HAPPENED.
ALL THIS WOULD DO IS CREATE A DIFFERENT PAPER THAT YOU WOULDN'T SEE UNTIL TOMORROW--
--THAT'S IF WE'RE NOT ALL DEAD. WHICH IS THE PATH WE'RE STILL ON.
DEAD?
BLARG.
MAN, I HATE TIME TRAVEL. SO MUCH.
SORRY, JOE. JUST FORGET I WAS EVER HERE.
THAT'S ACTUALLY GOOD ADVICE, MR. ROBERTSON.
FOR ALL OF OUR SAKES, IT'D BE BEST IF YOU COULD PRETEND THE LAST THREE MINUTES NEVER HAPPENED.
GOOD DAY.
WHAT?!

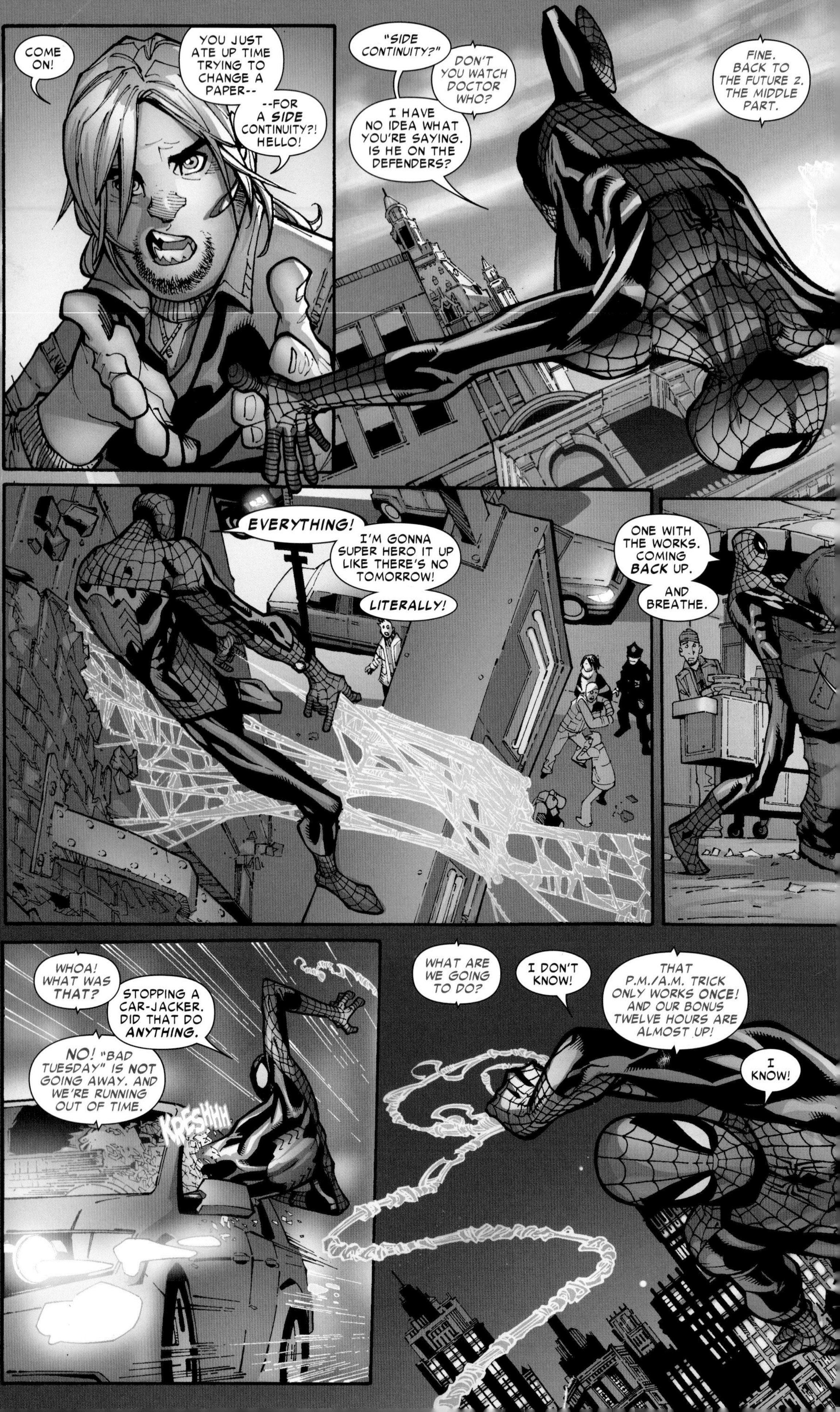
COME ON!
YOU JUST ATE UP TIME TRYING TO CHANGE A PAPER--
--FOR A SIDE CONTINUITY?! HELLO!
"SIDE CONTINUITY?"
DON'T YOU WATCH DOCTOR WHO?
I HAVE NO IDEA WHAT YOU'RE SAYING. IS HE ON THE DEFENDERS?
FINE. BACK TO THE FUTURE 2. THE MIDDLE PART.
EVERYTHING!
I'M GONNA SUPER HERO IT UP LIKE THERE'S NO TOMORROW!
LITERALLY!
ONE WITH THE WORKS. COMING BACK UP.
AND BREATHE.
WHOA! WHAT WAS THAT?
STOPPING A CAR-JACKER. DID THAT DO ANYTHING.
NO! "BAD TUESDAY" IS NOT GOING AWAY. AND WE'RE RUNNING OUT OF TIME.
KRESHHH
WHAT ARE WE GOING TO DO?
I DON'T KNOW!
THAT P.M./A.M. TRICK ONLY WORKS ONCE! AND OUR BONUS TWELVE HOURS ARE ALMOST UP!
I KNOW!

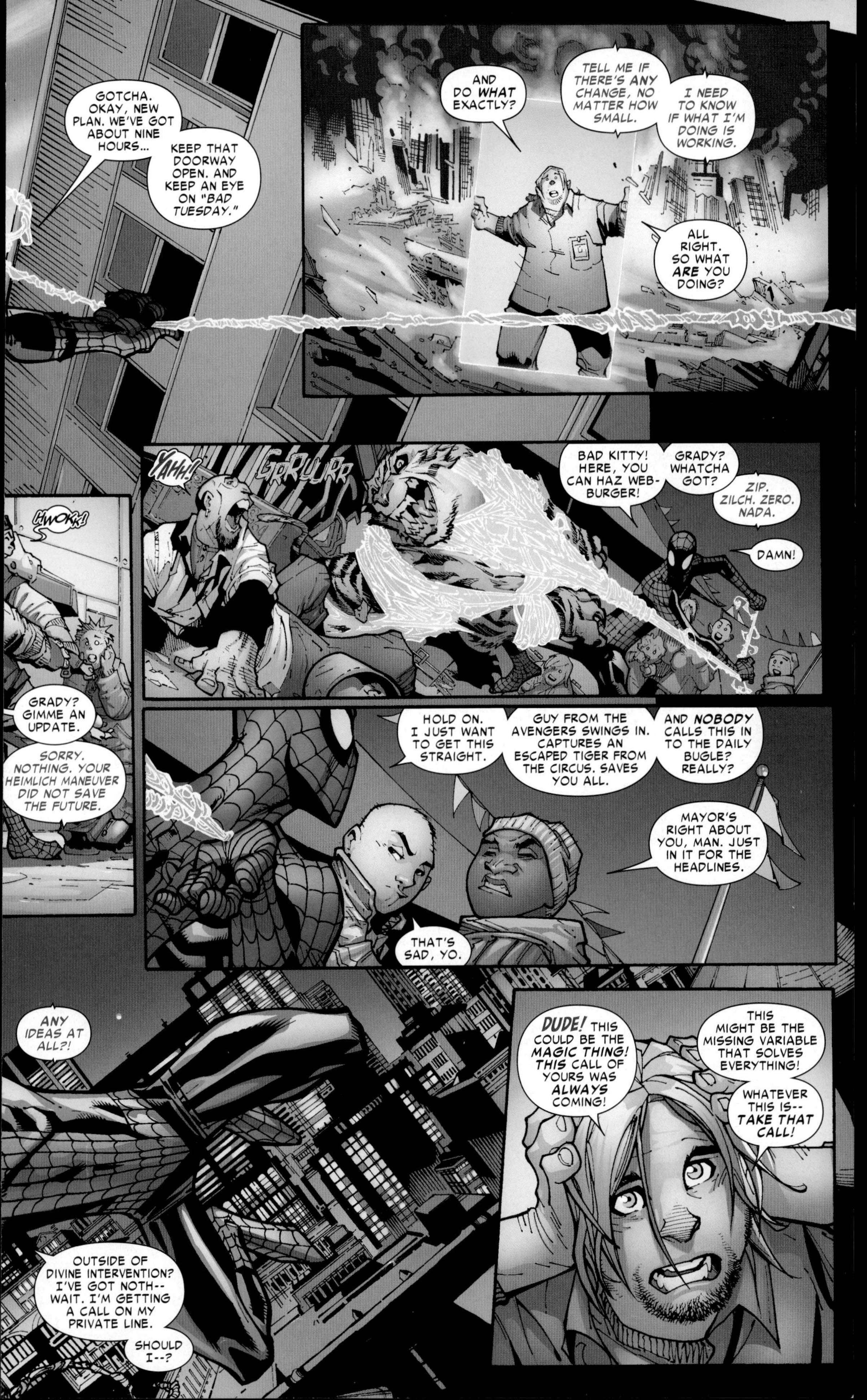
GOTCHA. OKAY, NEW PLAN. WE'VE GOT ABOUT NINE HOURS...
KEEP THAT DOORWAY OPEN. AND KEEP AN EYE ON "BAD TUESDAY."
AND DO WHAT EXACTLY?
TELL ME IF THERE'S ANY CHANGE, NO MATTER HOW SMALL.
I NEED TO KNOW IF WHAT I'M DOING IS WORKING.
ALL RIGHT. SO WHAT ARE YOU DOING?
HWOKK!
YAHH!
GRRUURR
BAD KITTY! HERE, YOU CAN HAZ WEB-BURGER!
GRADY? WHATCHA GOT?
ZIP. ZILCH. ZERO. NADA.
DAMN!
GRADY? GIMME AN UPDATE.
SORRY. NOTHING. YOUR HEIMLICH MANEUVER DID NOT SAVE THE FUTURE.
HOLD ON. I JUST WANT TO GET THIS STRAIGHT.
GUY FROM THE AVENGERS SWINGS IN. CAPTURES AN ESCAPED TIGER FROM THE CIRCUS. SAVES YOU ALL.
AND NOBODY CALLS THIS IN TO THE DAILY BUGLE? REALLY?
MAYOR'S RIGHT ABOUT YOU, MAN. JUST IN IT FOR THE HEADLINES.
THAT'S SAD, YO.
ANY IDEAS AT ALL?!
OUTSIDE OF DIVINE INTERVENTION? I'VE GOT NOTH-- WAIT. I'M GETTING A CALL ON MY PRIVATE LINE.
SHOULD I--?
DUDE! THIS COULD BE THE MAGIC THING! THIS CALL OF YOURS WAS ALWAYS COMING!
THIS MIGHT BE THE MISSING VARIABLE THAT SOLVES EVERYTHING!
WHATEVER THIS IS-- TAKE THAT CALL!

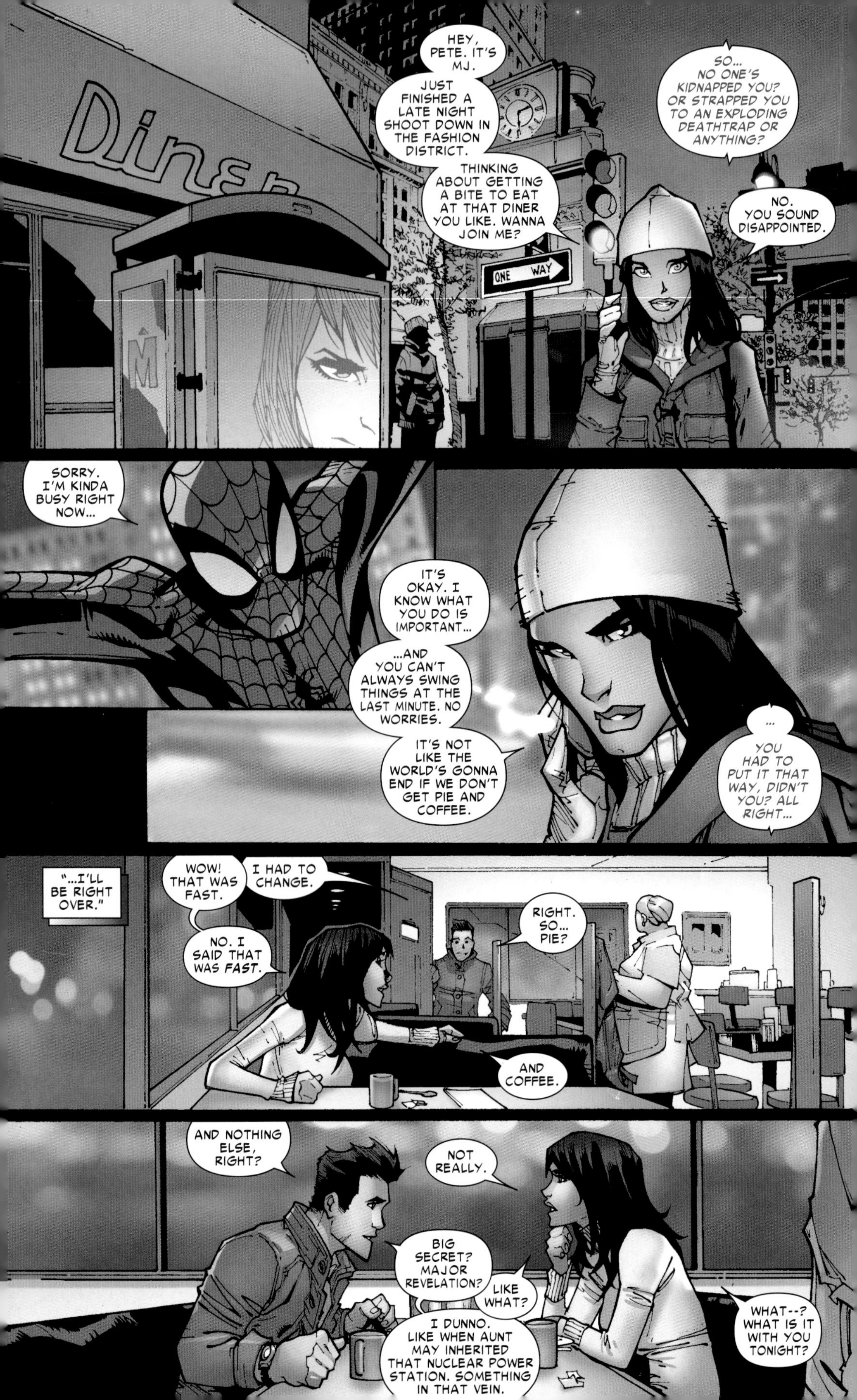

HEY, PETE. IT'S MJ.
JUST FINISHED A LATE NIGHT SHOOT DOWN IN THE FASHION DISTRICT.
THINKING ABOUT GETTING A BITE TO EAT AT THAT DINER YOU LIKE. WANNA JOIN ME?
SO... NO ONE'S KIDNAPPED YOU? OR STRAPPED YOU TO AN EXPLODING DEATHTRAP OR ANYTHING?
NO. YOU SOUND DISAPPOINTED.
Diner
ONE WAY
SORRY. I'M KINDA BUSY RIGHT NOW...
IT'S OKAY. I KNOW WHAT YOU DO IS IMPORTANT...
...AND YOU CAN'T ALWAYS SWING THINGS AT THE LAST MINUTE. NO WORRIES.
IT'S NOT LIKE THE WORLD'S GONNA END IF WE DON'T GET PIE AND COFFEE.
...
YOU HAD TO PUT IT THAT WAY, DIDN'T YOU? ALL RIGHT...
"...I'LL BE RIGHT OVER."
WOW! THAT WAS FAST.
I HAD TO CHANGE.
NO. I SAID THAT WAS FAST.
RIGHT. SO... PIE?
AND COFFEE.
AND NOTHING ELSE, RIGHT?
NOT REALLY.
BIG SECRET? MAJOR REVELATION?
LIKE WHAT?
I DUNNO. LIKE WHEN AUNT MAY INHERITED THAT NUCLEAR POWER STATION. SOMETHING IN THAT VEIN.
WHAT--? WHAT IS IT WITH YOU TONIGHT?

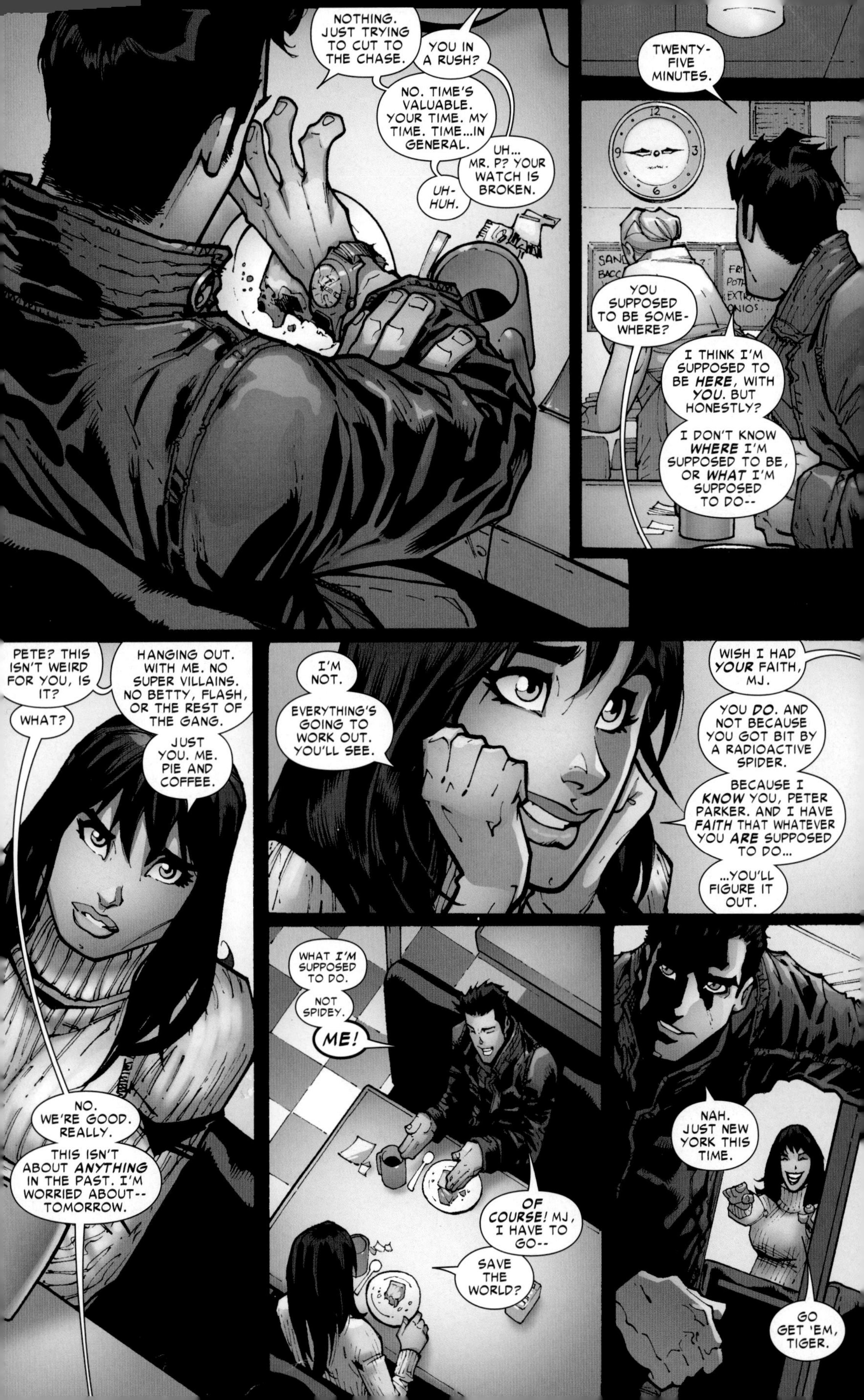

NOTHING. JUST TRYING TO CUT TO THE CHASE.
YOU IN A RUSH?
NO. TIME'S VALUABLE. YOUR TIME. MY TIME. TIME...IN GENERAL.
UH... MR. P? YOUR WATCH IS BROKEN.
UH-HUH.
TWENTY-FIVE MINUTES.
YOU SUPPOSED TO BE SOME-WHERE?
I THINK I'M SUPPOSED TO BE HERE, WITH YOU. BUT HONESTLY?
I DON'T KNOW WHERE I'M SUPPOSED TO BE, OR WHAT I'M SUPPOSED TO DO--
PETE? THIS ISN'T WEIRD FOR YOU, IS IT?
WHAT?
HANGING OUT. WITH ME. NO SUPER VILLAINS. NO BETTY, FLASH, OR THE REST OF THE GANG.
JUST YOU. ME. PIE AND COFFEE.
NO. WE'RE GOOD. REALLY.
THIS ISN'T ABOUT ANYTHING IN THE PAST. I'M WORRIED ABOUT-- TOMORROW.
I'M NOT.
EVERYTHING'S GOING TO WORK OUT. YOU'LL SEE.
WISH I HAD YOUR FAITH, MJ.
YOU DO. AND NOT BECAUSE YOU GOT BIT BY A RADIOACTIVE SPIDER.
BECAUSE I KNOW YOU, PETER PARKER. AND I HAVE FAITH THAT WHATEVER YOU ARE SUPPOSED TO DO...
...YOU'LL FIGURE IT OUT.
WHAT I'M SUPPOSED TO DO.
NOT SPIDEY.
ME!
OF COURSE! MJ, I HAVE TO GO--
SAVE THE WORLD?
NAH. JUST NEW YORK THIS TIME.
GO GET 'EM, TIGER.

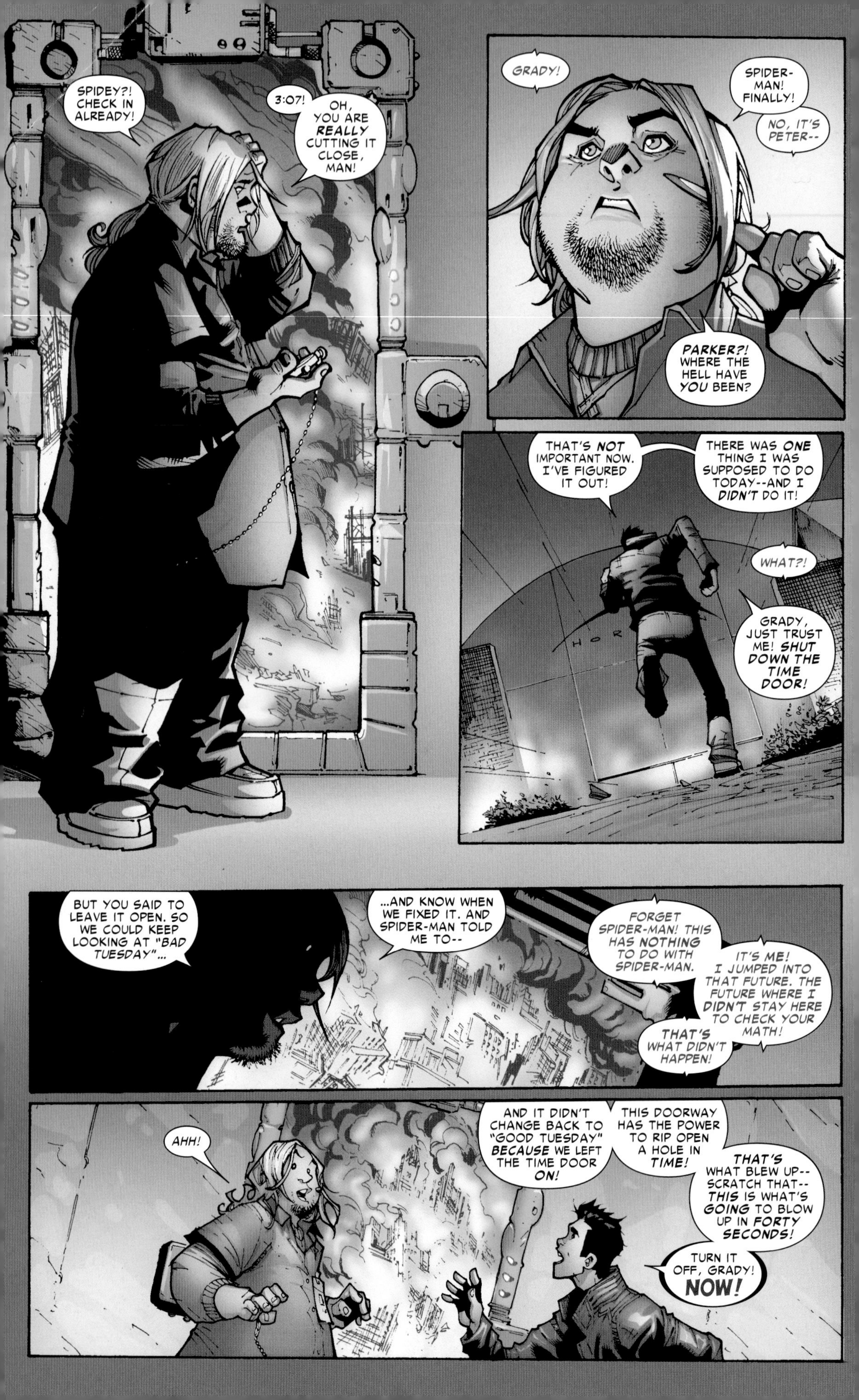
SPIDEY?! CHECK IN ALREADY!
3:07!
OH, YOU ARE REALLY CUTTING IT CLOSE, MAN!
GRADY!
SPIDER-MAN! FINALLY!
NO, IT'S PETER--
PARKER?! WHERE THE HELL HAVE YOU BEEN?
THAT'S NOT IMPORTANT NOW. I'VE FIGURED IT OUT!
THERE WAS ONE THING I WAS SUPPOSED TO DO TODAY--AND I DIDN'T DO IT!
WHAT?!
GRADY, JUST TRUST ME! SHUT DOWN THE TIME DOOR!
BUT YOU SAID TO LEAVE IT OPEN. SO WE COULD KEEP LOOKING AT "BAD TUESDAY"...
...AND KNOW WHEN WE FIXED IT. AND SPIDER-MAN TOLD ME TO--
FORGET SPIDER-MAN! THIS HAS NOTHING TO DO WITH SPIDER-MAN.
IT'S ME! I JUMPED INTO THAT FUTURE. THE FUTURE WHERE I DIDN'T STAY HERE TO CHECK YOUR MATH!
THAT'S WHAT DIDN'T HAPPEN!
AHH!
AND IT DIDN'T CHANGE BACK TO "GOOD TUESDAY" BECAUSE WE LEFT THE TIME DOOR ON!
THIS DOORWAY HAS THE POWER TO RIP OPEN A HOLE IN TIME!
THAT'S WHAT BLEW UP--SCRATCH THAT--THIS IS WHAT'S GOING TO BLOW UP IN FORTY SECONDS!
TURN IT OFF, GRADY! NOW!

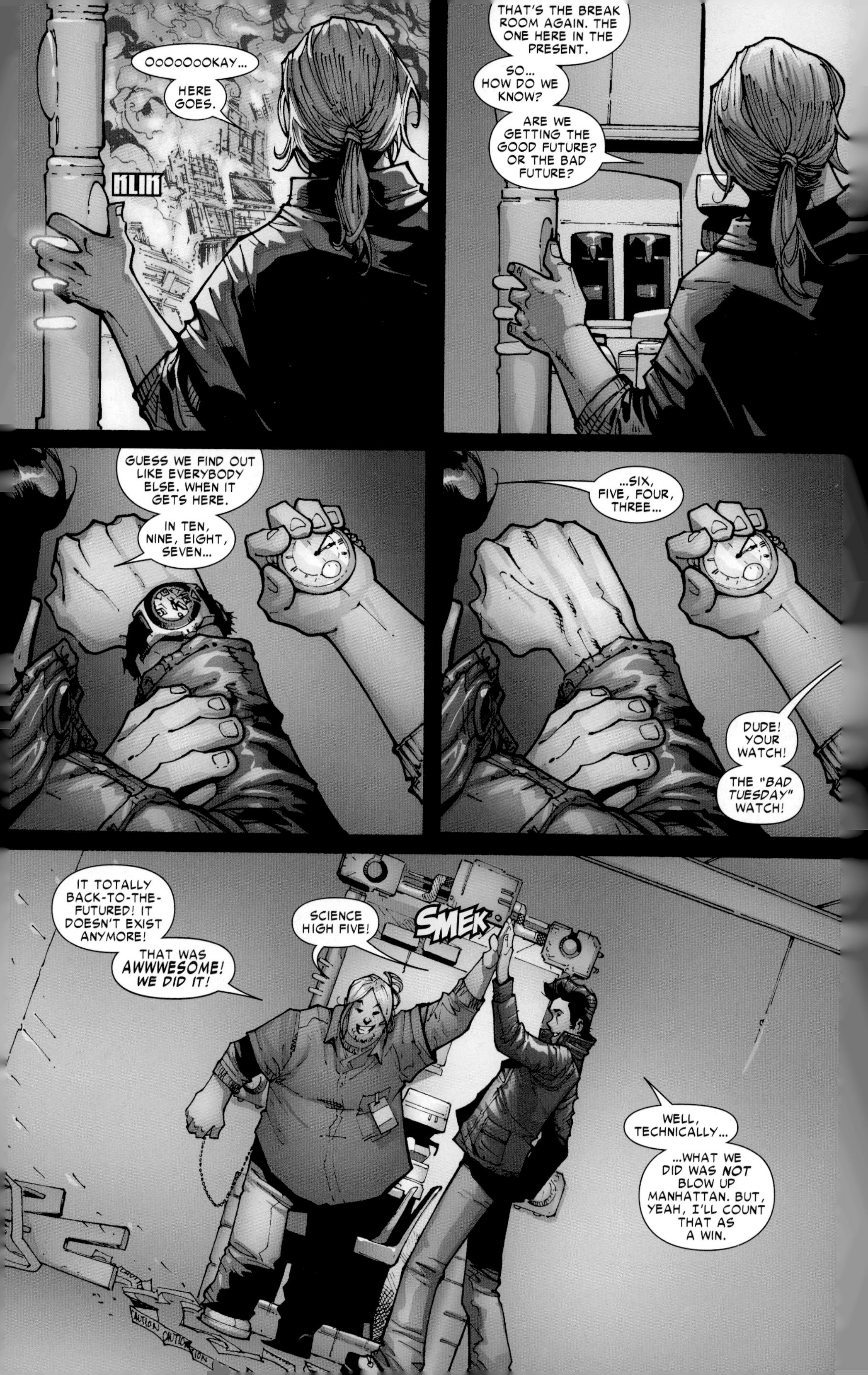

OOOOOOOKAY...
HERE GOES.
KLIK
THAT'S THE BREAK ROOM AGAIN. THE ONE HERE IN THE PRESENT.
SO... HOW DO WE KNOW?
ARE WE GETTING THE GOOD FUTURE? OR THE BAD FUTURE?
GUESS WE FIND OUT LIKE EVERYBODY ELSE. WHEN IT GETS HERE.
IN TEN, NINE, EIGHT, SEVEN...
...SIX, FIVE, FOUR, THREE...
DUDE! YOUR WATCH!
THE "*BAD TUESDAY*" WATCH!
IT TOTALLY BACK-TO-THE-FUTURED! IT DOESN'T EXIST ANYMORE!
THAT WAS ***AWWWESOME! WE DID IT!***
SCIENCE HIGH FIVE!
SMEK
WELL, TECHNICALLY...
...WHAT WE DID WAS ***NOT*** BLOW UP MANHATTAN. BUT, YEAH, I'LL COUNT THAT AS A WIN.
CAUTION CAUTION CAUTION

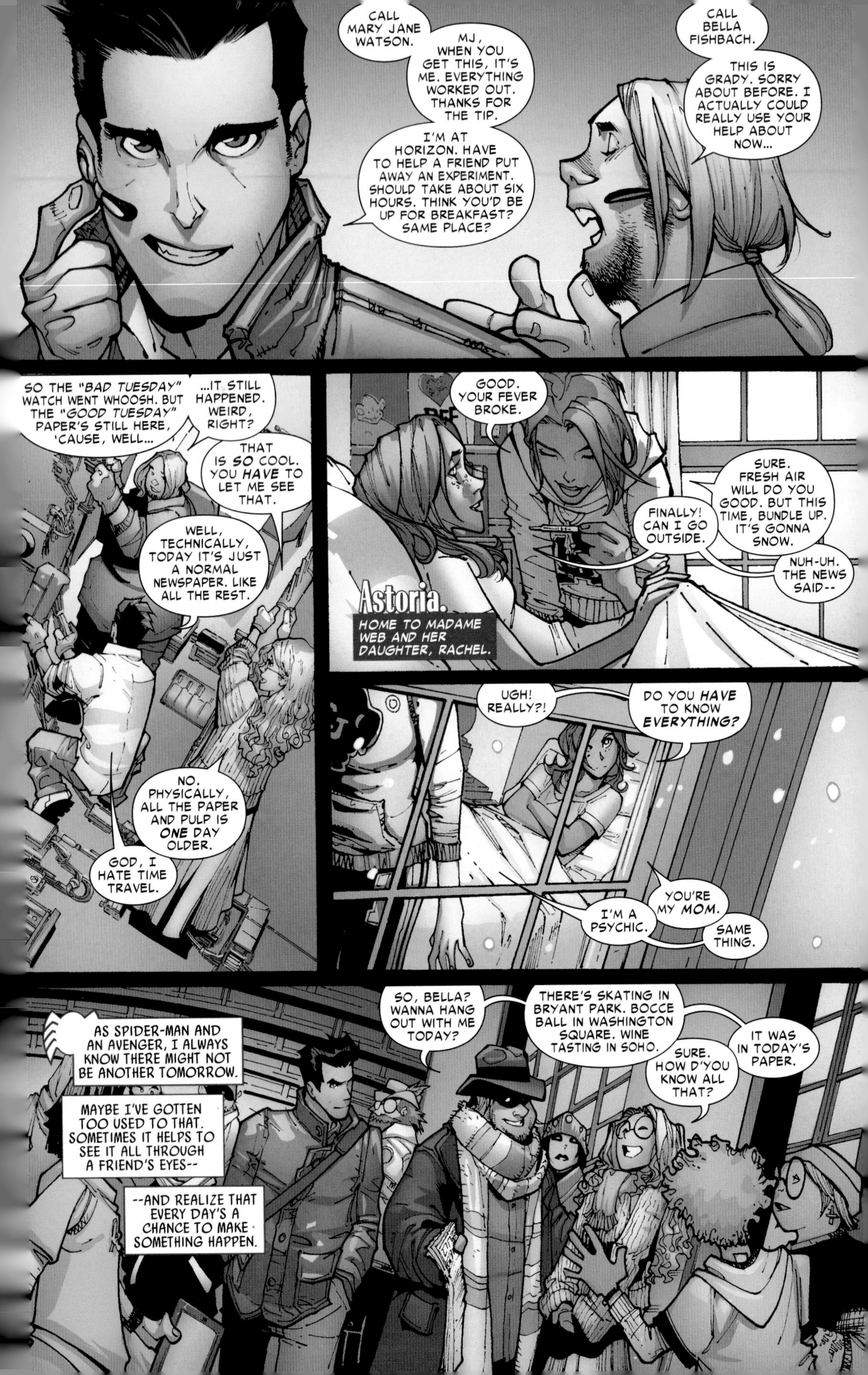
CALL MARY JANE WATSON.
MJ, WHEN YOU GET THIS, IT'S ME. EVERYTHING WORKED OUT. THANKS FOR THE TIP.
I'M AT HORIZON. HAVE TO HELP A FRIEND PUT AWAY AN EXPERIMENT. SHOULD TAKE ABOUT SIX HOURS. THINK YOU'D BE UP FOR BREAKFAST? SAME PLACE?
CALL BELLA FISHBACH.
THIS IS GRADY. SORRY ABOUT BEFORE. I ACTUALLY COULD REALLY USE YOUR HELP ABOUT NOW...
SO THE "BAD TUESDAY" WATCH WENT WHOOSH. BUT THE "GOOD TUESDAY" PAPER'S STILL HERE, 'CAUSE, WELL...
...IT STILL HAPPENED. WEIRD, RIGHT?
THAT IS SO COOL. YOU HAVE TO LET ME SEE THAT.
WELL, TECHNICALLY, TODAY IT'S JUST A NORMAL NEWSPAPER. LIKE ALL THE REST.
NO. PHYSICALLY, ALL THE PAPER AND PULP IS ONE DAY OLDER.
GOD, I HATE TIME TRAVEL.
Astoria.
HOME TO MADAME WEB AND HER DAUGHTER, RACHEL.
GOOD. YOUR FEVER BROKE.
FINALLY! CAN I GO OUTSIDE.
SURE. FRESH AIR WILL DO YOU GOOD. BUT THIS TIME, BUNDLE UP. IT'S GONNA SNOW.
NUH-UH. THE NEWS SAID--
UGH! REALLY?!
DO YOU HAVE TO KNOW EVERYTHING?
I'M A PSYCHIC.
YOU'RE MY MOM.
SAME THING.
AS SPIDER-MAN AND AN AVENGER, I ALWAYS KNOW THERE MIGHT NOT BE ANOTHER TOMORROW.
MAYBE I'VE GOTTEN TOO USED TO THAT. SOMETIMES IT HELPS TO SEE IT ALL THROUGH A FRIEND'S EYES--
--AND REALIZE THAT EVERY DAY'S A CHANCE TO MAKE SOMETHING HAPPEN.
SO, BELLA? WANNA HANG OUT WITH ME TODAY?
THERE'S SKATING IN BRYANT PARK. BOCCE BALL IN WASHINGTON SQUARE. WINE TASTING IN SOHO.
SURE. HOW D'YOU KNOW ALL THAT?
IT WAS IN TODAY'S PAPER.

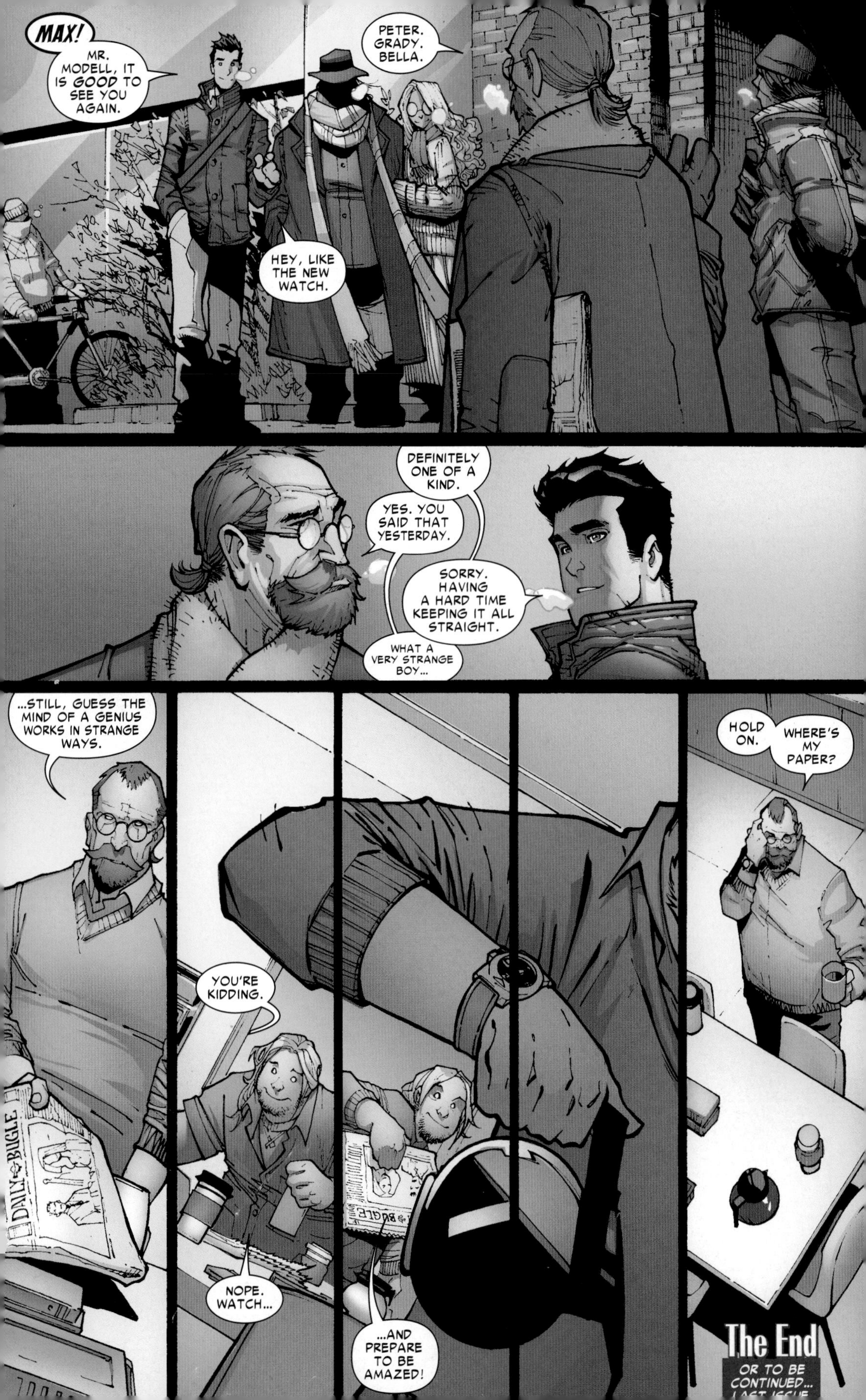
MAX!
MR. MODELL, IT IS GOOD TO SEE YOU AGAIN.
PETER. GRADY. BELLA.
HEY, LIKE THE NEW WATCH.
DEFINITELY ONE OF A KIND.
YES. YOU SAID THAT YESTERDAY.
SORRY. HAVING A HARD TIME KEEPING IT ALL STRAIGHT.
WHAT A VERY STRANGE BOY...
...STILL, GUESS THE MIND OF A GENIUS WORKS IN STRANGE WAYS.
DAILY BUGLE
YOU'RE KIDDING.
NOPE. WATCH...
...AND PREPARE TO BE AMAZED!
HOLD ON.
WHERE'S MY PAPER?
The End
OR TO BE CONTINUED...

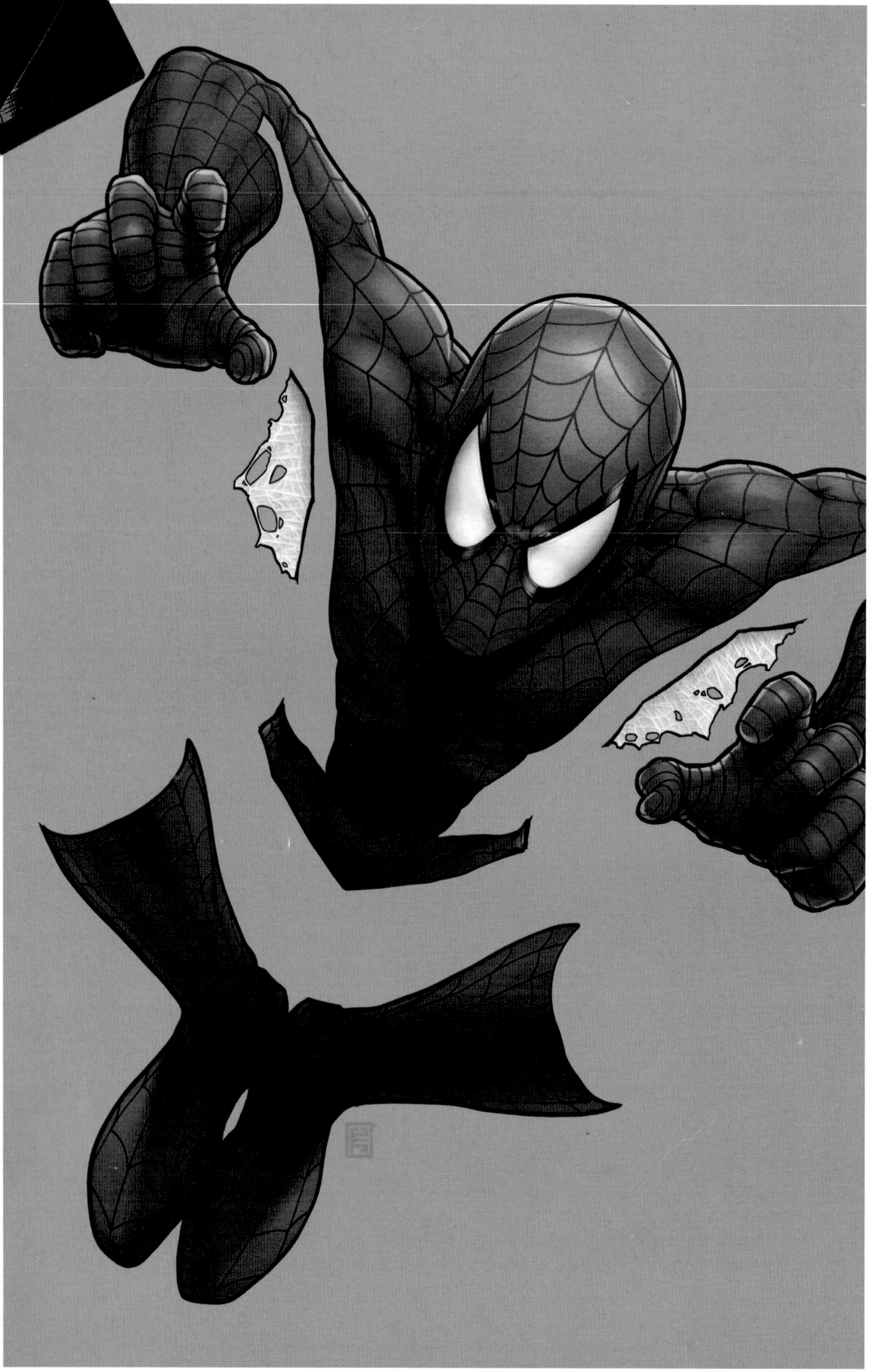

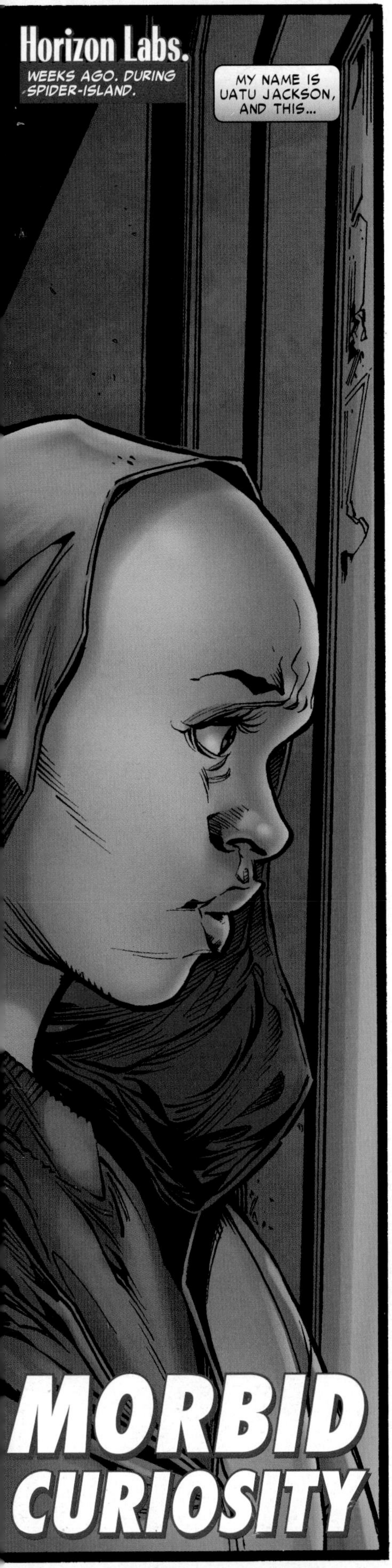
Horizon Labs.
WEEKS AGO. DURING SPIDER-ISLAND.
MY NAME IS UATU JACKSON, AND THIS...
MORBID CURIOSITY

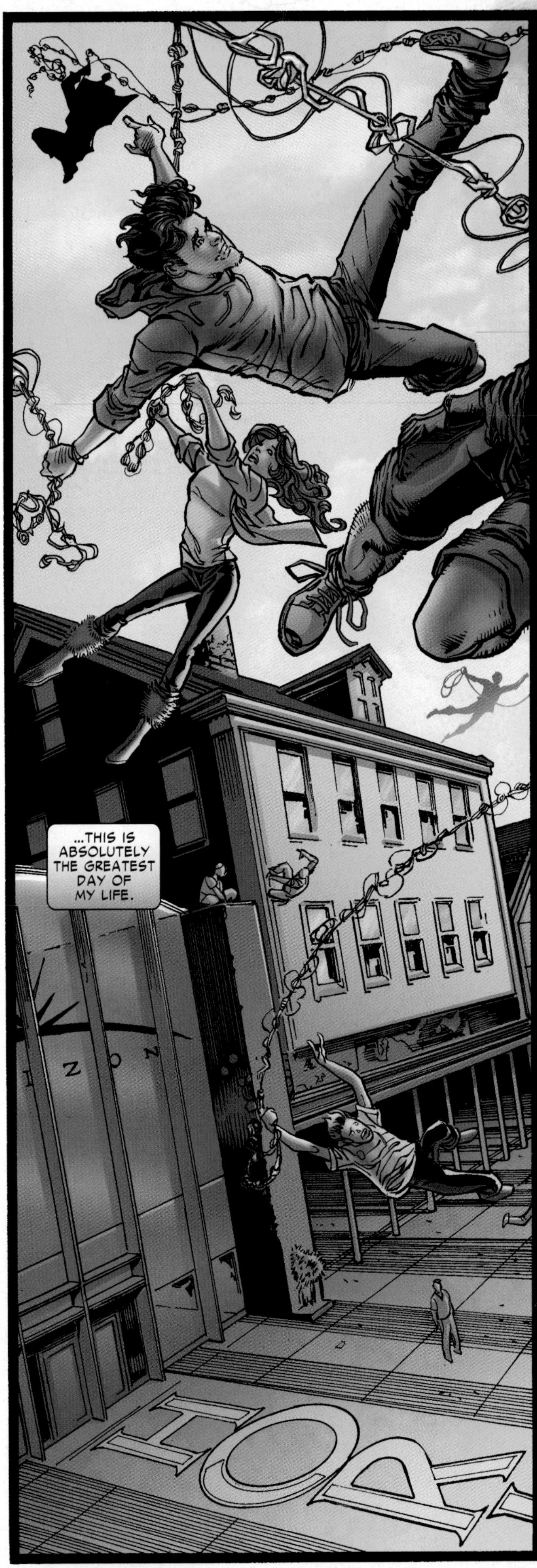
...THIS IS ABSOLUTELY THE GREATEST DAY OF MY LIFE.

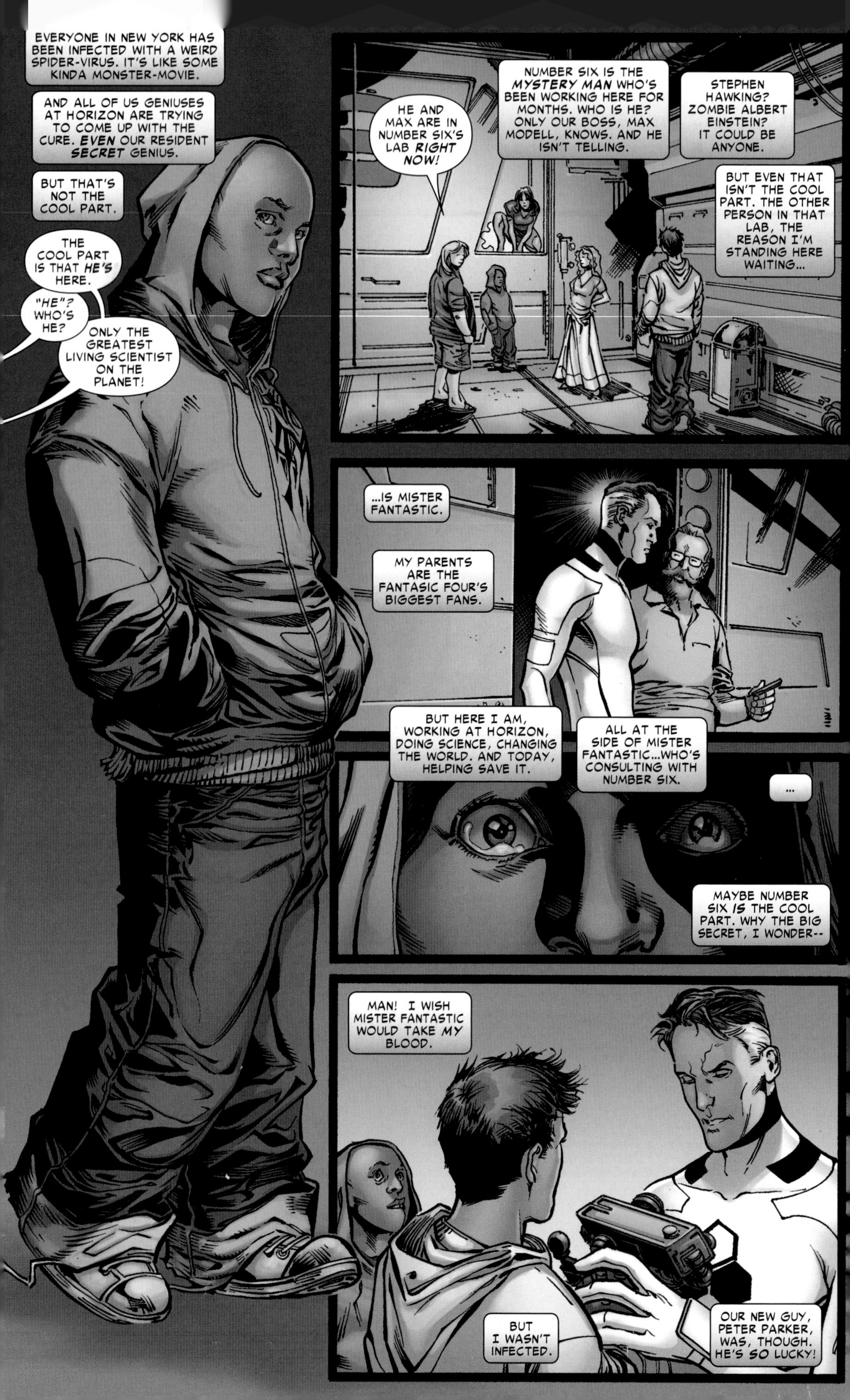
EVERYONE IN NEW YORK HAS BEEN INFECTED WITH A WEIRD SPIDER-VIRUS. IT'S LIKE SOME KINDA MONSTER-MOVIE.
AND ALL OF US GENIUSES AT HORIZON ARE TRYING TO COME UP WITH THE CURE. EVEN OUR RESIDENT SECRET GENIUS.
BUT THAT'S NOT THE COOL PART.
THE COOL PART IS THAT HE'S HERE.
"HE"? WHO'S HE?
ONLY THE GREATEST LIVING SCIENTIST ON THE PLANET!
HE AND MAX ARE IN NUMBER SIX'S LAB RIGHT NOW!
NUMBER SIX IS THE MYSTERY MAN WHO'S BEEN WORKING HERE FOR MONTHS. WHO IS HE? ONLY OUR BOSS, MAX MODELL, KNOWS. AND HE ISN'T TELLING.
STEPHEN HAWKING? ZOMBIE ALBERT EINSTEIN? IT COULD BE ANYONE.
BUT EVEN THAT ISN'T THE COOL PART. THE OTHER PERSON IN THAT LAB, THE REASON I'M STANDING HERE WAITING...
...IS MISTER FANTASTIC.
MY PARENTS ARE THE FANTASIC FOUR'S BIGGEST FANS.
BUT HERE I AM, WORKING AT HORIZON, DOING SCIENCE, CHANGING THE WORLD. AND TODAY, HELPING SAVE IT.
ALL AT THE SIDE OF MISTER FANTASTIC...WHO'S CONSULTING WITH NUMBER SIX.
...
MAYBE NUMBER SIX IS THE COOL PART. WHY THE BIG SECRET, I WONDER--
MAN! I WISH MISTER FANTASTIC WOULD TAKE MY BLOOD.
BUT I WASN'T INFECTED.
OUR NEW GUY, PETER PARKER, WAS, THOUGH. HE'S SO LUCKY!

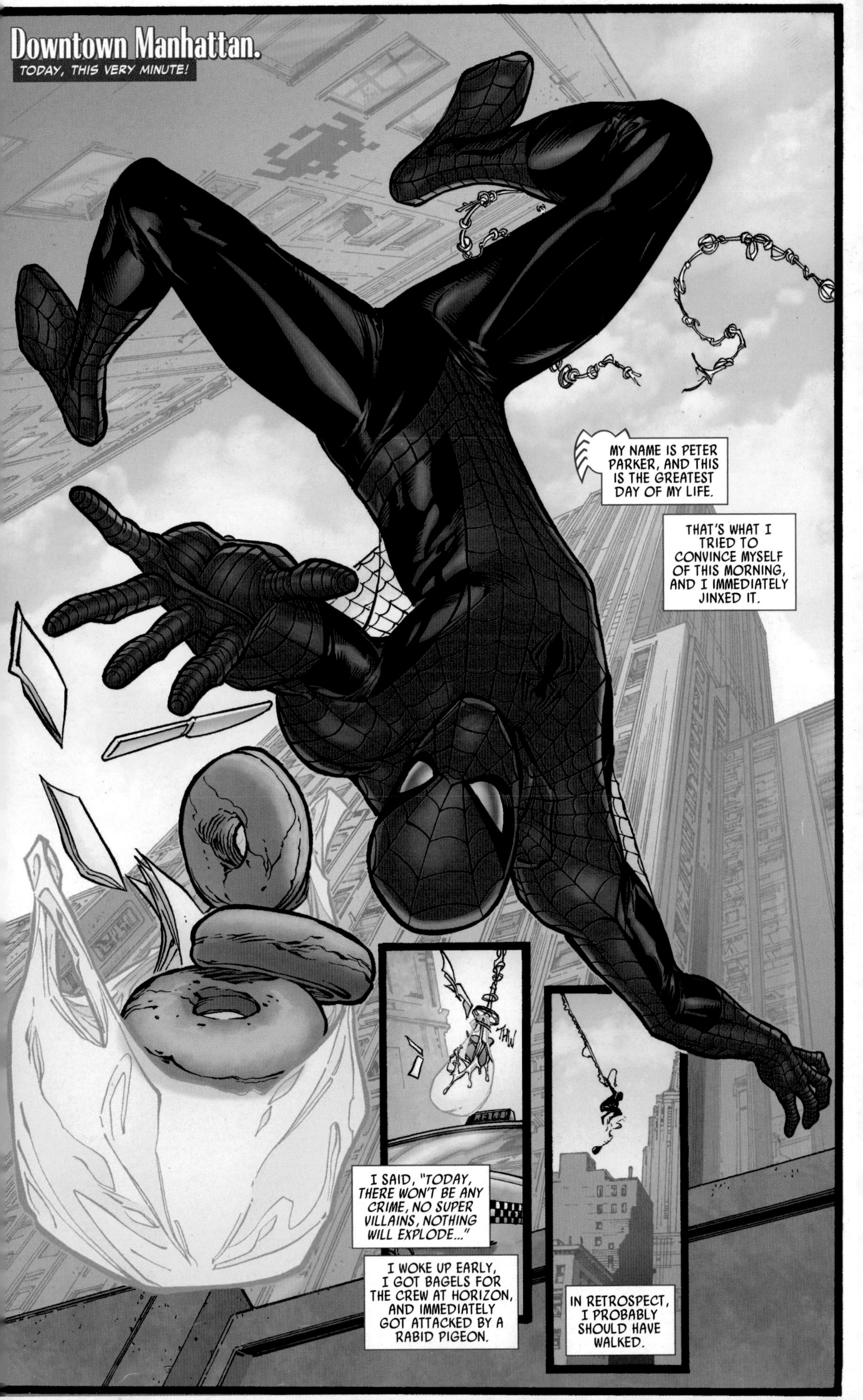
Downtown Manhattan.
TODAY, THIS VERY MINUTE!
MY NAME IS PETER PARKER, AND THIS IS THE GREATEST DAY OF MY LIFE.
THAT'S WHAT I TRIED TO CONVINCE MYSELF OF THIS MORNING, AND I IMMEDIATELY JINXED IT.
I SAID, "TODAY, THERE WON'T BE ANY CRIME, NO SUPER VILLAINS, NOTHING WILL EXPLODE..."
I WOKE UP EARLY, I GOT BAGELS FOR THE CREW AT HORIZON, AND IMMEDIATELY GOT ATTACKED BY A RABID PIGEON.
IN RETROSPECT, I PROBABLY SHOULD HAVE WALKED.

NO! STAY POSITIVE!

ALL THE SPIDER-INSANITY IS OVER. TIME FOR A LITTLE PETER PARKER TIME. I LOVE MY JOB.

MY OWN LAB, ALL THE SCIENCE TOYS I COULD WANT, THEY ACTUALLY *PAY* ME, AND BEST OF ALL...

...EASY ACCESS AS SPIDER-MAN.

A LITTLE REWIRING HERE, SOME BYPASSING THERE... MY OWN LITTLE PRIVATE SECURITY DOOR, JUST FOR ME.

Lab 7.
WORKPLACE OF PETER PARKER.

LIFE IS GOO- *BZZZ! BZZZ!*

AND OF COURSE. SOMEONE'S AT THE DOOR, MID-COSTUME CHANGE. I DID JINX IT.

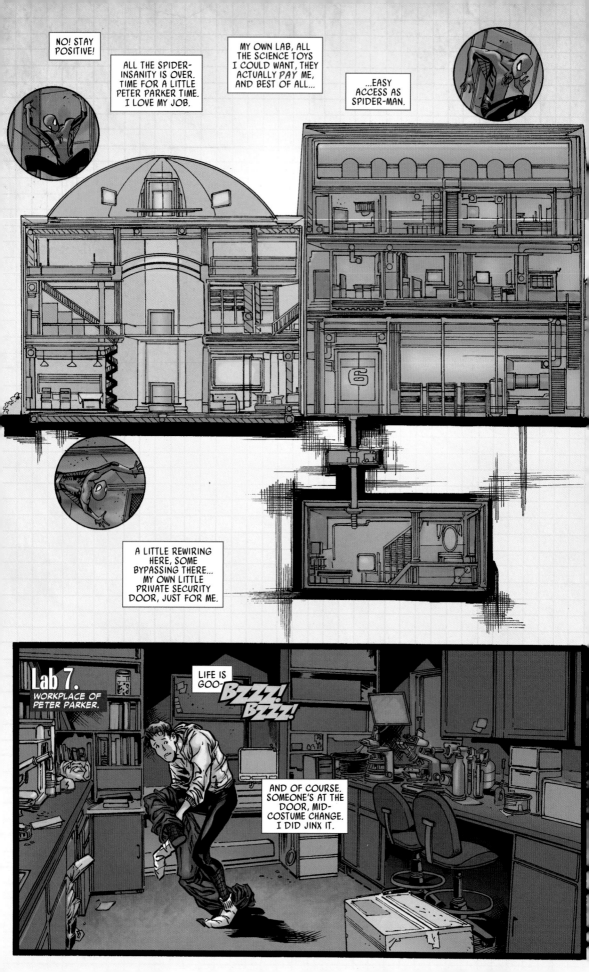

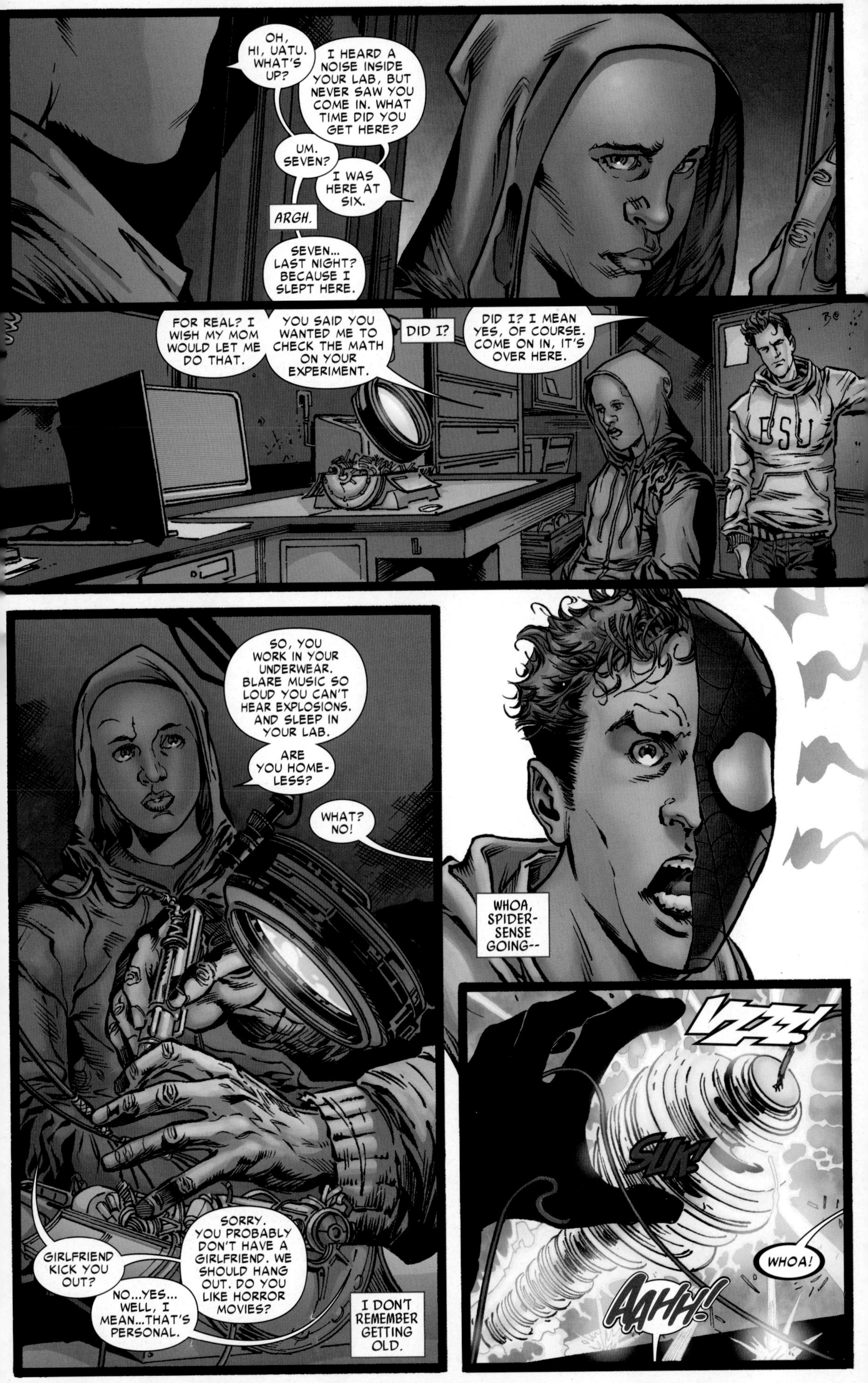

OH, HI, UATU. WHAT'S UP?
I HEARD A NOISE INSIDE YOUR LAB, BUT NEVER SAW YOU COME IN. WHAT TIME DID YOU GET HERE?
UM. SEVEN?
I WAS HERE AT SIX.
ARGH.
SEVEN... LAST NIGHT? BECAUSE I SLEPT HERE.
FOR REAL? I WISH MY MOM WOULD LET ME DO THAT.
YOU SAID YOU WANTED ME TO CHECK THE MATH ON YOUR EXPERIMENT.
DID I?
DID I? I MEAN YES, OF COURSE. COME ON IN, IT'S OVER HERE.
BSU
SO, YOU WORK IN YOUR UNDERWEAR. BLARE MUSIC SO LOUD YOU CAN'T HEAR EXPLOSIONS. AND SLEEP IN YOUR LAB.
ARE YOU HOMELESS?
WHAT? NO!
GIRLFRIEND KICK YOU OUT?
NO...YES... WELL, I MEAN...THAT'S PERSONAL.
SORRY. YOU PROBABLY DON'T HAVE A GIRLFRIEND. WE SHOULD HANG OUT. DO YOU LIKE HORROR MOVIES?
I DON'T REMEMBER GETTING OLD.
WHOA, SPIDER-SENSE GOING--
VZZZ!
SLAK!
WHOA!
AAHH!

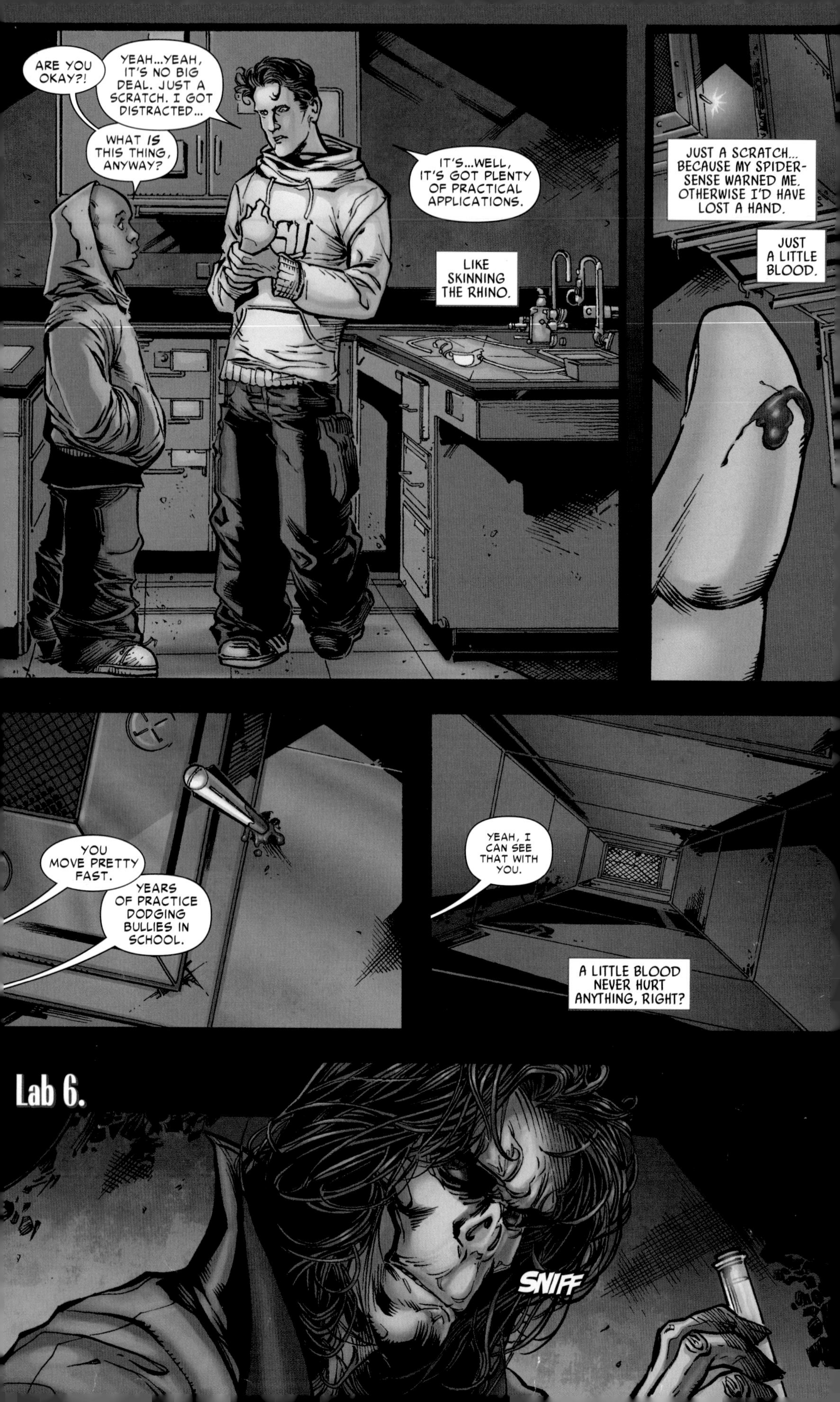
ARE YOU OKAY?!
YEAH...YEAH, IT'S NO BIG DEAL. JUST A SCRATCH. I GOT DISTRACTED...
WHAT IS THIS THING, ANYWAY?
IT'S...WELL, IT'S GOT PLENTY OF PRACTICAL APPLICATIONS.
LIKE SKINNING THE RHINO.
JUST A SCRATCH... BECAUSE MY SPIDER-SENSE WARNED ME. OTHERWISE I'D HAVE LOST A HAND.
JUST A LITTLE BLOOD.
YOU MOVE PRETTY FAST.
YEARS OF PRACTICE DODGING BULLIES IN SCHOOL.
YEAH, I CAN SEE THAT WITH YOU.
A LITTLE BLOOD NEVER HURT ANYTHING, RIGHT?
Lab 6.
SNIFF

The Next Day.

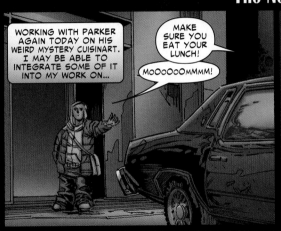

WORKING WITH PARKER AGAIN TODAY ON HIS WEIRD MYSTERY CUISINART. I MAY BE ABLE TO INTEGRATE SOME OF IT INTO MY WORK ON...

MAKE SURE YOU EAT YOUR LUNCH!

MOOOOOOMMMM!

WORKING WITH UATU AGAIN TODAY ON MY ANTI-RHINO GIZMO. DE-RHINO-ER? RHINO-OFF? I'M BAD AT NAMES.

WAIT. I FORGOT MY LUNCH.

MAX MODELL. COMING OUT OF LAB 6 AGAIN. HE DOESN'T LOOK HAPPY.

I WANT TO NOT BE HAPPY IN LAB 6, TOO! MAN, THIS IS UNFAIR!

HUH. SPIDER-SENSE. NOT REALLY TINGLING, MORE LIKE ITCHING. AND RIGHT OUTSIDE LAB 6.

THERE'S SOMETHING DANGEROUS IN THERE... AND BECAUSE I'M AN IDIOT, MY FIRST INSTINCT IS TO GET *CLOSER* TO IT.

WHAT IS GOING ON IN THERE?

SOMETHING AWESOME, I BET.

WHAT IS GOING *ON* IN THERE?!

SOMETHING HORRIBLE, I BET.

Lab 7.

THAT...IS CREEPY. AND IT'S COMING FROM LAB 6.

OKAY. FOR REAL. WE HAVE TO FIND OUT WHO'S IN THERE.

AGREED.

SKRTCH! SKRTCH!

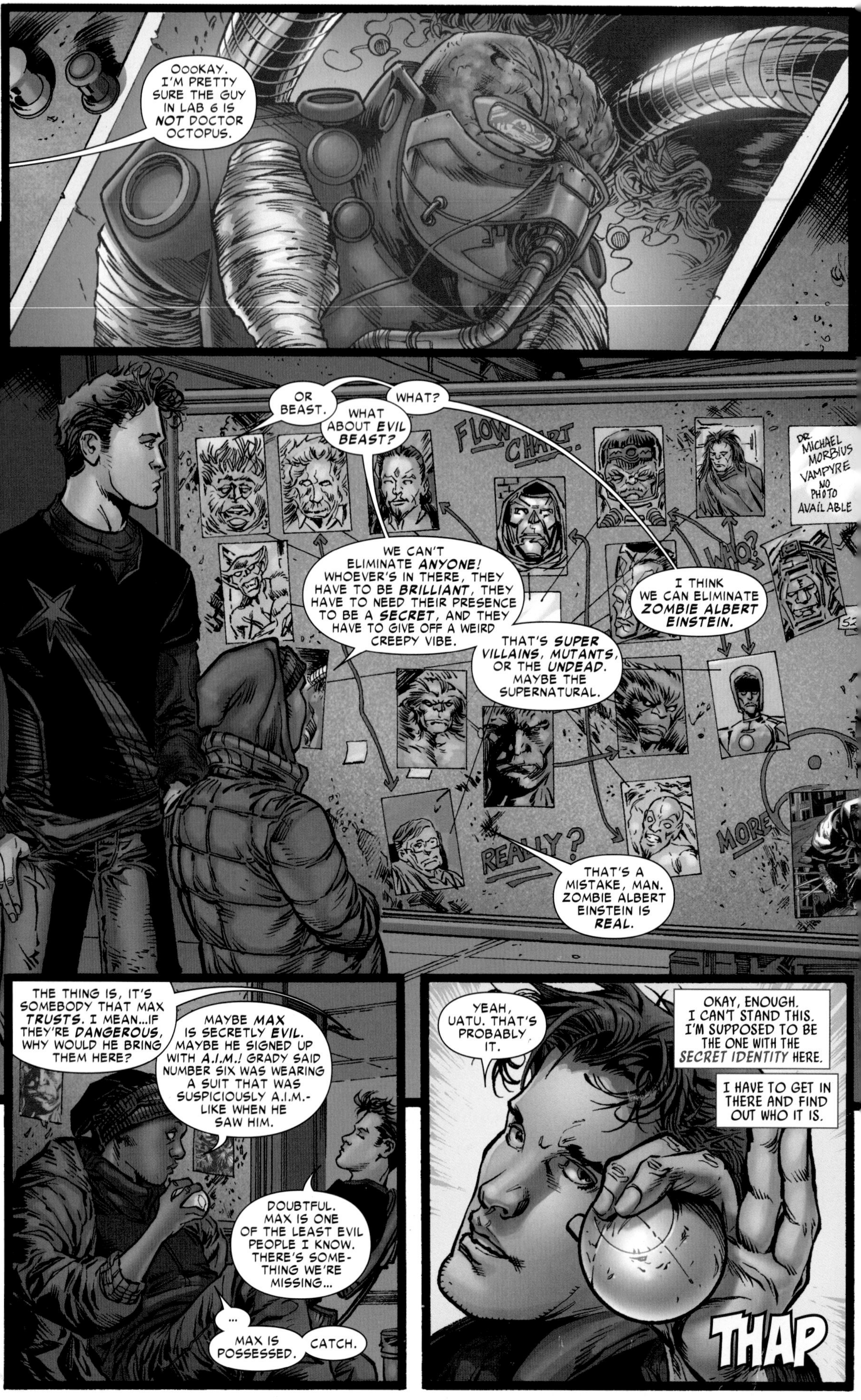
OOOKAY. I'M PRETTY SURE THE GUY IN LAB 6 IS NOT DOCTOR OCTOPUS.
OR BEAST.
WHAT?
WHAT ABOUT EVIL BEAST?
FLOW CHART.
DR. MICHAEL MORBIUS VAMPYRE NO PHOTO AVAILABLE
WHO?
WE CAN'T ELIMINATE ANYONE! WHOEVER'S IN THERE, THEY HAVE TO BE BRILLIANT, THEY HAVE TO NEED THEIR PRESENCE TO BE A SECRET, AND THEY HAVE TO GIVE OFF A WEIRD CREEPY VIBE.
I THINK WE CAN ELIMINATE ZOMBIE ALBERT EINSTEIN.
THAT'S SUPER VILLAINS, MUTANTS, OR THE UNDEAD. MAYBE THE SUPERNATURAL.
REALLY?
MORE
THAT'S A MISTAKE, MAN. ZOMBIE ALBERT EINSTEIN IS REAL.
THE THING IS, IT'S SOMEBODY THAT MAX TRUSTS. I MEAN...IF THEY'RE DANGEROUS, WHY WOULD HE BRING THEM HERE?
MAYBE MAX IS SECRETLY EVIL. MAYBE HE SIGNED UP WITH A.I.M.! GRADY SAID NUMBER SIX WAS WEARING A SUIT THAT WAS SUSPICIOUSLY A.I.M.-LIKE WHEN HE SAW HIM.
DOUBTFUL. MAX IS ONE OF THE LEAST EVIL PEOPLE I KNOW. THERE'S SOME-THING WE'RE MISSING...
...
MAX IS POSSESSED.
CATCH.
YEAH, UATU. THAT'S PROBABLY IT.
OKAY, ENOUGH. I CAN'T STAND THIS. I'M SUPPOSED TO BE THE ONE WITH THE SECRET IDENTITY HERE.
I HAVE TO GET IN THERE AND FIND OUT WHO IT IS.
THAP

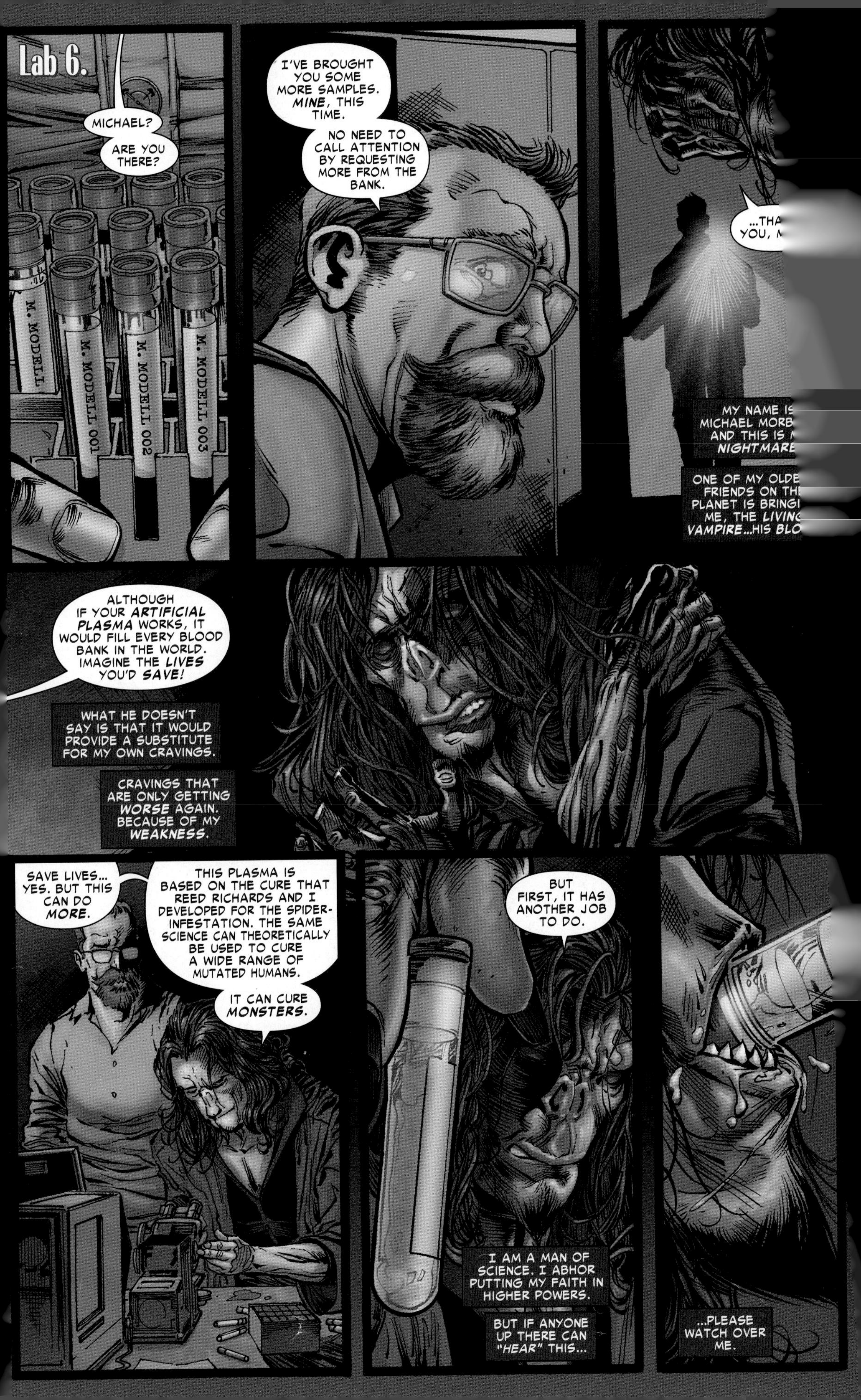

Lab 6.
MICHAEL?
ARE YOU THERE?
M. MODELL
M. MODELL 001
M. MODELL 002
M. MODELL 003
I'VE BROUGHT YOU SOME MORE SAMPLES. *MINE*, THIS TIME.
NO NEED TO CALL ATTENTION BY REQUESTING MORE FROM THE BANK.
...THA YOU, M
MY NAME IS MICHAEL MORB AND THIS IS NIGHTMARE
ONE OF MY OLDE FRIENDS ON THE PLANET IS BRINGI ME, THE *LIVING VAMPIRE*...HIS BLO
ALTHOUGH IF YOUR *ARTIFICIAL PLASMA* WORKS, IT WOULD FILL EVERY BLOOD BANK IN THE WORLD. IMAGINE THE *LIVES* YOU'D *SAVE!*
WHAT HE DOESN'T SAY IS THAT IT WOULD PROVIDE A SUBSTITUTE FOR MY OWN CRAVINGS.
CRAVINGS THAT ARE ONLY GETTING *WORSE* AGAIN. BECAUSE OF MY *WEAKNESS*.
SAVE LIVES... YES. BUT THIS CAN DO *MORE*.
THIS PLASMA IS BASED ON THE CURE THAT REED RICHARDS AND I DEVELOPED FOR THE SPIDER-INFESTATION. THE SAME SCIENCE CAN THEORETICALLY BE USED TO CURE A WIDE RANGE OF MUTATED HUMANS.
IT CAN CURE *MONSTERS*.
BUT FIRST, IT HAS ANOTHER JOB TO DO.
I AM A MAN OF SCIENCE. I ABHOR PUTTING MY FAITH IN HIGHER POWERS.
BUT IF ANYONE UP THERE CAN *"HEAR"* THIS...
...PLEASE WATCH OVER ME.

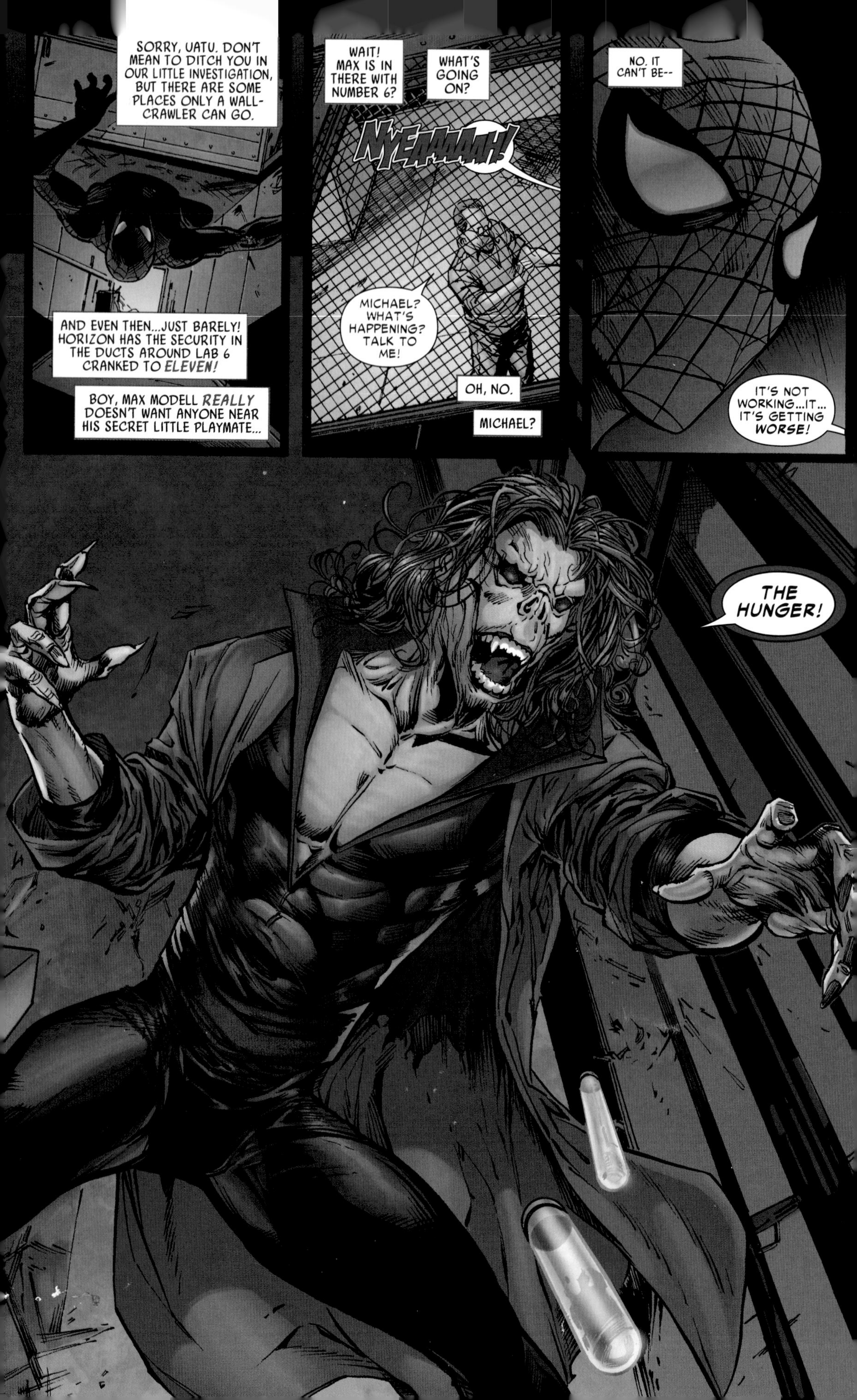
SORRY, UATU. DON'T MEAN TO DITCH YOU IN OUR LITTLE INVESTIGATION, BUT THERE ARE SOME PLACES ONLY A WALL-CRAWLER CAN GO.
AND EVEN THEN...JUST BARELY! HORIZON HAS THE SECURITY IN THE DUCTS AROUND LAB 6 CRANKED TO ELEVEN!
BOY, MAX MODELL REALLY DOESN'T WANT ANYONE NEAR HIS SECRET LITTLE PLAYMATE...
WAIT! MAX IS IN THERE WITH NUMBER 6?
WHAT'S GOING ON?
NYEAAAAAH!
MICHAEL? WHAT'S HAPPENING? TALK TO ME!
OH, NO.
MICHAEL?
NO. IT CAN'T BE--
IT'S NOT WORKING...IT... IT'S GETTING WORSE!
THE HUNGER!

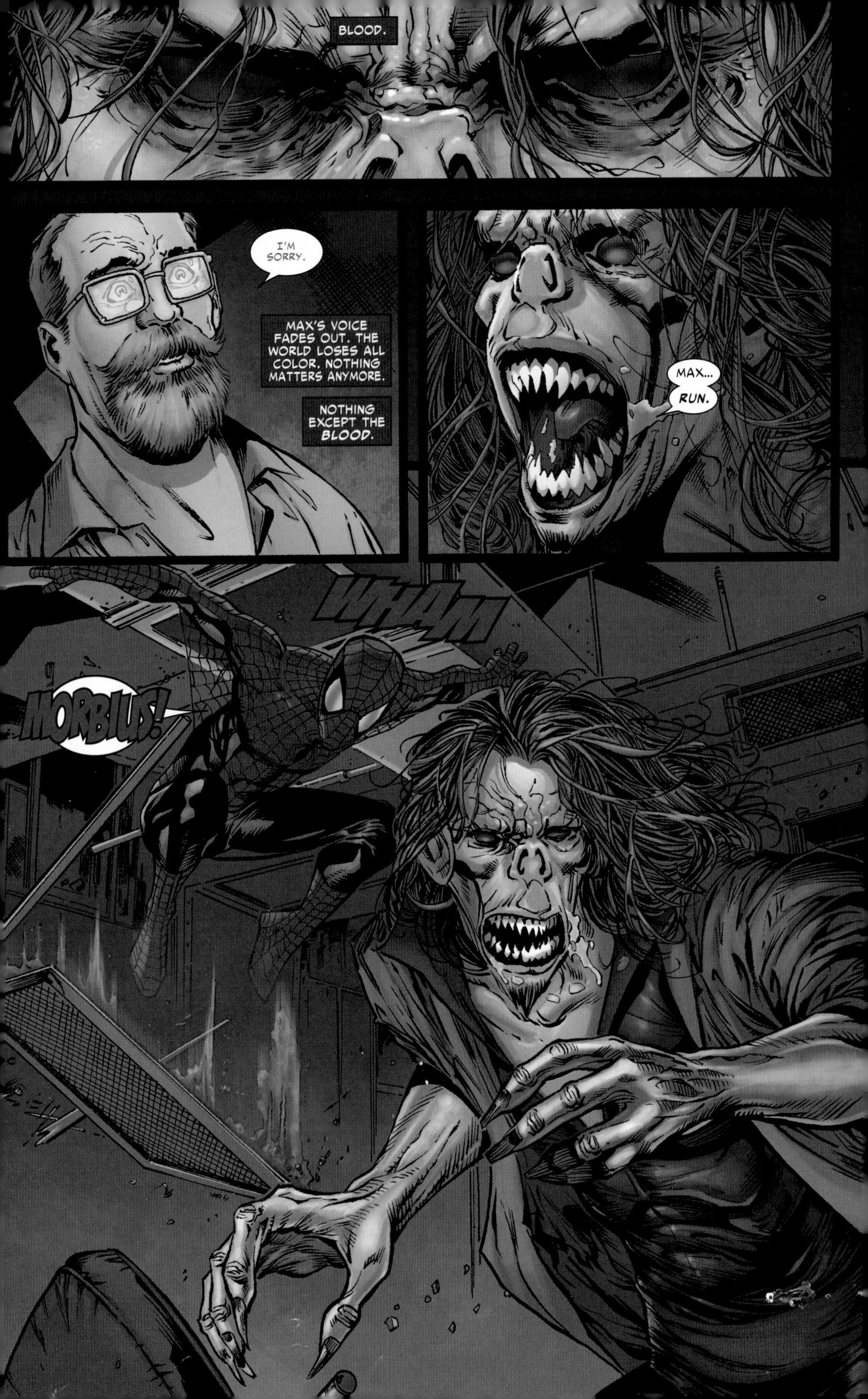
BLOOD.
I'M SORRY.
MAX'S VOICE FADES OUT. THE WORLD LOSES ALL COLOR. NOTHING MATTERS ANYMORE.
NOTHING EXCEPT THE *BLOOD*.
MAX...
RUN.
WHAM
MORBIUS!

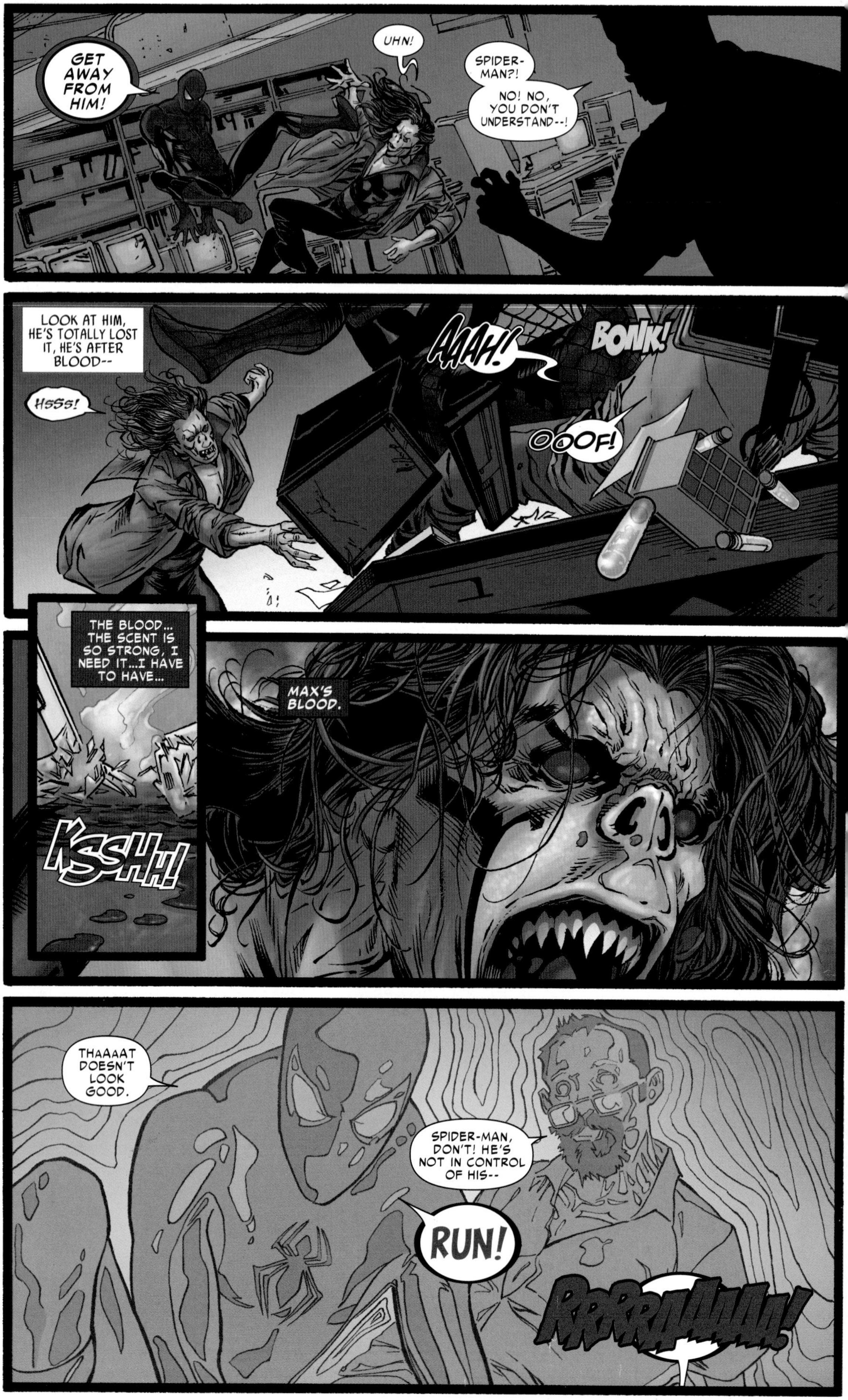
GET AWAY FROM HIM!
UHN!
SPIDER-MAN?!
NO! NO, YOU DON'T UNDERSTAND--!
LOOK AT HIM, HE'S TOTALLY LOST IT, HE'S AFTER BLOOD--
HSSS!
AAAH!
BONK!
OOOF!
THE BLOOD... THE SCENT IS SO STRONG, I NEED IT...I HAVE TO HAVE...
KSSHH!
MAX'S BLOOD.
THAAAAT DOESN'T LOOK GOOD.
SPIDER-MAN, DON'T! HE'S NOT IN CONTROL OF HIS--
RUN!
RRRRAAAAH!

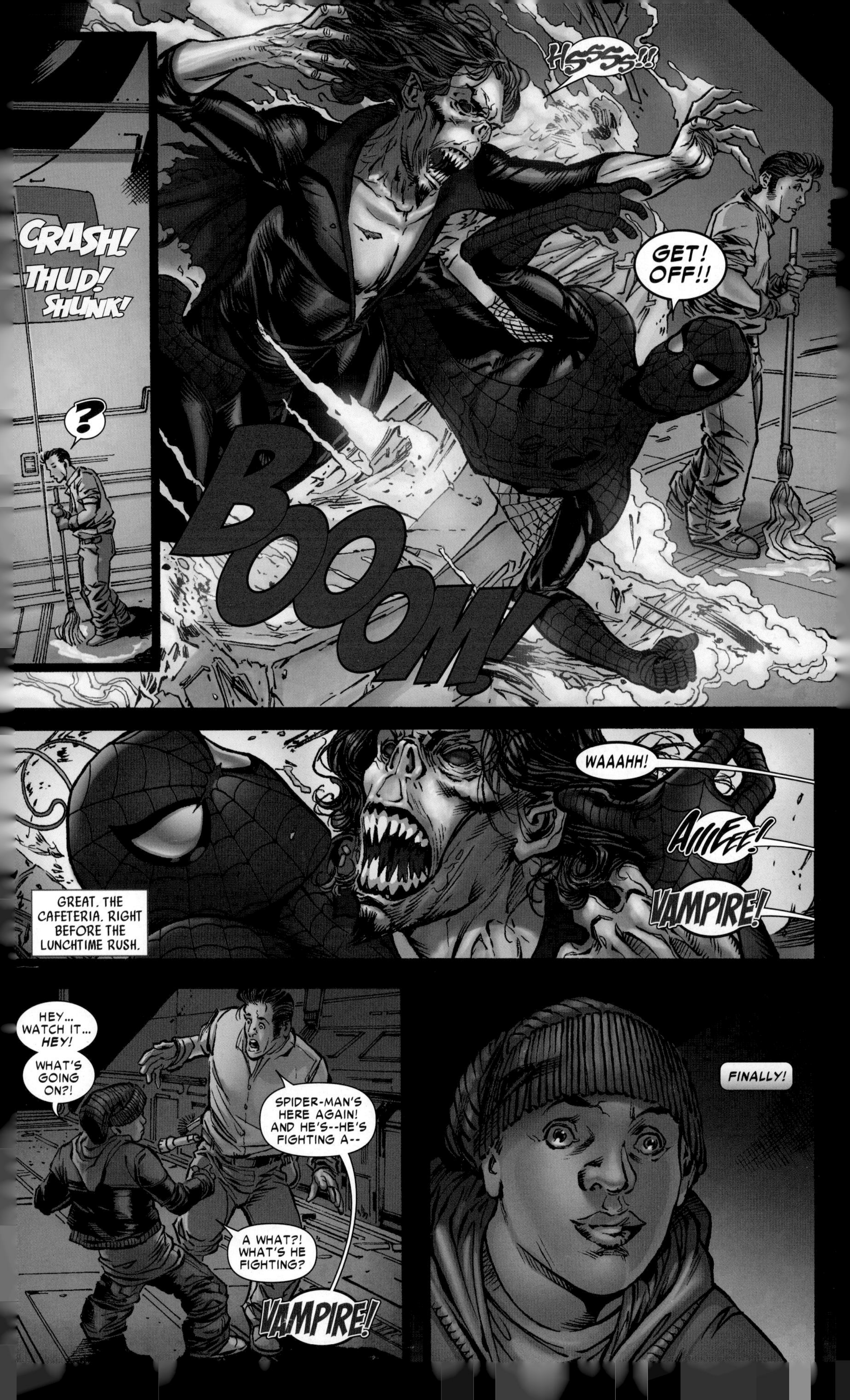
HSSSS!!
CRASH!
THUD!
SHUNK!
?
GET! OFF!!
BOOOOM!
GREAT. THE CAFETERIA. RIGHT BEFORE THE LUNCHTIME RUSH.
WAAAHH!
AIIIEEE!
VAMPIRE!
HEY... WATCH IT... HEY!
WHAT'S GOING ON?!
SPIDER-MAN'S HERE AGAIN! AND HE'S--HE'S FIGHTING A--
A WHAT?! WHAT'S HE FIGHTING?
VAMPIRE!
FINALLY!

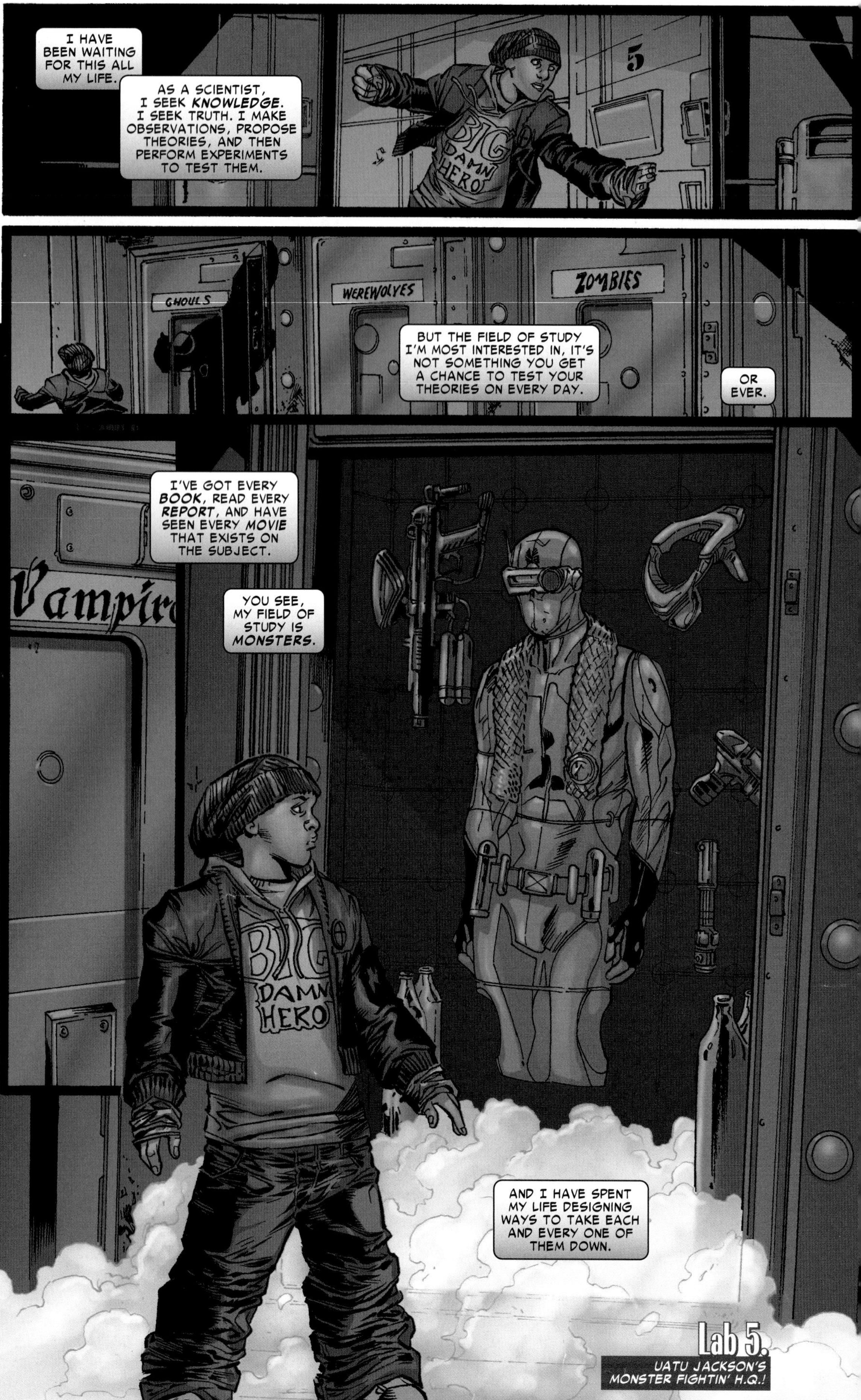
I HAVE BEEN WAITING FOR THIS ALL MY LIFE.
AS A SCIENTIST, I SEEK KNOWLEDGE. I SEEK TRUTH. I MAKE OBSERVATIONS, PROPOSE THEORIES, AND THEN PERFORM EXPERIMENTS TO TEST THEM.
BIG DAMN HERO
5
GHOULS
WEREWOLVES
ZOMBIES
BUT THE FIELD OF STUDY I'M MOST INTERESTED IN, IT'S NOT SOMETHING YOU GET A CHANCE TO TEST YOUR THEORIES ON EVERY DAY.
OR EVER.
I'VE GOT EVERY BOOK, READ EVERY REPORT, AND HAVE SEEN EVERY MOVIE THAT EXISTS ON THE SUBJECT.
Vampire
YOU SEE, MY FIELD OF STUDY IS MONSTERS.
BIG DAMN HERO
AND I HAVE SPENT MY LIFE DESIGNING WAYS TO TAKE EACH AND EVERY ONE OF THEM DOWN.
Lab 5.
UATU JACKSON'S MONSTER FIGHTIN' H.Q.!

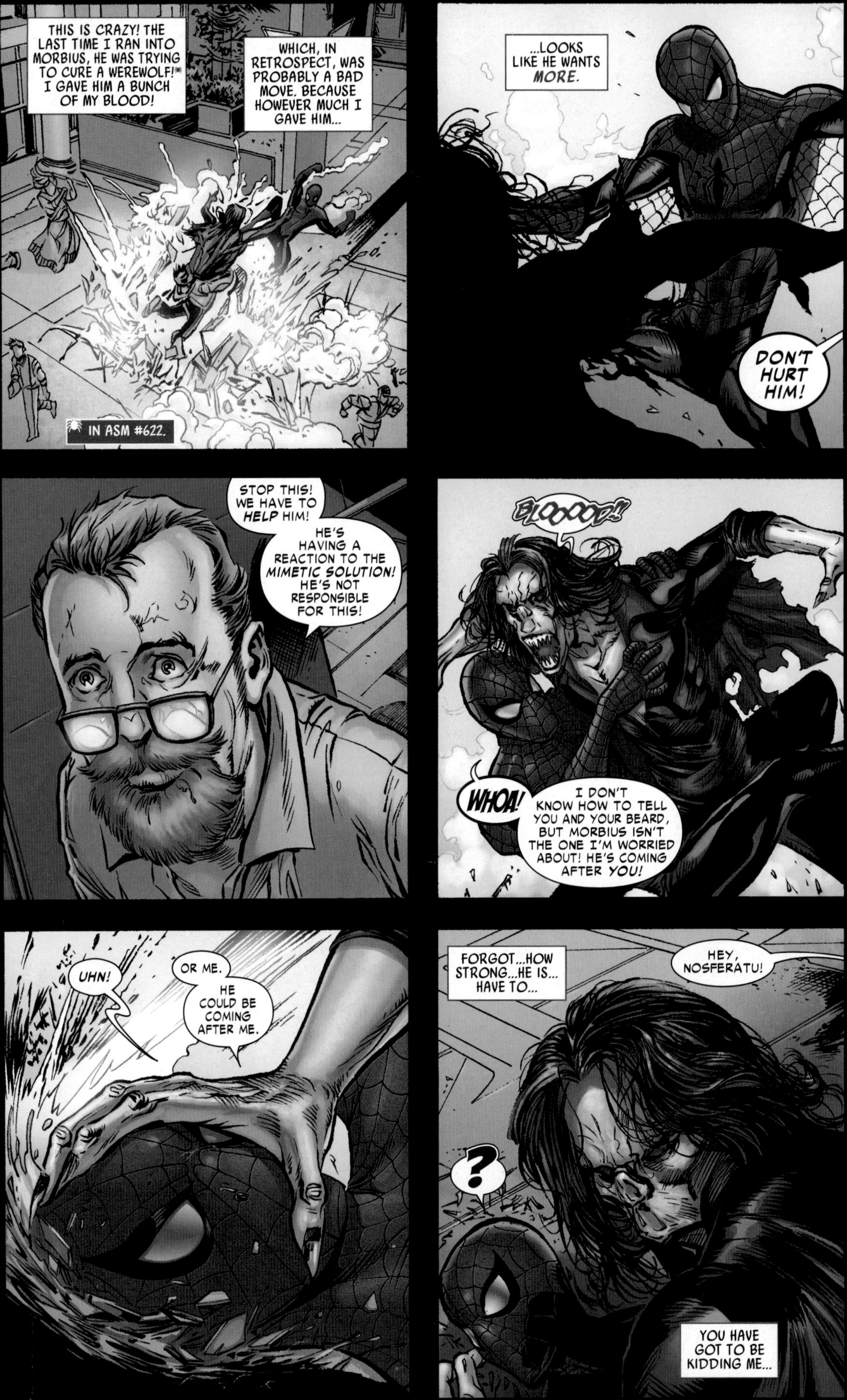
THIS IS CRAZY! THE LAST TIME I RAN INTO MORBIUS, HE WAS TRYING TO CURE A WEREWOLF!* I GAVE HIM A BUNCH OF MY BLOOD!
WHICH, IN RETROSPECT, WAS PROBABLY A BAD MOVE. BECAUSE HOWEVER MUCH I GAVE HIM...
*IN ASM #622.
...LOOKS LIKE HE WANTS MORE.
DON'T HURT HIM!
STOP THIS! WE HAVE TO HELP HIM!
HE'S HAVING A REACTION TO THE MIMETIC SOLUTION! HE'S NOT RESPONSIBLE FOR THIS!
BLOOOOD!!
WHOA!
I DON'T KNOW HOW TO TELL YOU AND YOUR BEARD, BUT MORBIUS ISN'T THE ONE I'M WORRIED ABOUT! HE'S COMING AFTER YOU!
UHN!
OR ME.
HE COULD BE COMING AFTER ME.
FORGOT...HOW STRONG...HE IS... HAVE TO...
HEY, NOSFERATU!
?
YOU HAVE GOT TO BE KIDDING ME...

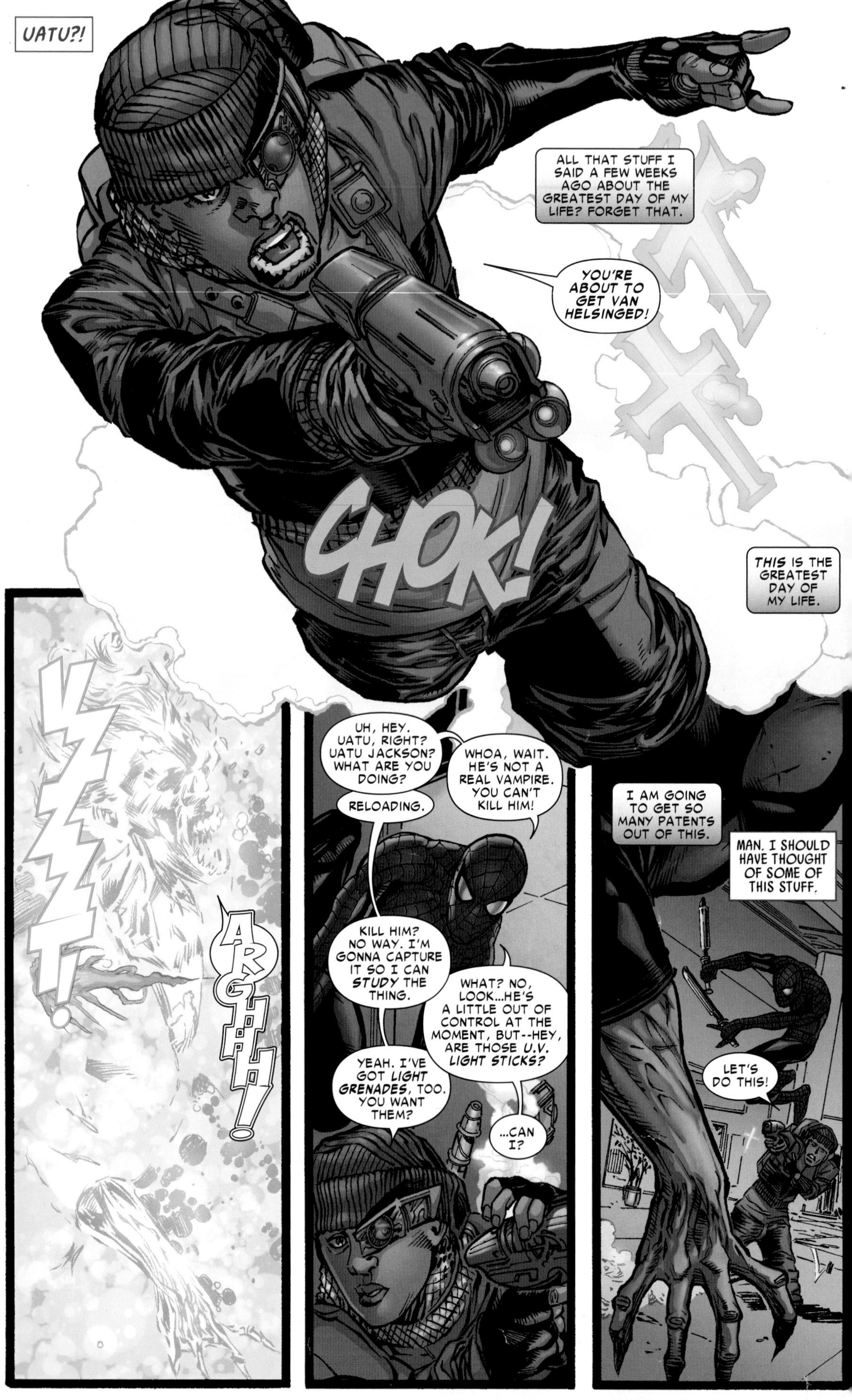
UATU?!
ALL THAT STUFF I SAID A FEW WEEKS AGO ABOUT THE GREATEST DAY OF MY LIFE? FORGET THAT.
YOU'RE ABOUT TO GET VAN HELSINGED!
CHOK!
THIS IS THE GREATEST DAY OF MY LIFE.
VZZZT!
ARGHHH!
UH, HEY. UATU, RIGHT? UATU JACKSON? WHAT ARE YOU DOING?
RELOADING.
WHOA, WAIT. HE'S NOT A REAL VAMPIRE. YOU CAN'T KILL HIM!
KILL HIM? NO WAY. I'M GONNA CAPTURE IT SO I CAN STUDY THE THING.
WHAT? NO, LOOK...HE'S A LITTLE OUT OF CONTROL AT THE MOMENT, BUT--HEY, ARE THOSE U.V. LIGHT STICKS?
YEAH. I'VE GOT LIGHT GRENADES, TOO. YOU WANT THEM?
...CAN I?
I AM GOING TO GET SO MANY PATENTS OUT OF THIS.
MAN. I SHOULD HAVE THOUGHT OF SOME OF THIS STUFF.
LET'S DO THIS!

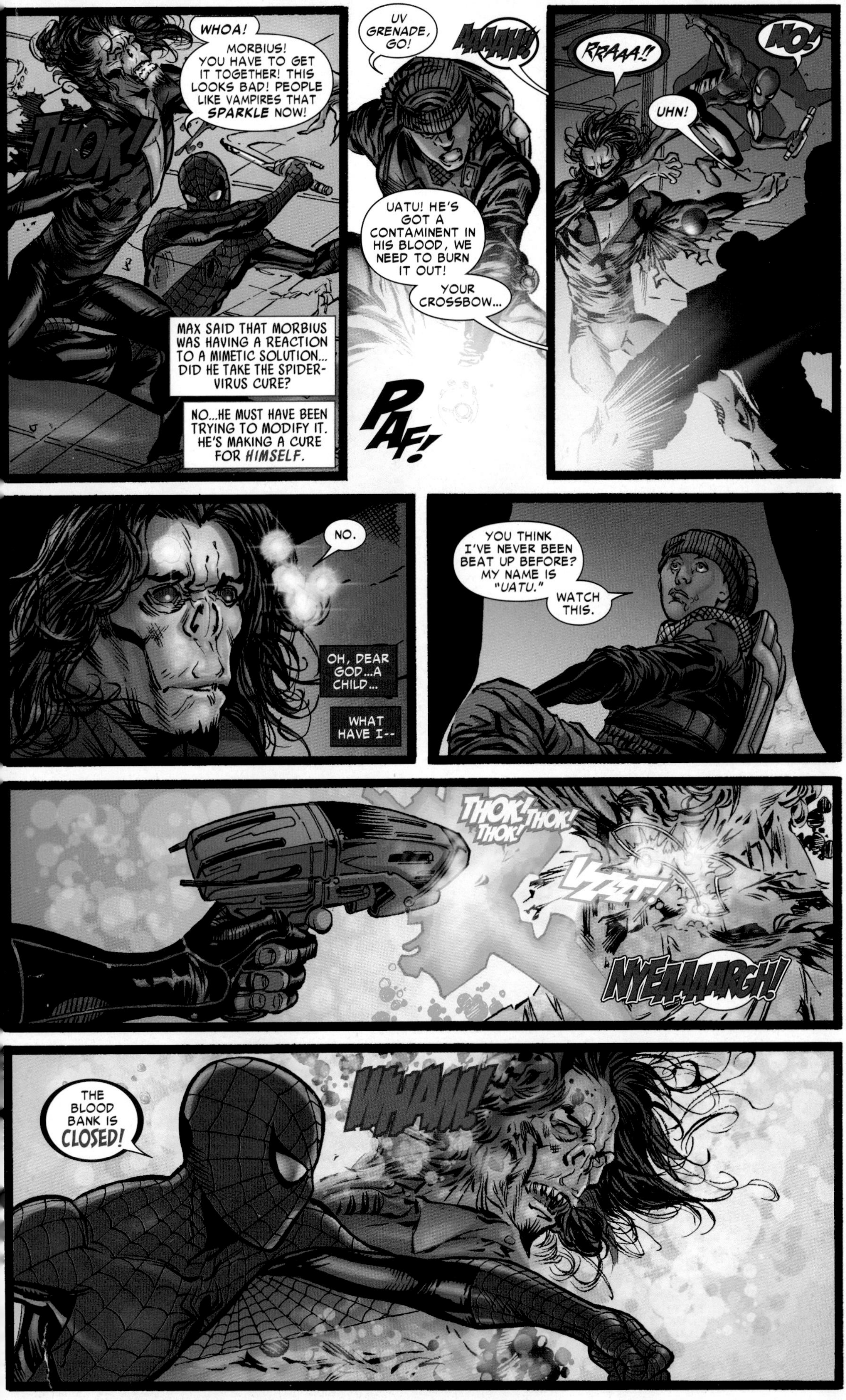
WHOA!
MORBIUS! YOU HAVE TO GET IT TOGETHER! THIS LOOKS BAD! PEOPLE LIKE VAMPIRES THAT SPARKLE NOW!
THOK!
MAX SAID THAT MORBIUS WAS HAVING A REACTION TO A MIMETIC SOLUTION... DID HE TAKE THE SPIDER-VIRUS CURE?
NO...HE MUST HAVE BEEN TRYING TO MODIFY IT. HE'S MAKING A CURE FOR HIMSELF.
UV GRENADE, GO!
AAAAH!
UATU! HE'S GOT A CONTAMINENT IN HIS BLOOD, WE NEED TO BURN IT OUT!
YOUR CROSSBOW...
PAF!
RRAAA!!
NO!
UHN!
NO.
OH, DEAR GOD...A CHILD...
WHAT HAVE I--
YOU THINK I'VE NEVER BEEN BEAT UP BEFORE? MY NAME IS "UATU."
WATCH THIS.
THOK! THOK! THOK!
VZZT!
NYEAAAARGH!
THE BLOOD BANK IS CLOSED!
WHAM!

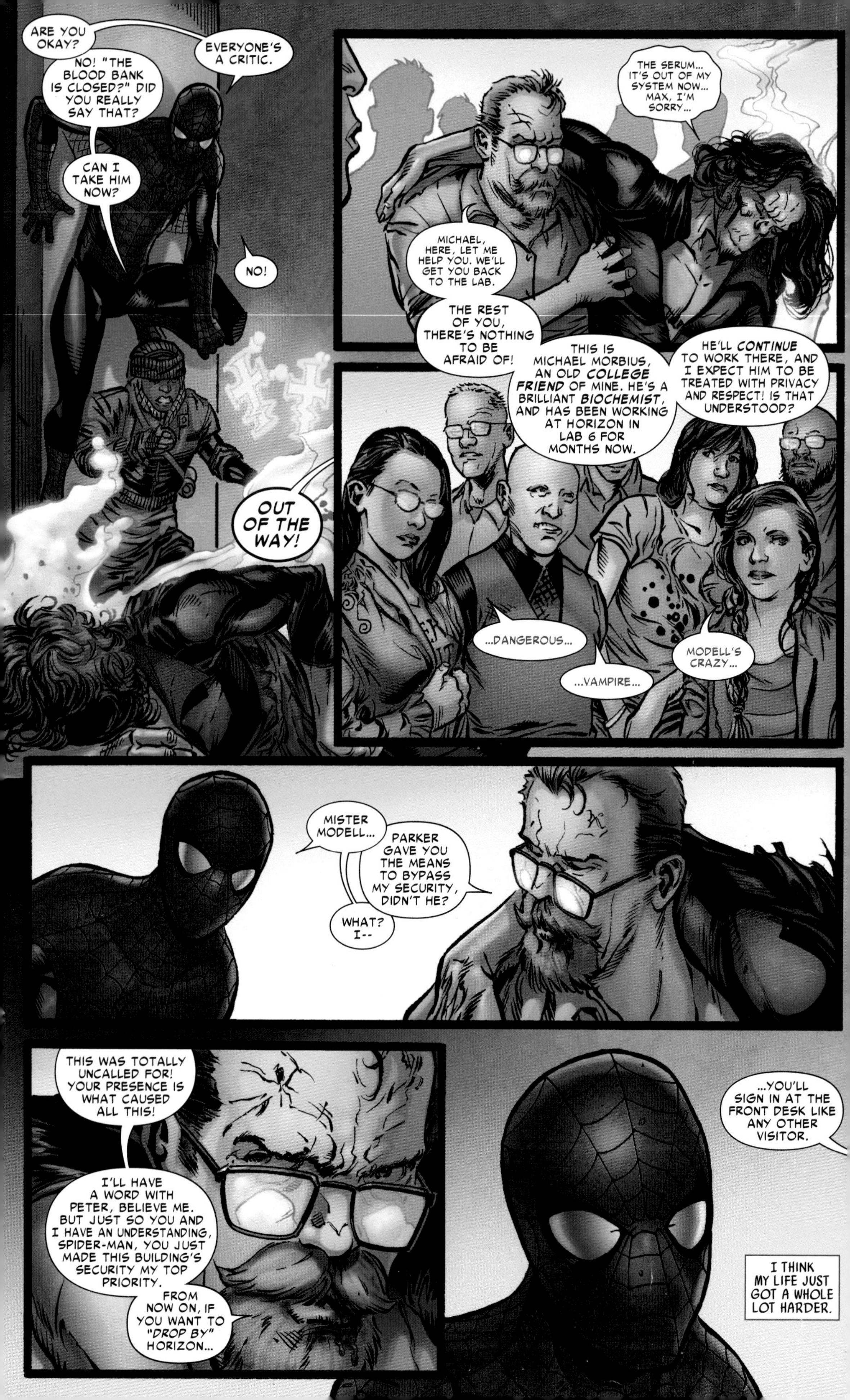
ARE YOU OKAY?
EVERYONE'S A CRITIC.
NO! "THE BLOOD BANK IS CLOSED?" DID YOU REALLY SAY THAT?
CAN I TAKE HIM NOW?
NO!
OUT OF THE WAY!
THE SERUM... IT'S OUT OF MY SYSTEM NOW... MAX, I'M SORRY...
MICHAEL, HERE, LET ME HELP YOU. WE'LL GET YOU BACK TO THE LAB.
THE REST OF YOU, THERE'S NOTHING TO BE AFRAID OF!
THIS IS MICHAEL MORBIUS, AN OLD COLLEGE FRIEND OF MINE. HE'S A BRILLIANT BIOCHEMIST, AND HAS BEEN WORKING AT HORIZON IN LAB 6 FOR MONTHS NOW.
HE'LL CONTINUE TO WORK THERE, AND I EXPECT HIM TO BE TREATED WITH PRIVACY AND RESPECT! IS THAT UNDERSTOOD?
...DANGEROUS...
...VAMPIRE...
MODELL'S CRAZY...
MISTER MODELL...
PARKER GAVE YOU THE MEANS TO BYPASS MY SECURITY, DIDN'T HE?
WHAT? I--
THIS WAS TOTALLY UNCALLED FOR! YOUR PRESENCE IS WHAT CAUSED ALL THIS!
I'LL HAVE A WORD WITH PETER, BELIEVE ME. BUT JUST SO YOU AND I HAVE AN UNDERSTANDING, SPIDER-MAN, YOU JUST MADE THIS BUILDING'S SECURITY MY TOP PRIORITY.
FROM NOW ON, IF YOU WANT TO "DROP BY" HORIZON...
...YOU'LL SIGN IN AT THE FRONT DESK LIKE ANY OTHER VISITOR.
I THINK MY LIFE JUST GOT A WHOLE LOT HARDER.

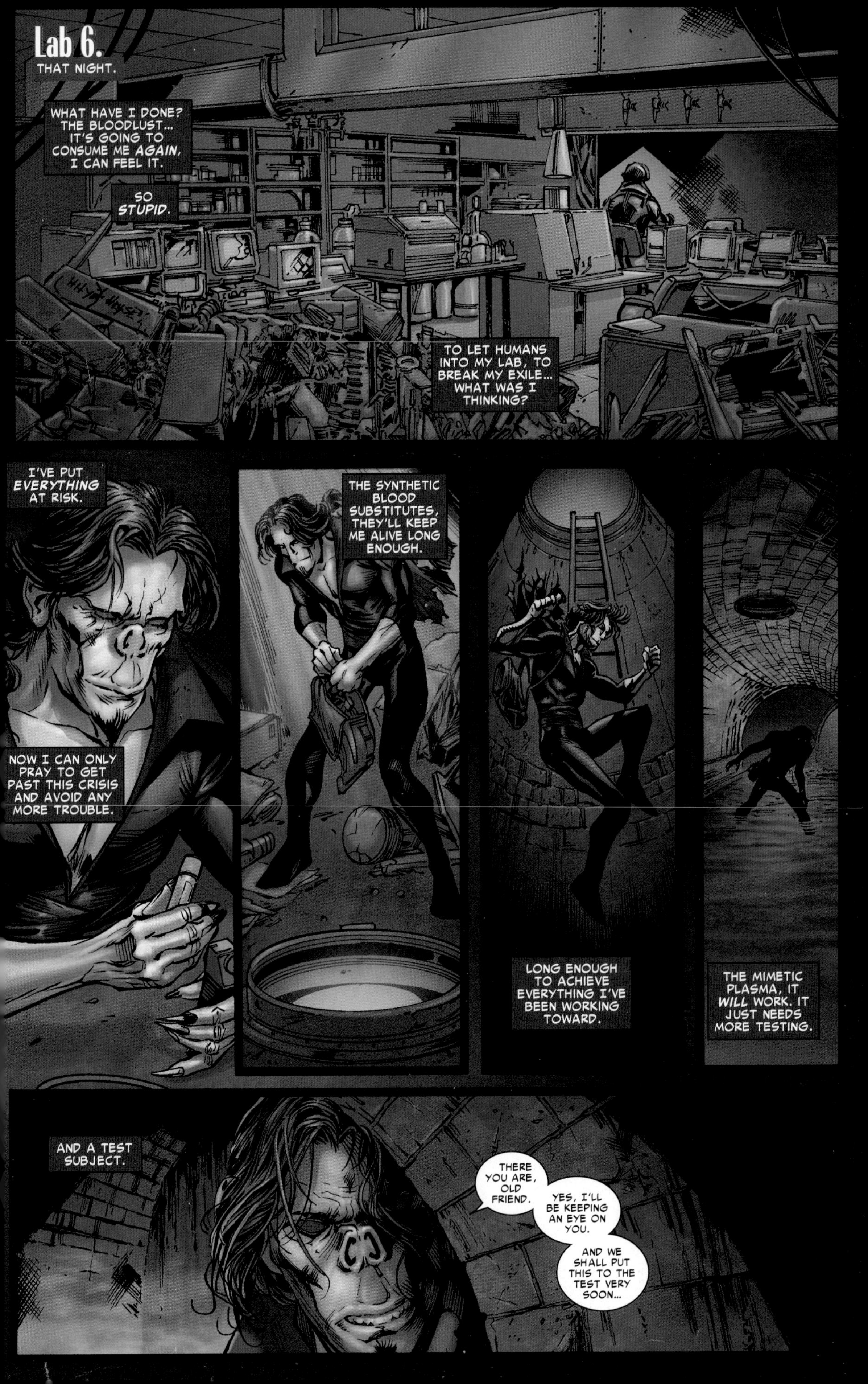
Lab 6.
THAT NIGHT.
WHAT HAVE I DONE? THE BLOODLUST... IT'S GOING TO CONSUME ME AGAIN, I CAN FEEL IT.
SO STUPID.
TO LET HUMANS INTO MY LAB, TO BREAK MY EXILE... WHAT WAS I THINKING?
I'VE PUT EVERYTHING AT RISK.
NOW I CAN ONLY PRAY TO GET PAST THIS CRISIS AND AVOID ANY MORE TROUBLE.
THE SYNTHETIC BLOOD SUBSTITUTES, THEY'LL KEEP ME ALIVE LONG ENOUGH.
LONG ENOUGH TO ACHIEVE EVERYTHING I'VE BEEN WORKING TOWARD.
THE MIMETIC PLASMA, IT WILL WORK. IT JUST NEEDS MORE TESTING.
AND A TEST SUBJECT.
THERE YOU ARE, OLD FRIEND.
YES, I'LL BE KEEPING AN EYE ON YOU.
AND WE SHALL PUT THIS TO THE TEST VERY SOON...

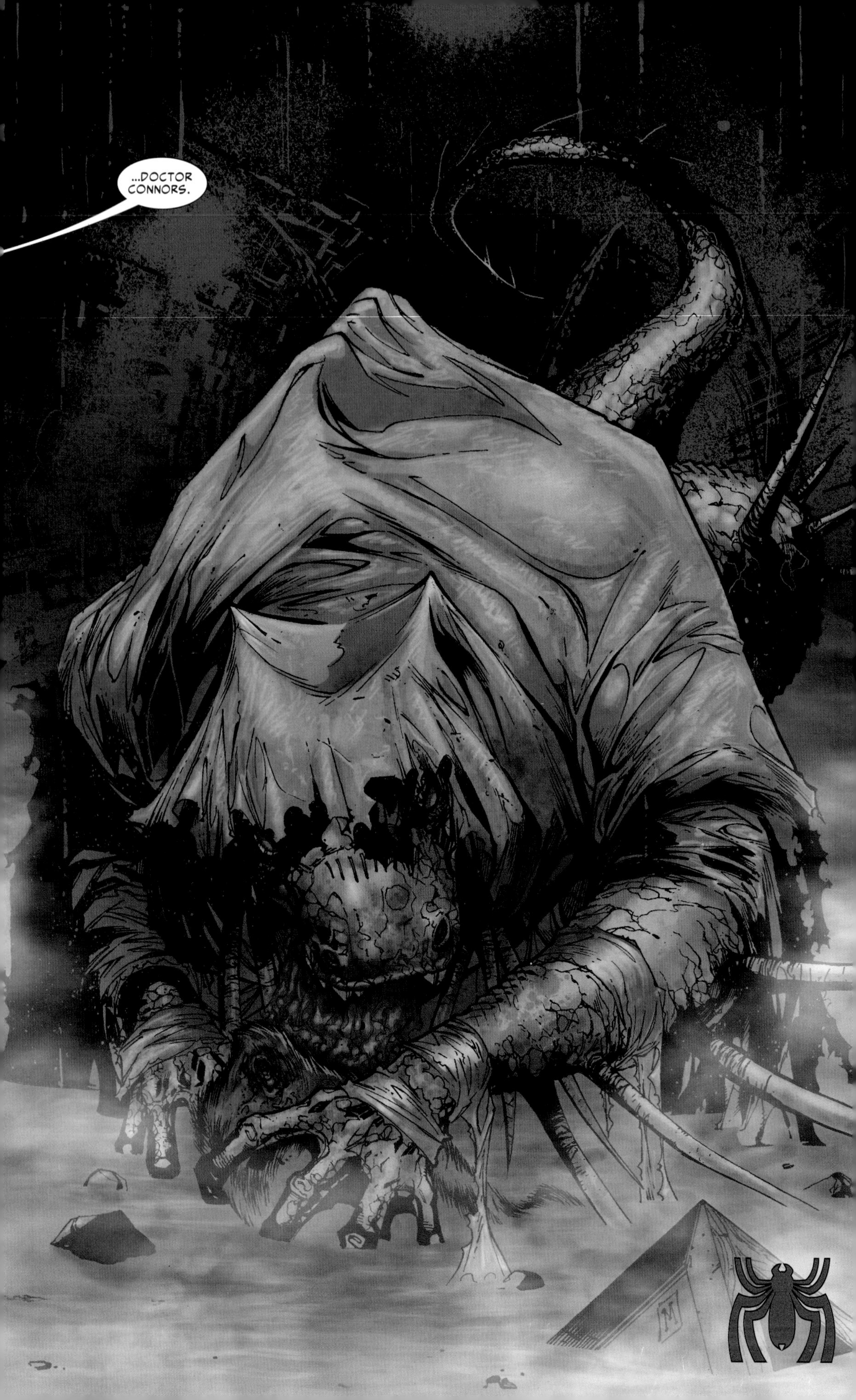
...DOCTOR CONNORS.

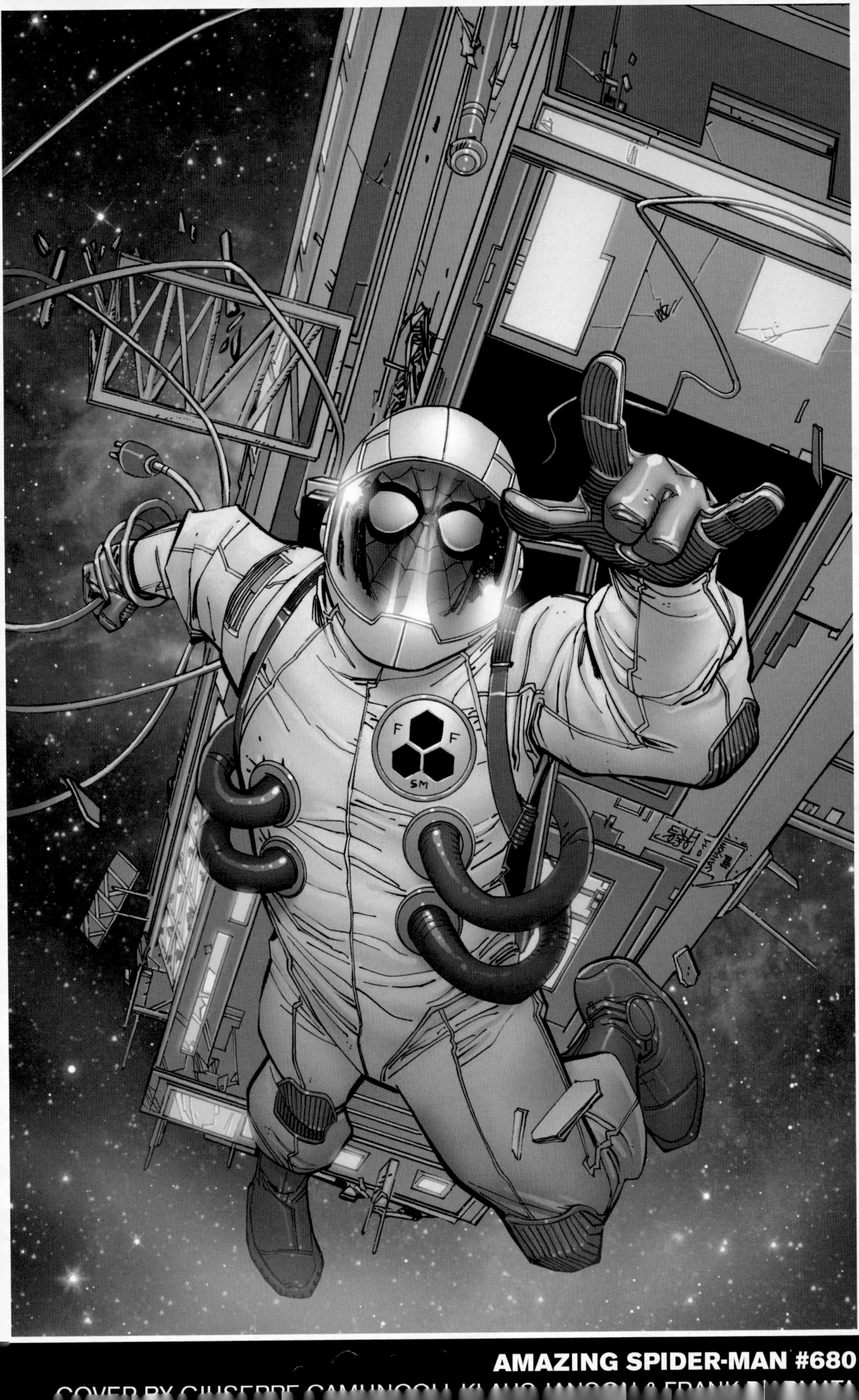

AMAZING SPIDER-MAN #680

COVER BY GIUSEPPE CAMUNCOLI, KLAUS JANSON & FRANK D'ARMATA

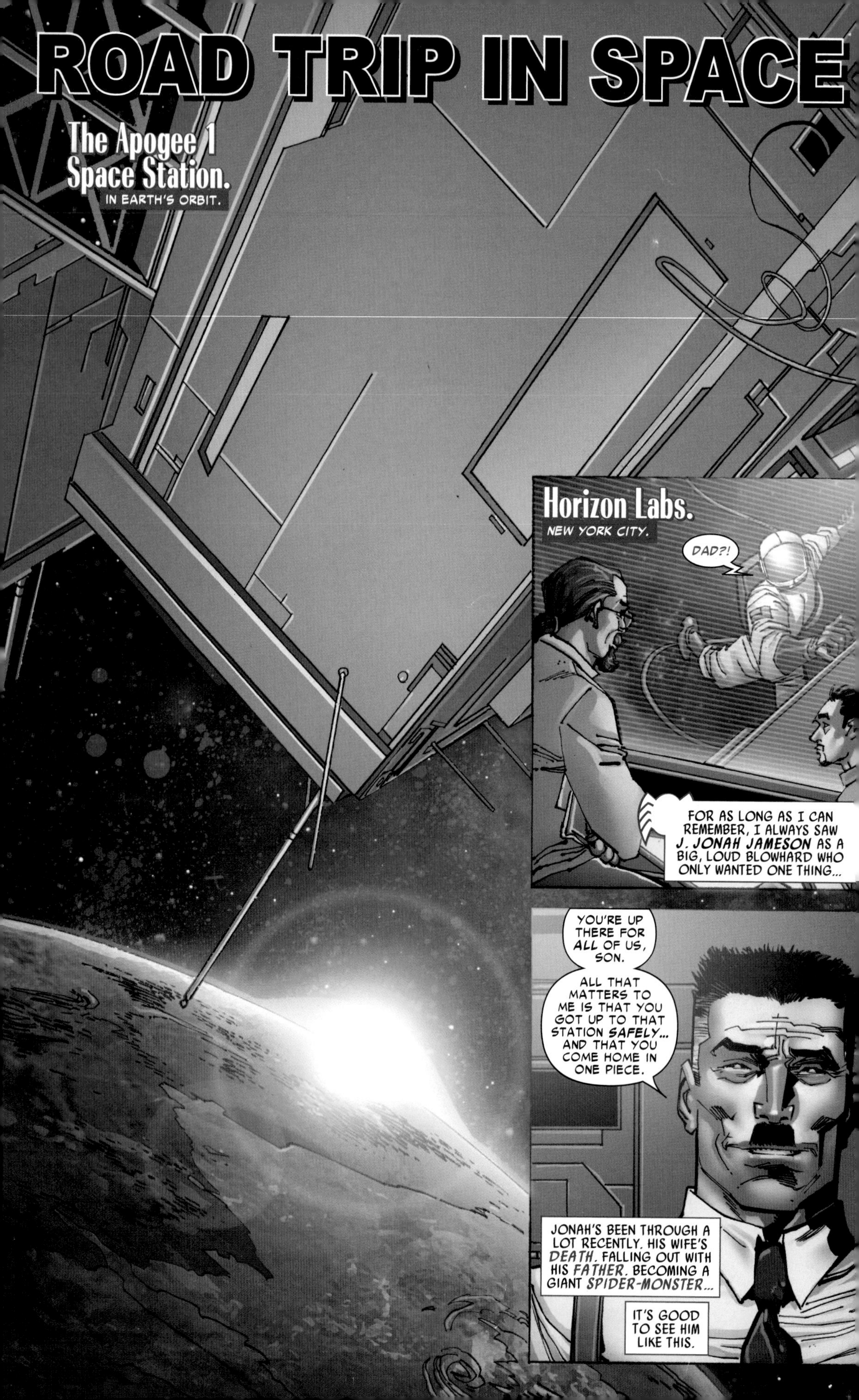
ROAD TRIP IN SPACE
The Apogee 1 Space Station.
IN EARTH'S ORBIT.
Horizon Labs.
NEW YORK CITY.
DAD?!
FOR AS LONG AS I CAN REMEMBER, I ALWAYS SAW J. JONAH JAMESON AS A BIG, LOUD BLOWHARD WHO ONLY WANTED ONE THING...
YOU'RE UP THERE FOR ALL OF US, SON.
ALL THAT MATTERS TO ME IS THAT YOU GOT UP TO THAT STATION SAFELY... AND THAT YOU COME HOME IN ONE PIECE.
JONAH'S BEEN THROUGH A LOT RECENTLY. HIS WIFE'S DEATH. FALLING OUT WITH HIS FATHER. BECOMING A GIANT SPIDER-MONSTER...
IT'S GOOD TO SEE HIM LIKE THIS.

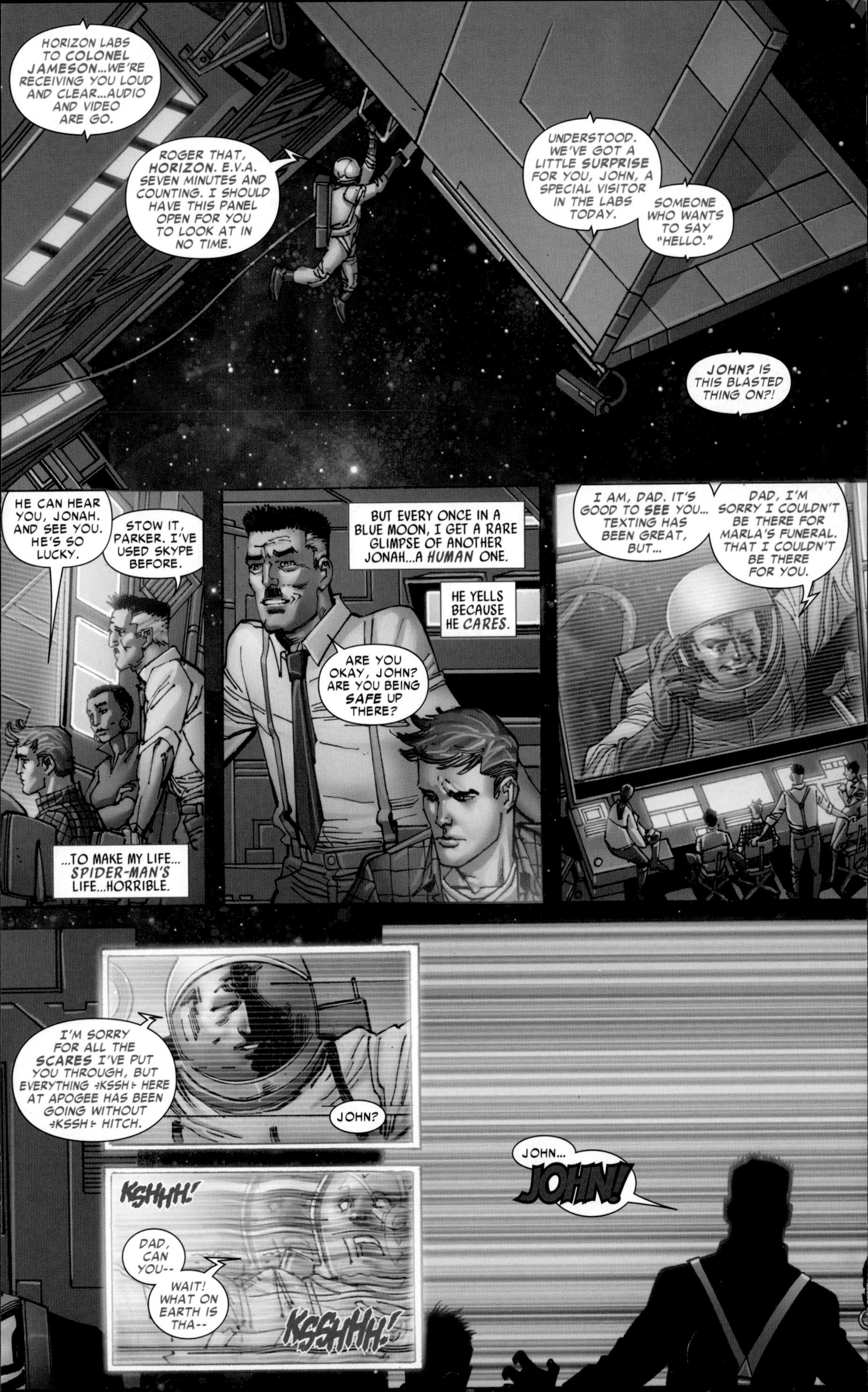
HORIZON LABS TO COLONEL JAMESON...WE'RE RECEIVING YOU LOUD AND CLEAR...AUDIO AND VIDEO ARE GO.
ROGER THAT, HORIZON. E.V.A. SEVEN MINUTES AND COUNTING. I SHOULD HAVE THIS PANEL OPEN FOR YOU TO LOOK AT IN NO TIME.
UNDERSTOOD. WE'VE GOT A LITTLE SURPRISE FOR YOU, JOHN, A SPECIAL VISITOR IN THE LABS TODAY.
SOMEONE WHO WANTS TO SAY "HELLO."
JOHN? IS THIS BLASTED THING ON?!
HE CAN HEAR YOU, JONAH. AND SEE YOU. HE'S SO LUCKY.
STOW IT, PARKER. I'VE USED SKYPE BEFORE.
...TO MAKE MY LIFE... SPIDER-MAN'S LIFE...HORRIBLE.
BUT EVERY ONCE IN A BLUE MOON, I GET A RARE GLIMPSE OF ANOTHER JONAH...A HUMAN ONE.
HE YELLS BECAUSE HE CARES.
ARE YOU OKAY, JOHN? ARE YOU BEING SAFE UP THERE?
I AM, DAD. IT'S GOOD TO SEE YOU... TEXTING HAS BEEN GREAT, BUT...
DAD, I'M SORRY I COULDN'T BE THERE FOR MARLA'S FUNERAL. THAT I COULDN'T BE THERE FOR YOU.
I'M SORRY FOR ALL THE SCARES I'VE PUT YOU THROUGH, BUT EVERYTHING ≠KSSH≠ HERE AT APOGEE HAS BEEN GOING WITHOUT ≠KSSH≠ HITCH.
JOHN?
KSHHH!
DAD, CAN YOU--
WAIT! WHAT ON EARTH IS THA--
KSSHHH!
JOHN... JOHN!

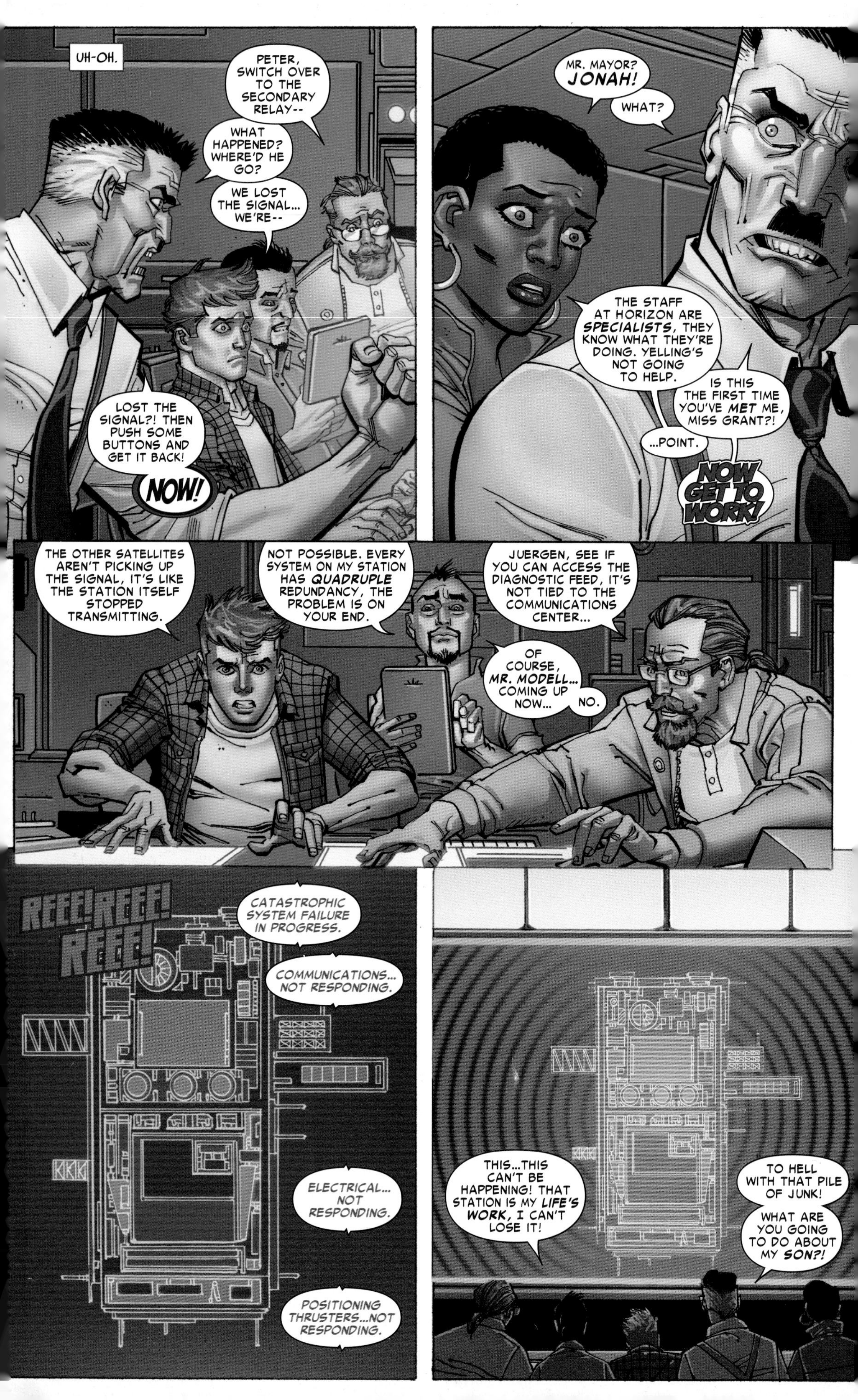
UH-OH.
PETER, SWITCH OVER TO THE SECONDARY RELAY--
WHAT HAPPENED? WHERE'D HE GO?
WE LOST THE SIGNAL... WE'RE--
LOST THE SIGNAL?! THEN PUSH SOME BUTTONS AND GET IT BACK!
NOW!
MR. MAYOR? JONAH!
WHAT?
THE STAFF AT HORIZON ARE SPECIALISTS, THEY KNOW WHAT THEY'RE DOING. YELLING'S NOT GOING TO HELP.
IS THIS THE FIRST TIME YOU'VE MET ME, MISS GRANT?!
...POINT.
NOW GET TO WORK!
THE OTHER SATELLITES AREN'T PICKING UP THE SIGNAL, IT'S LIKE THE STATION ITSELF STOPPED TRANSMITTING.
NOT POSSIBLE. EVERY SYSTEM ON MY STATION HAS QUADRUPLE REDUNDANCY, THE PROBLEM IS ON YOUR END.
JUERGEN, SEE IF YOU CAN ACCESS THE DIAGNOSTIC FEED, IT'S NOT TIED TO THE COMMUNICATIONS CENTER...
OF COURSE, MR. MODELL... COMING UP NOW...
NO.
REEE! REEE! REEE!
CATASTROPHIC SYSTEM FAILURE IN PROGRESS.
COMMUNICATIONS... NOT RESPONDING.
ELECTRICAL... NOT RESPONDING.
POSITIONING THRUSTERS...NOT RESPONDING.
THIS...THIS CAN'T BE HAPPENING! THAT STATION IS MY LIFE'S WORK, I CAN'T LOSE IT!
TO HELL WITH THAT PILE OF JUNK!
WHAT ARE YOU GOING TO DO ABOUT MY SON?!

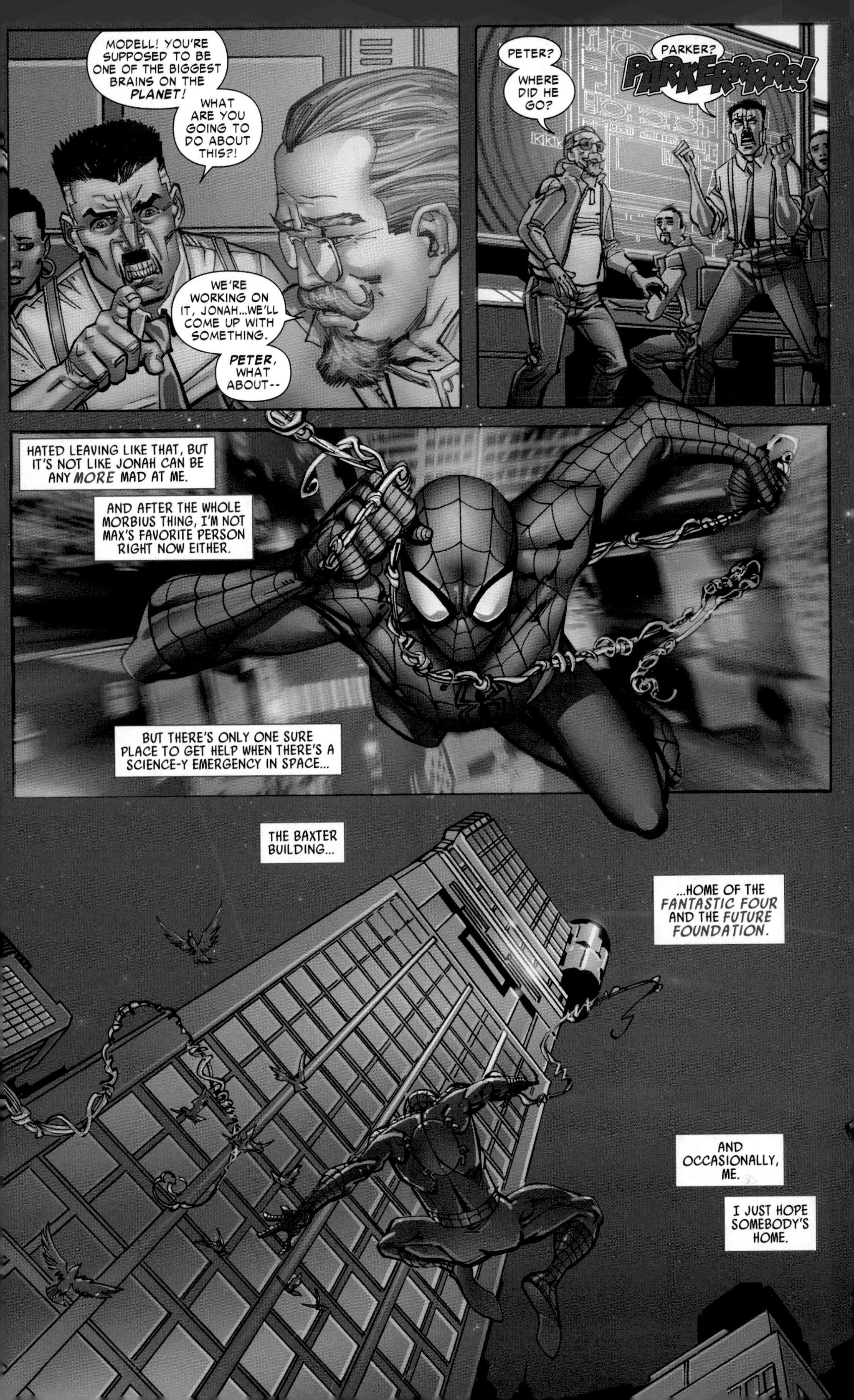
MODELL! YOU'RE SUPPOSED TO BE ONE OF THE BIGGEST BRAINS ON THE PLANET!
WHAT ARE YOU GOING TO DO ABOUT THIS?!
WE'RE WORKING ON IT, JONAH...WE'LL COME UP WITH SOMETHING.
PETER, WHAT ABOUT--
PETER?
WHERE DID HE GO?
PARKER?
PARKERRRRR!
HATED LEAVING LIKE THAT, BUT IT'S NOT LIKE JONAH CAN BE ANY MORE MAD AT ME.
AND AFTER THE WHOLE MORBIUS THING, I'M NOT MAX'S FAVORITE PERSON RIGHT NOW EITHER.
BUT THERE'S ONLY ONE SURE PLACE TO GET HELP WHEN THERE'S A SCIENCE-Y EMERGENCY IN SPACE...
THE BAXTER BUILDING...
...HOME OF THE FANTASTIC FOUR AND THE FUTURE FOUNDATION.
AND OCCASIONALLY, ME.
I JUST HOPE SOMEBODY'S HOME.

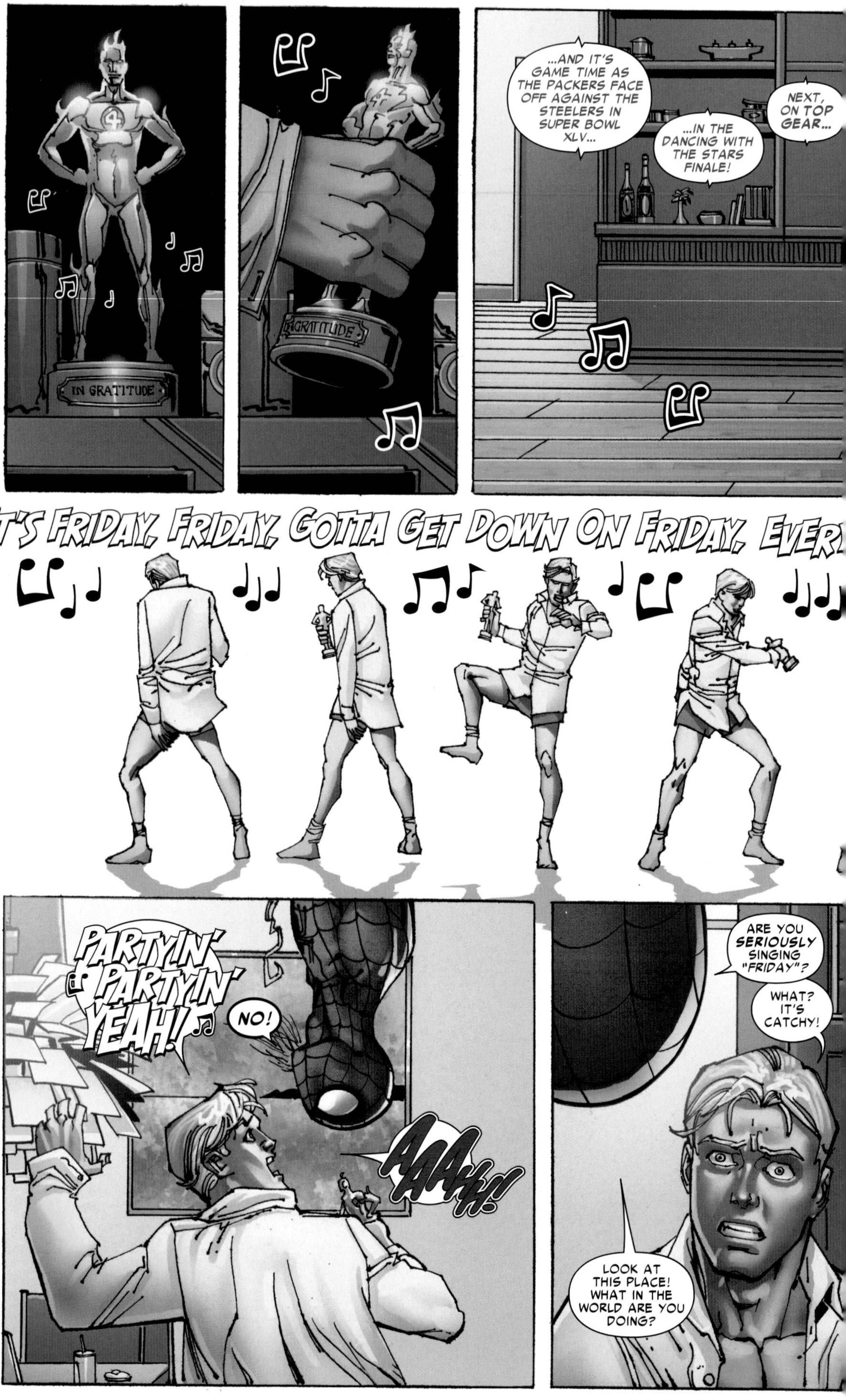
IN GRATITUDE
GRATITUDE
...AND IT'S GAME TIME AS THE PACKERS FACE OFF AGAINST THE STEELERS IN SUPER BOWL XLV...
...IN THE DANCING WITH THE STARS FINALE!
NEXT, ON TOP GEAR...
IT'S FRIDAY, FRIDAY, GOTTA GET DOWN ON FRIDAY, EVER
PARTYIN' PARTYIN' YEAH!
NO!
AAAAH!
ARE YOU SERIOUSLY SINGING "FRIDAY"?
WHAT? IT'S CATCHY!
LOOK AT THIS PLACE! WHAT IN THE WORLD ARE YOU DOING?

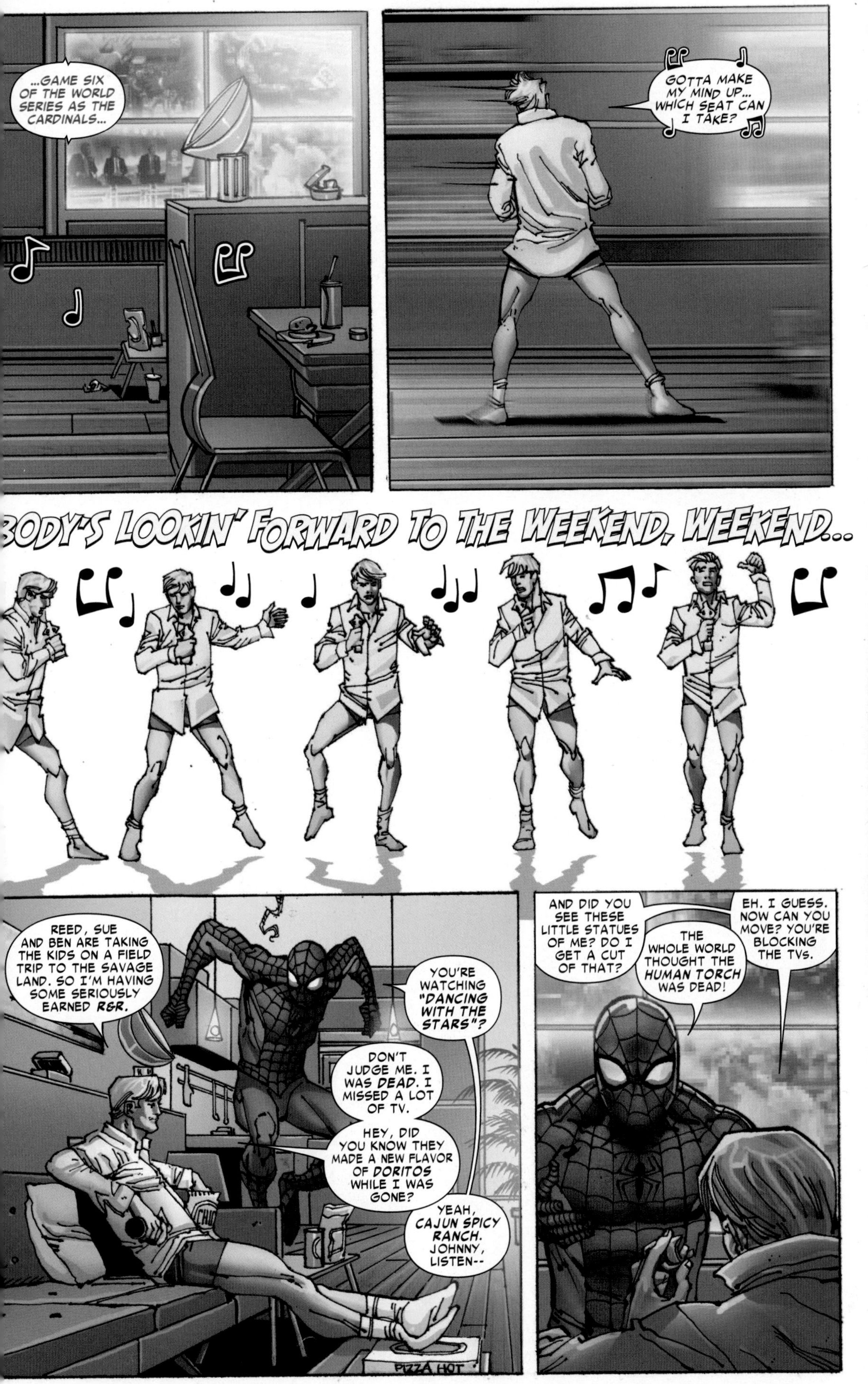

...GAME SIX OF THE WORLD SERIES AS THE CARDINALS...
GOTTA MAKE MY MIND UP... WHICH SEAT CAN I TAKE?
BODY'S LOOKIN' FORWARD TO THE WEEKEND, WEEKEND...
REED, SUE AND BEN ARE TAKING THE KIDS ON A FIELD TRIP TO THE SAVAGE LAND. SO I'M HAVING SOME SERIOUSLY EARNED R&R.
YOU'RE WATCHING "DANCING WITH THE STARS"?
DON'T JUDGE ME. I WAS DEAD. I MISSED A LOT OF TV.
HEY, DID YOU KNOW THEY MADE A NEW FLAVOR OF DORITOS WHILE I WAS GONE?
YEAH, CAJUN SPICY RANCH. JOHNNY, LISTEN--
PIZZA HOT
AND DID YOU SEE THESE LITTLE STATUES OF ME? DO I GET A CUT OF THAT?
EH. I GUESS. NOW CAN YOU MOVE? YOU'RE BLOCKING THE TVs.
THE WHOLE WORLD THOUGHT THE HUMAN TORCH WAS DEAD!

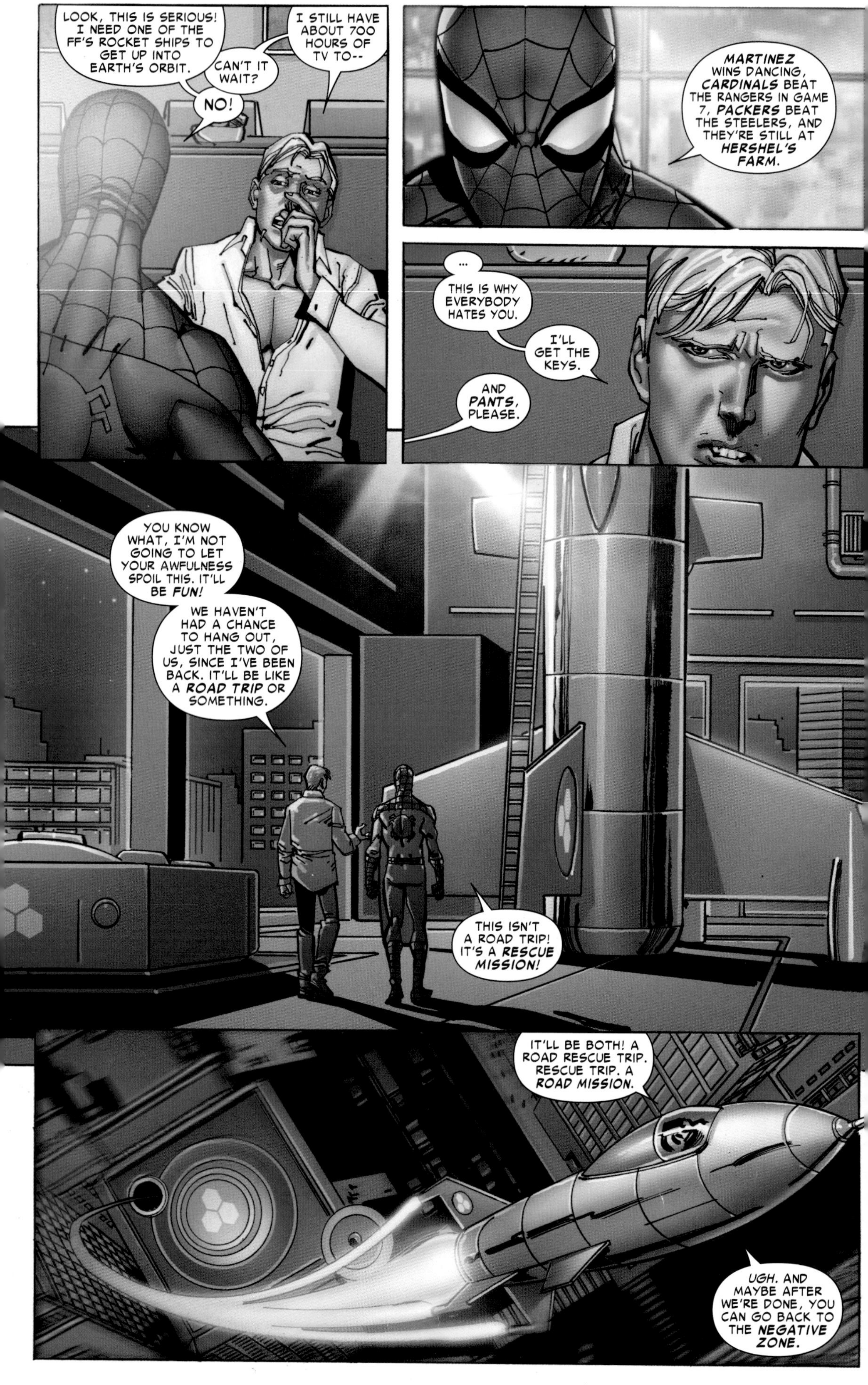
LOOK, THIS IS SERIOUS! I NEED ONE OF THE FF'S ROCKET SHIPS TO GET UP INTO EARTH'S ORBIT.
I STILL HAVE ABOUT 700 HOURS OF TV TO--
CAN'T IT WAIT?
NO!
MARTINEZ WINS DANCING, CARDINALS BEAT THE RANGERS IN GAME 7, PACKERS BEAT THE STEELERS, AND THEY'RE STILL AT HERSHEL'S FARM.
...
THIS IS WHY EVERYBODY HATES YOU.
I'LL GET THE KEYS.
AND PANTS, PLEASE.
YOU KNOW WHAT, I'M NOT GOING TO LET YOUR AWFULNESS SPOIL THIS. IT'LL BE FUN!
WE HAVEN'T HAD A CHANCE TO HANG OUT, JUST THE TWO OF US, SINCE I'VE BEEN BACK. IT'LL BE LIKE A ROAD TRIP OR SOMETHING.
THIS ISN'T A ROAD TRIP! IT'S A RESCUE MISSION!
IT'LL BE BOTH! A ROAD RESCUE TRIP. RESCUE TRIP. A ROAD MISSION.
UGH. AND MAYBE AFTER WE'RE DONE, YOU CAN GO BACK TO THE NEGATIVE ZONE.

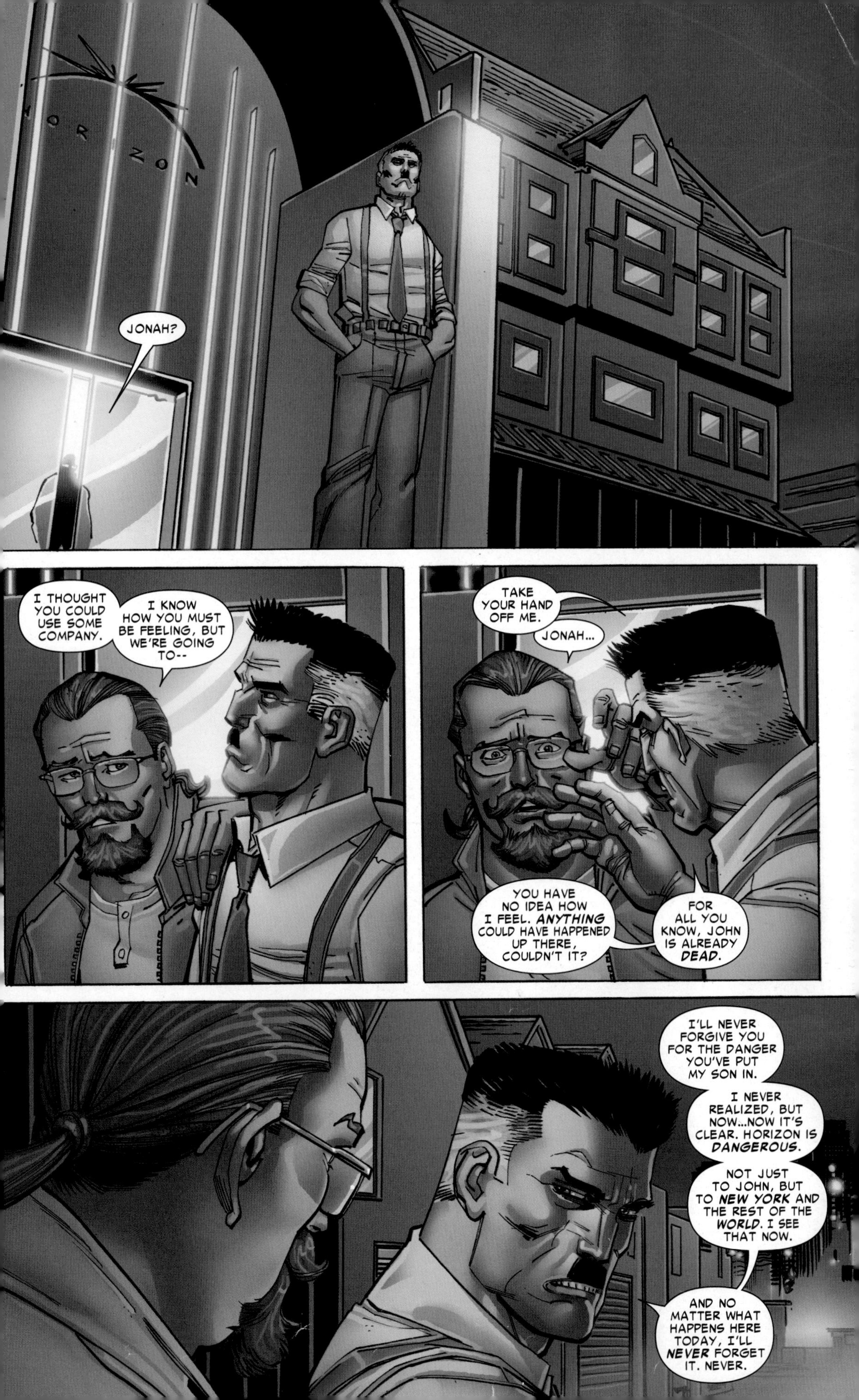
HORIZON
JONAH?
I THOUGHT YOU COULD USE SOME COMPANY.
I KNOW HOW YOU MUST BE FEELING, BUT WE'RE GOING TO--
TAKE YOUR HAND OFF ME.
JONAH...
YOU HAVE NO IDEA HOW I FEEL. ANYTHING COULD HAVE HAPPENED UP THERE, COULDN'T IT?
FOR ALL YOU KNOW, JOHN IS ALREADY DEAD.
I'LL NEVER FORGIVE YOU FOR THE DANGER YOU'VE PUT MY SON IN.
I NEVER REALIZED, BUT NOW...NOW IT'S CLEAR. HORIZON IS DANGEROUS.
NOT JUST TO JOHN, BUT TO NEW YORK AND THE REST OF THE WORLD. I SEE THAT NOW.
AND NO MATTER WHAT HAPPENS HERE TODAY, I'LL NEVER FORGET IT. NEVER.

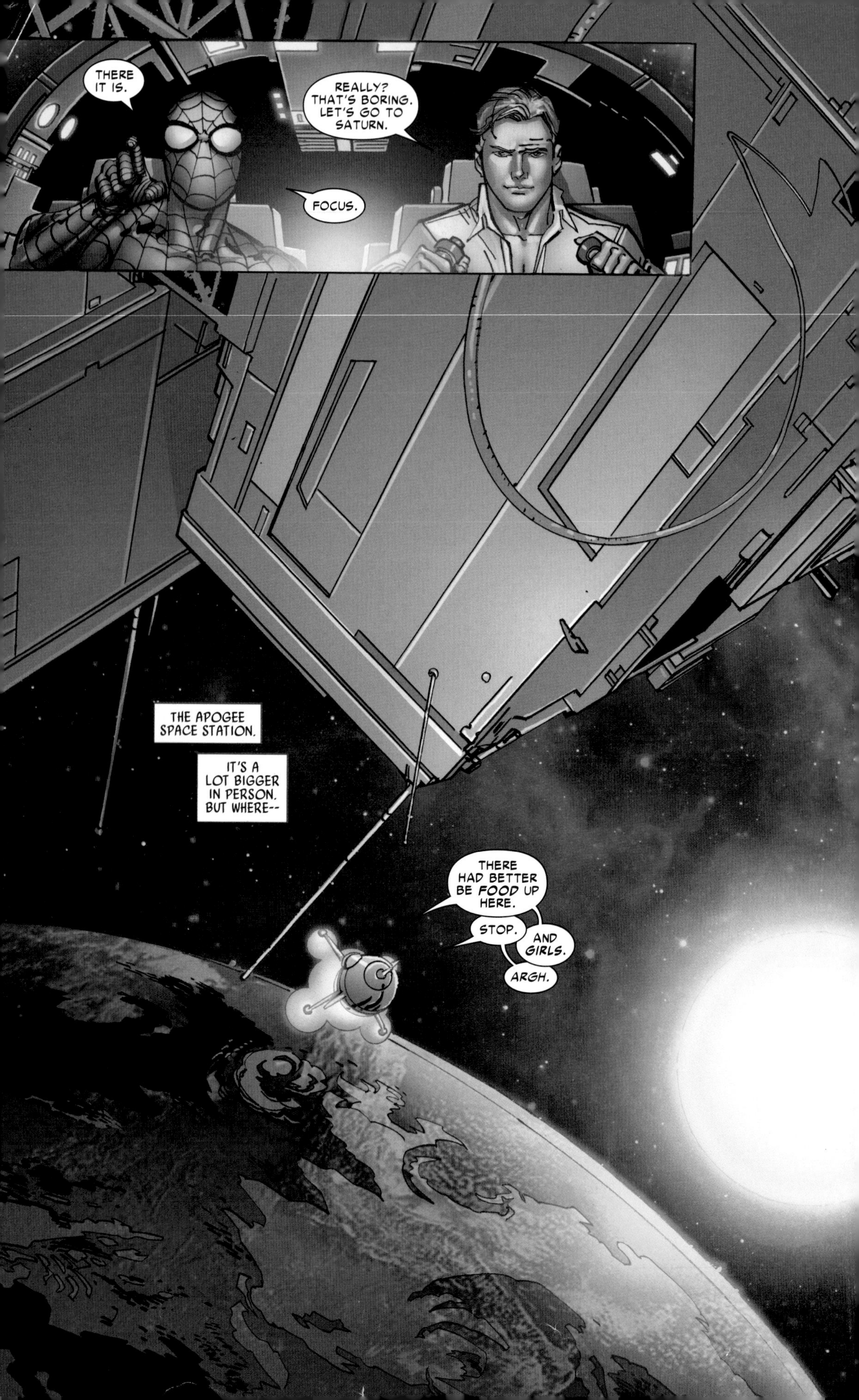
THERE IT IS.
REALLY? THAT'S BORING. LET'S GO TO SATURN.
FOCUS.
THE APOGEE SPACE STATION.
IT'S A LOT BIGGER IN PERSON. BUT WHERE--
THERE HAD BETTER BE FOOD UP HERE.
STOP.
AND GIRLS.
ARGH.

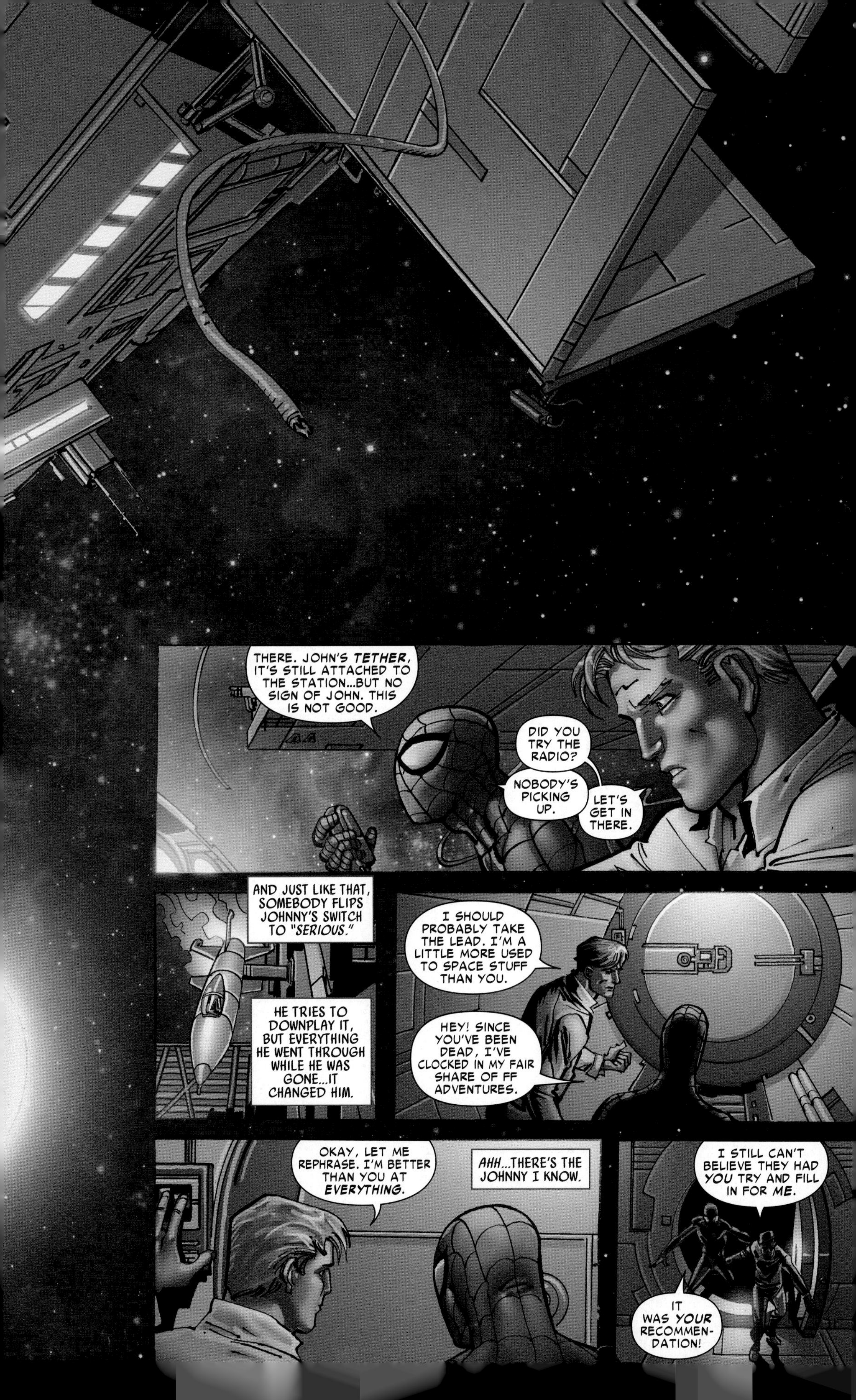
THERE. JOHN'S TETHER, IT'S STILL ATTACHED TO THE STATION...BUT NO SIGN OF JOHN. THIS IS NOT GOOD.
DID YOU TRY THE RADIO?
NOBODY'S PICKING UP.
LET'S GET IN THERE.
AND JUST LIKE THAT, SOMEBODY FLIPS JOHNNY'S SWITCH TO "SERIOUS."
HE TRIES TO DOWNPLAY IT, BUT EVERYTHING HE WENT THROUGH WHILE HE WAS GONE...IT CHANGED HIM.
I SHOULD PROBABLY TAKE THE LEAD. I'M A LITTLE MORE USED TO SPACE STUFF THAN YOU.
HEY! SINCE YOU'VE BEEN DEAD, I'VE CLOCKED IN MY FAIR SHARE OF FF ADVENTURES.
OKAY, LET ME REPHRASE. I'M BETTER THAN YOU AT EVERYTHING.
AHH...THERE'S THE JOHNNY I KNOW.
I STILL CAN'T BELIEVE THEY HAD YOU TRY AND FILL IN FOR ME.
IT WAS YOUR RECOMMEN-DATION!

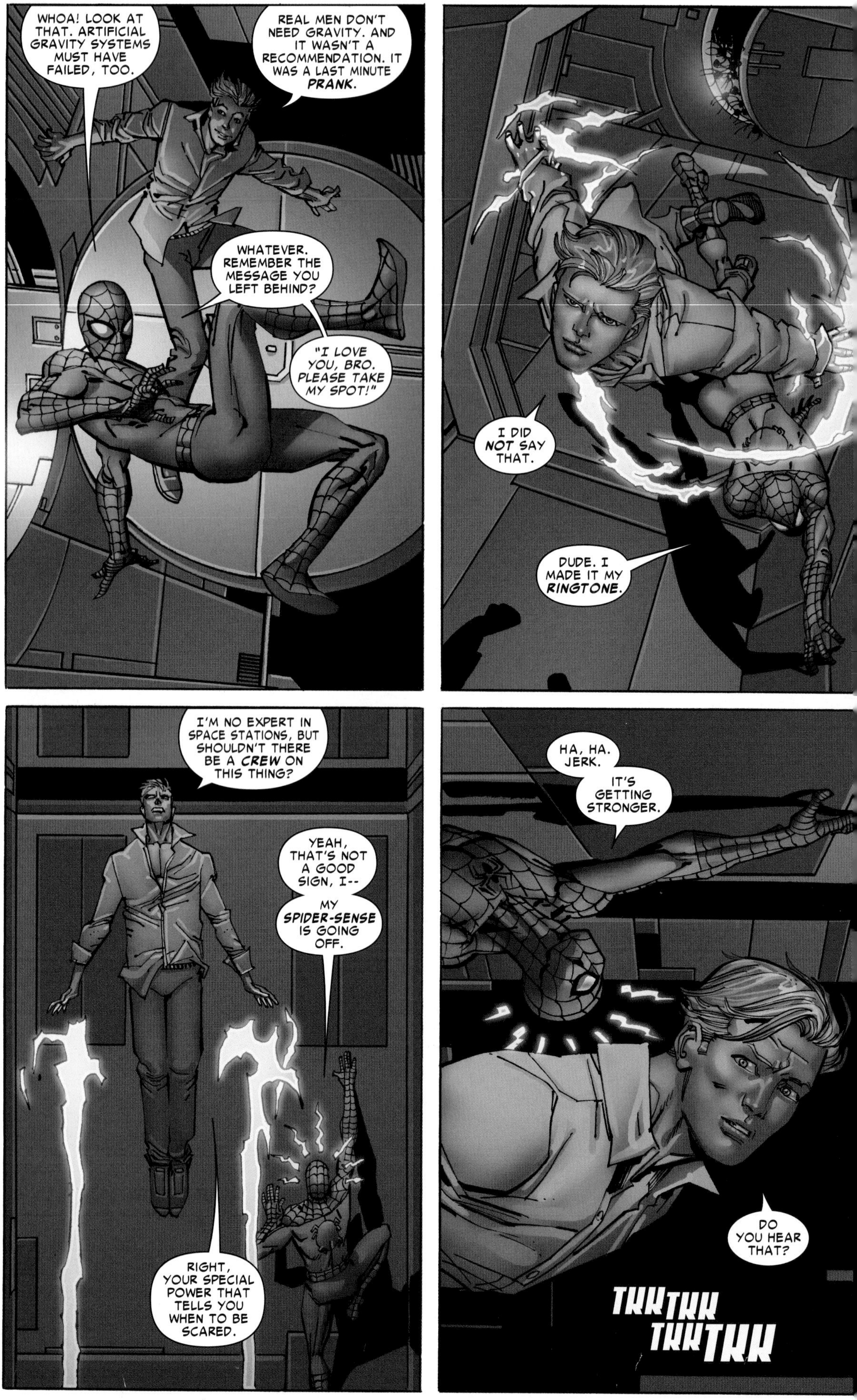
WHOA! LOOK AT THAT. ARTIFICIAL GRAVITY SYSTEMS MUST HAVE FAILED, TOO.
REAL MEN DON'T NEED GRAVITY. AND IT WASN'T A RECOMMENDATION. IT WAS A LAST MINUTE PRANK.
WHATEVER. REMEMBER THE MESSAGE YOU LEFT BEHIND?
"I LOVE YOU, BRO. PLEASE TAKE MY SPOT!"
I DID NOT SAY THAT.
DUDE. I MADE IT MY RINGTONE.
I'M NO EXPERT IN SPACE STATIONS, BUT SHOULDN'T THERE BE A CREW ON THIS THING?
YEAH, THAT'S NOT A GOOD SIGN, I--
MY SPIDER-SENSE IS GOING OFF.
RIGHT, YOUR SPECIAL POWER THAT TELLS YOU WHEN TO BE SCARED.
HA, HA. JERK.
IT'S GETTING STRONGER.
DO YOU HEAR THAT?
TKKTKK TKKTKK

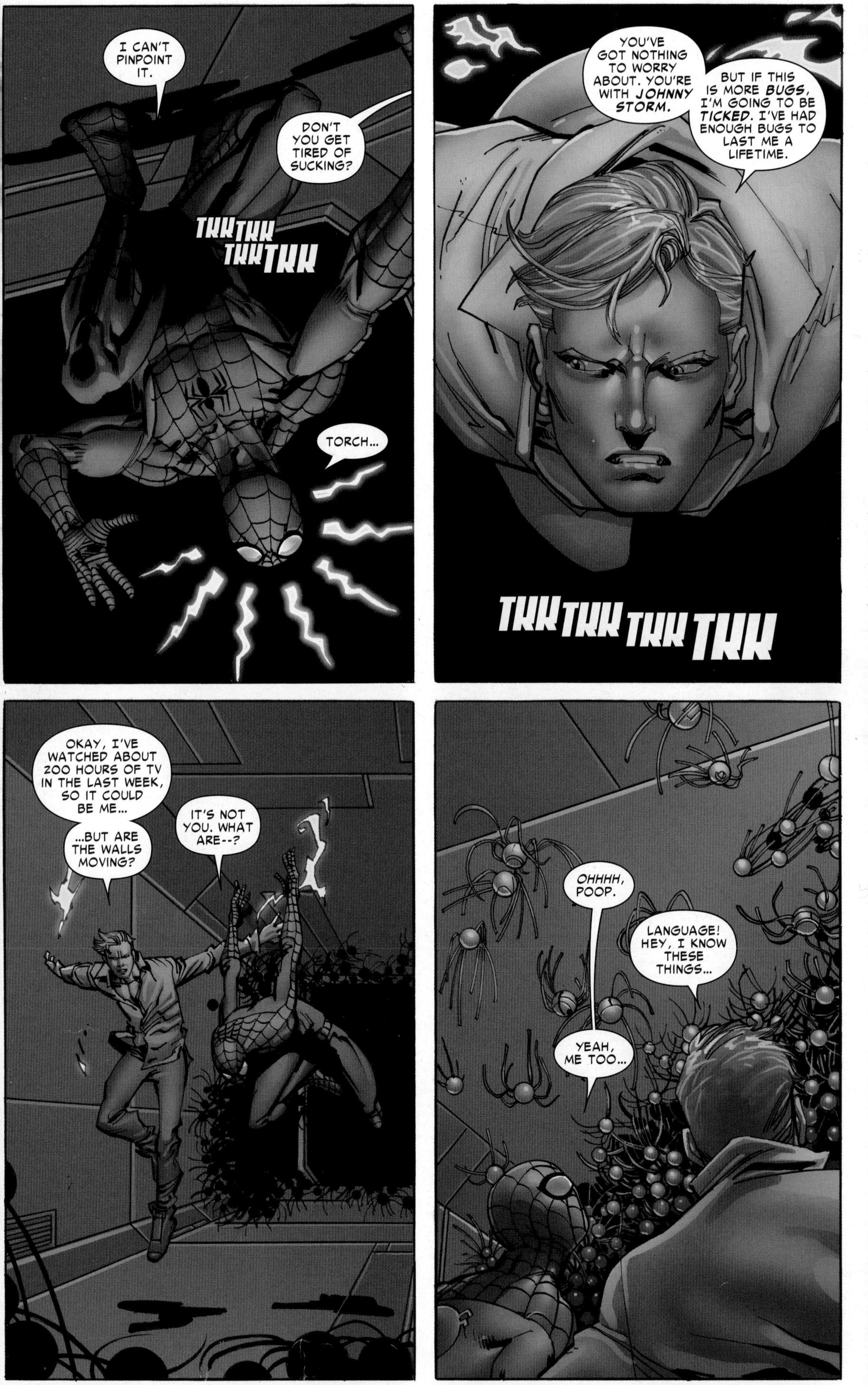
I CAN'T PINPOINT IT.
DON'T YOU GET TIRED OF SUCKING?
TKKTKK TKKTKK
TORCH...
YOU'VE GOT NOTHING TO WORRY ABOUT. YOU'RE WITH *JOHNNY STORM.*
BUT IF THIS IS MORE *BUGS,* I'M GOING TO BE *TICKED.* I'VE HAD ENOUGH BUGS TO LAST ME A LIFETIME.
TKKTKK TKK TKK
OKAY, I'VE WATCHED ABOUT 200 HOURS OF TV IN THE LAST WEEK, SO IT COULD BE ME...
...BUT ARE THE WALLS MOVING?
IT'S NOT YOU. WHAT ARE--?
OHHHH, POOP.
LANGUAGE! HEY, I KNOW THESE THINGS...
YEAH, ME TOO...

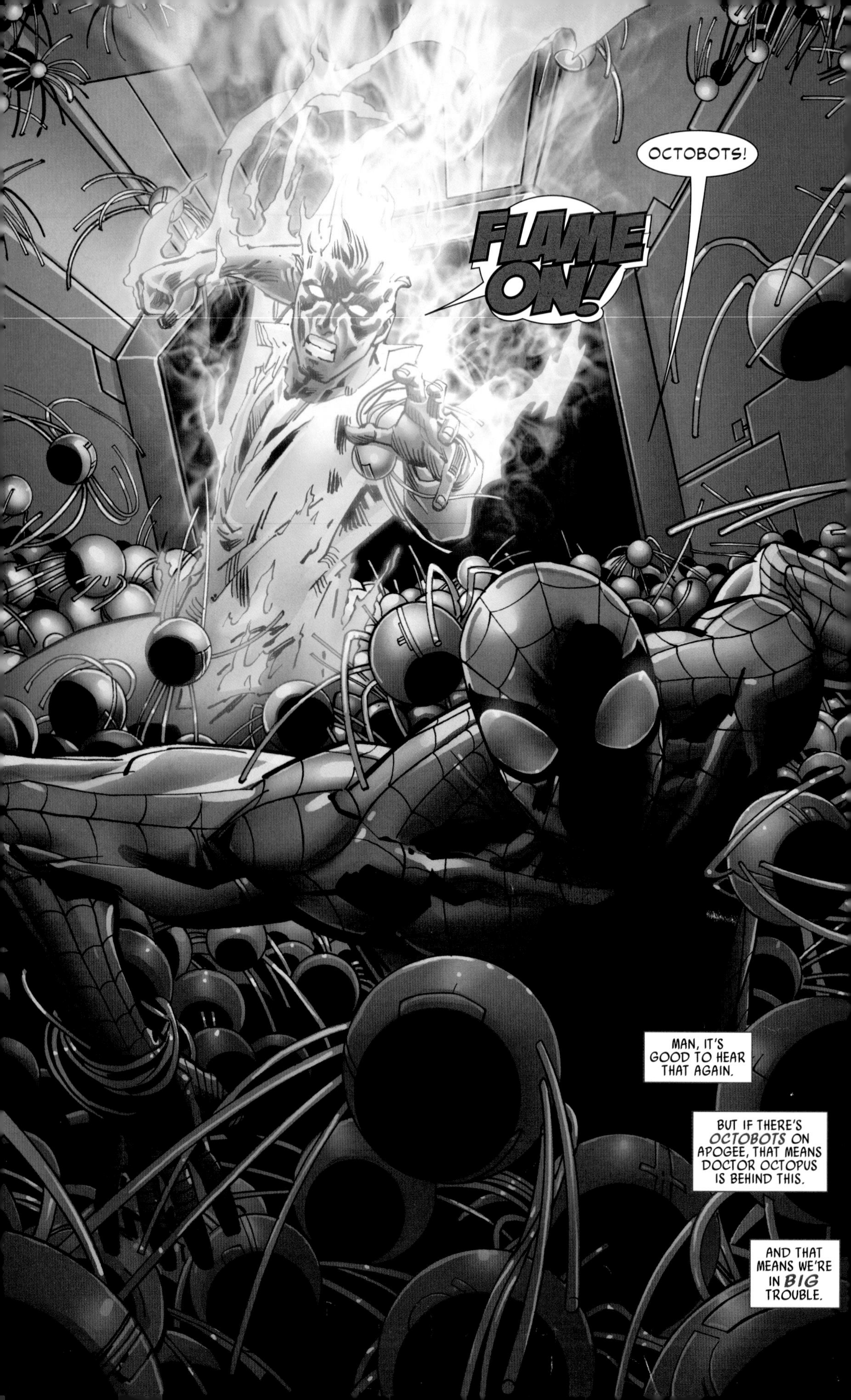
FLAME ON!
OCTOBOTS!
MAN, IT'S GOOD TO HEAR THAT AGAIN.
BUT IF THERE'S *OCTOBOTS* ON APOGEE, THAT MEANS DOCTOR OCTOPUS IS BEHIND THIS.
AND THAT MEANS WE'RE IN *BIG* TROUBLE.

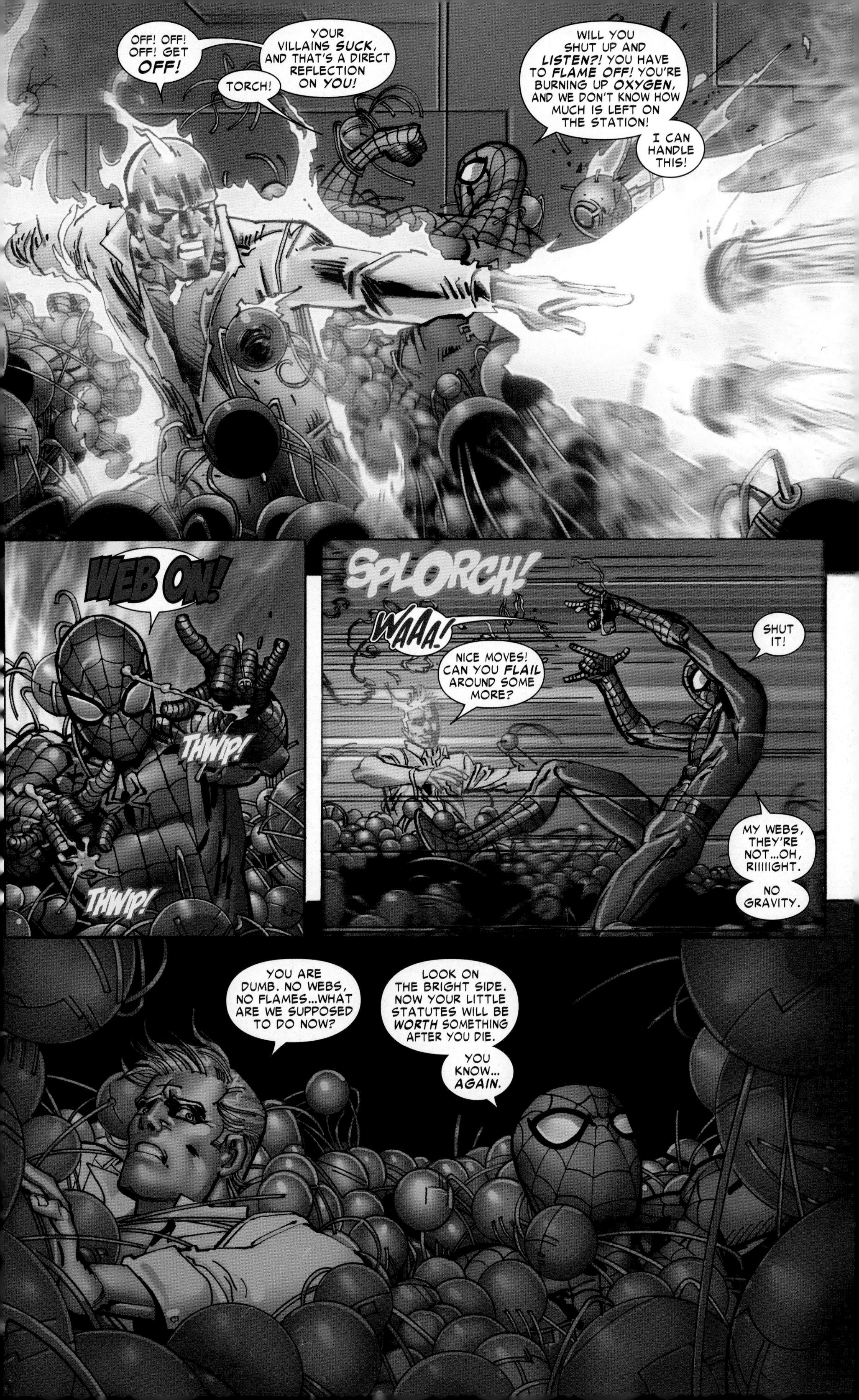

OFF! OFF! OFF! GET **OFF!**
YOUR VILLAINS **SUCK**, AND THAT'S A DIRECT REFLECTION ON **YOU!**
TORCH!
WILL YOU SHUT UP AND **LISTEN?!** YOU HAVE TO **FLAME OFF!** YOU'RE BURNING UP **OXYGEN**, AND WE DON'T KNOW HOW MUCH IS LEFT ON THE STATION!
I CAN HANDLE THIS!
WEB ON!
THWIP!
THWIP!
SPLORCH!
WAAA!
NICE MOVES! CAN YOU **FLAIL** AROUND SOME MORE?
SHUT IT!
MY WEBS, THEY'RE NOT...OH, RIIIIIGHT.
NO GRAVITY.
YOU ARE DUMB. NO WEBS, NO FLAMES...WHAT ARE WE SUPPOSED TO DO NOW?
LOOK ON THE BRIGHT SIDE. NOW YOUR LITTLE STATUTES WILL BE **WORTH** SOMETHING AFTER YOU DIE.
YOU KNOW... **AGAIN**.

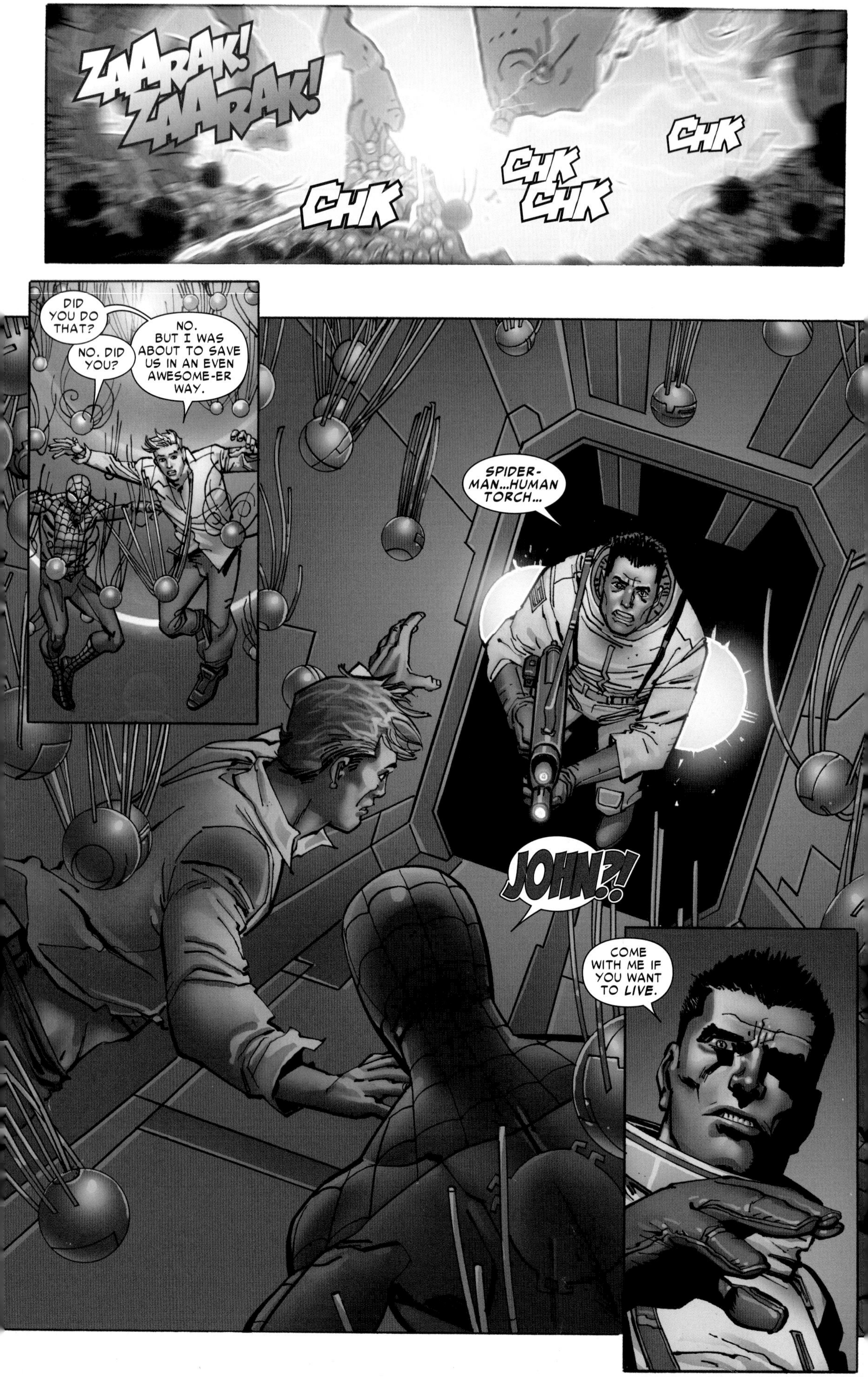
ZAARAK! ZAARAK!
CHK
CHK CHK
CHK
DID YOU DO THAT?
NO. DID YOU?
NO. BUT I WAS ABOUT TO SAVE US IN AN EVEN AWESOME-ER WAY.
SPIDER-MAN...HUMAN TORCH...
JOHN?!
COME WITH ME IF YOU WANT TO LIVE.

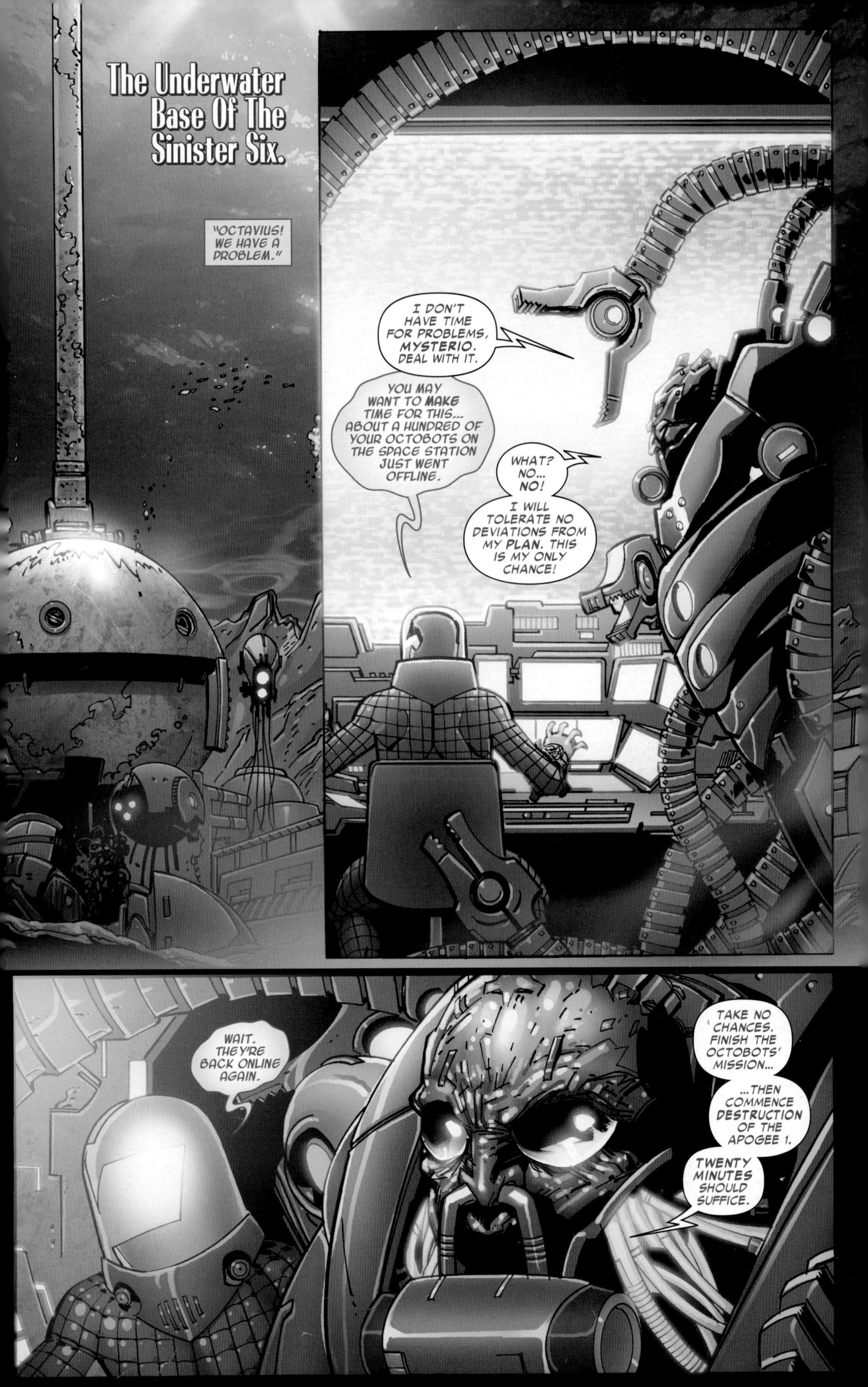
The Underwater Base Of The Sinister Six.
"OCTAVIUS! WE HAVE A PROBLEM."
I DON'T HAVE TIME FOR PROBLEMS, MYSTERIO. DEAL WITH IT.
YOU MAY WANT TO MAKE TIME FOR THIS... ABOUT A HUNDRED OF YOUR OCTOBOTS ON THE SPACE STATION JUST WENT OFFLINE.
WHAT? NO... NO!
I WILL TOLERATE NO DEVIATIONS FROM MY PLAN. THIS IS MY ONLY CHANCE!
WAIT. THEY'RE BACK ONLINE AGAIN.
TAKE NO CHANCES. FINISH THE OCTOBOTS' MISSION...
...THEN COMMENCE DESTRUCTION OF THE APOGEE 1.
TWENTY MINUTES SHOULD SUFFICE.

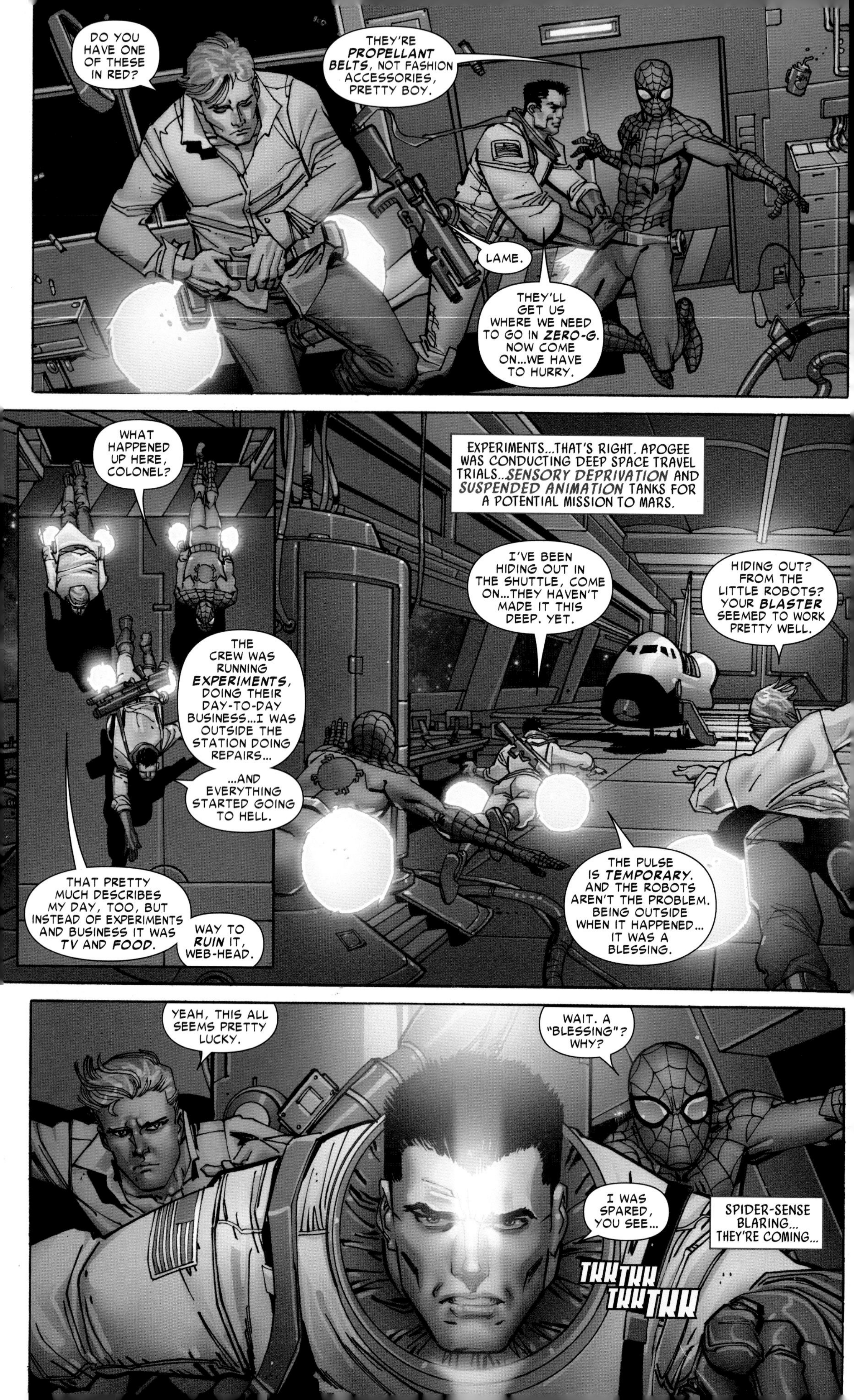
DO YOU HAVE ONE OF THESE IN RED?
THEY'RE PROPELLANT BELTS, NOT FASHION ACCESSORIES, PRETTY BOY.
LAME.
THEY'LL GET US WHERE WE NEED TO GO IN ZERO-G. NOW COME ON...WE HAVE TO HURRY.
WHAT HAPPENED UP HERE, COLONEL?
THE CREW WAS RUNNING EXPERIMENTS, DOING THEIR DAY-TO-DAY BUSINESS...I WAS OUTSIDE THE STATION DOING REPAIRS...
...AND EVERYTHING STARTED GOING TO HELL.
THAT PRETTY MUCH DESCRIBES MY DAY, TOO, BUT INSTEAD OF EXPERIMENTS AND BUSINESS IT WAS TV AND FOOD.
WAY TO RUIN IT, WEB-HEAD.
EXPERIMENTS...THAT'S RIGHT. APOGEE WAS CONDUCTING DEEP SPACE TRAVEL TRIALS...SENSORY DEPRIVATION AND SUSPENDED ANIMATION TANKS FOR A POTENTIAL MISSION TO MARS.
I'VE BEEN HIDING OUT IN THE SHUTTLE, COME ON...THEY HAVEN'T MADE IT THIS DEEP. YET.
HIDING OUT? FROM THE LITTLE ROBOTS? YOUR BLASTER SEEMED TO WORK PRETTY WELL.
THE PULSE IS TEMPORARY. AND THE ROBOTS AREN'T THE PROBLEM. BEING OUTSIDE WHEN IT HAPPENED... IT WAS A BLESSING.
YEAH, THIS ALL SEEMS PRETTY LUCKY.
WAIT. A "BLESSING"? WHY?
I WAS SPARED, YOU SEE...
SPIDER-SENSE BLARING... THEY'RE COMING...
TKKTKK TKKTKK

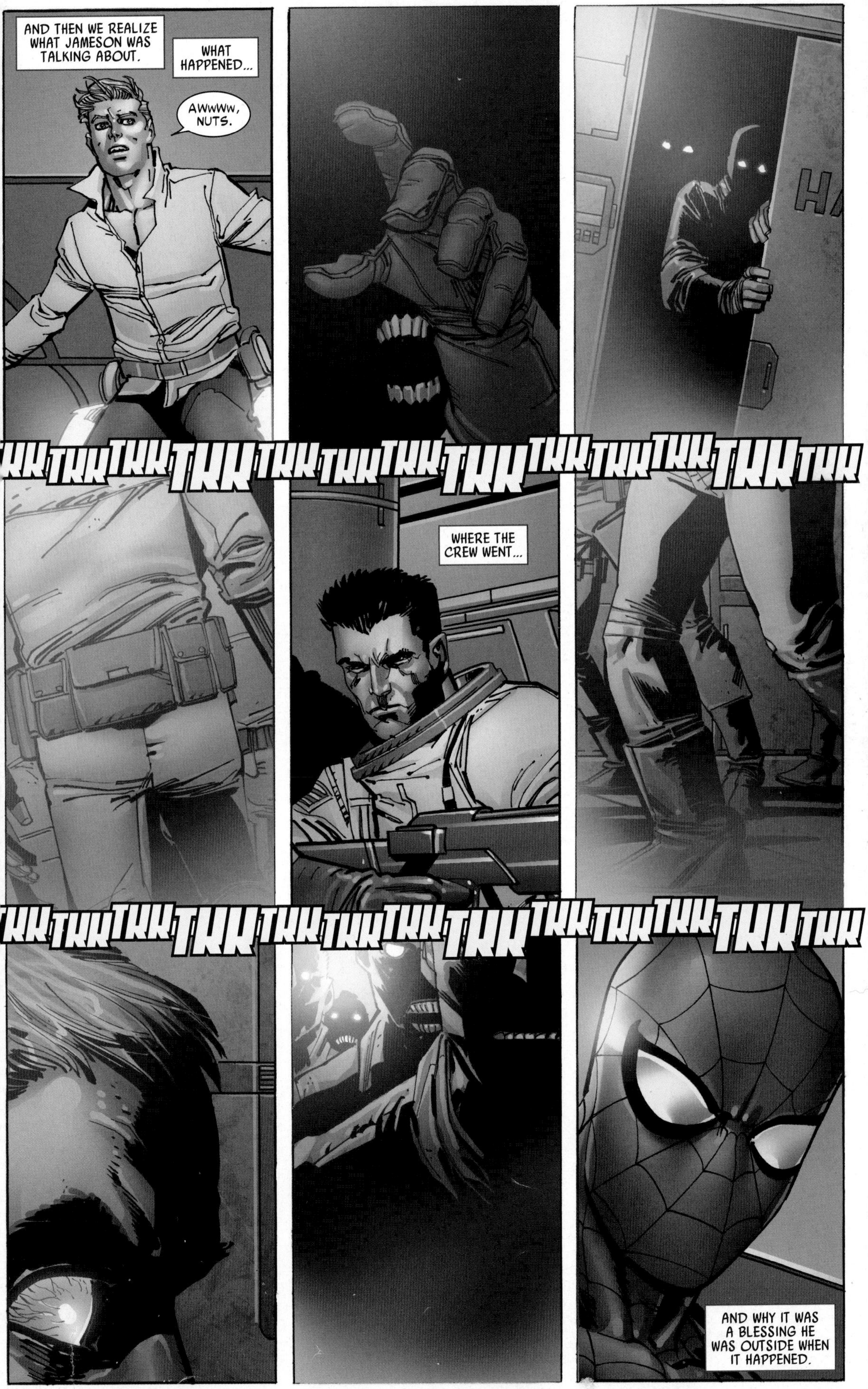
AND THEN WE REALIZE WHAT JAMESON WAS TALKING ABOUT.
WHAT HAPPENED...
AWWWW, NUTS.
TRK TRK TRK TRK TRK TRK TRK TRK TRK TRK TRK TRK
WHERE THE CREW WENT...
TRK TRK TRK TRK TRK TRK TRK TRK TRK TRK TRK TRK
AND WHY IT WAS A BLESSING HE WAS OUTSIDE WHEN IT HAPPENED.

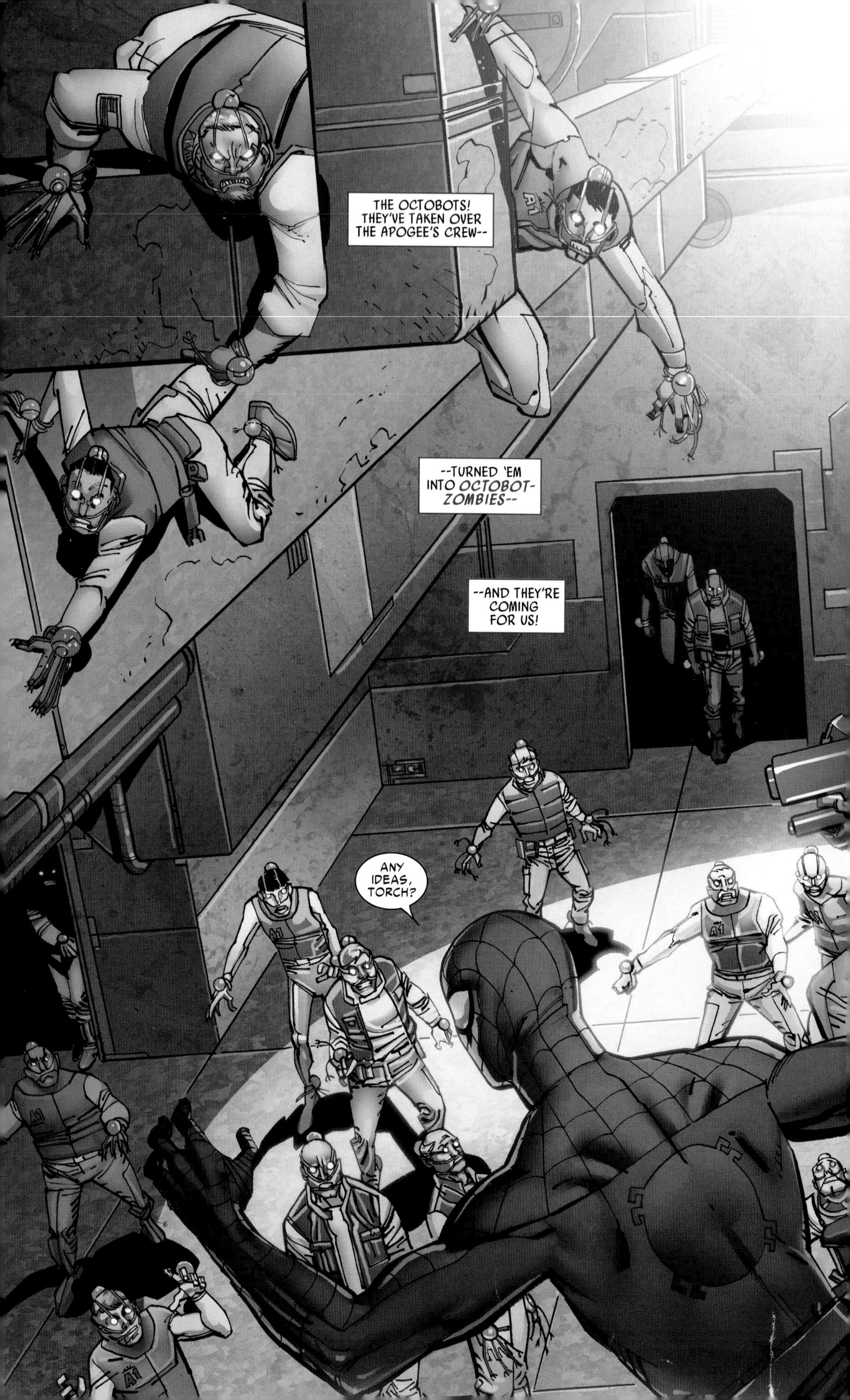
THE OCTOBOTS! THEY'VE TAKEN OVER THE APOGEE'S CREW--
--TURNED 'EM INTO *OCTOBOT-ZOMBIES*--
--AND THEY'RE COMING FOR US!
ANY IDEAS, TORCH?

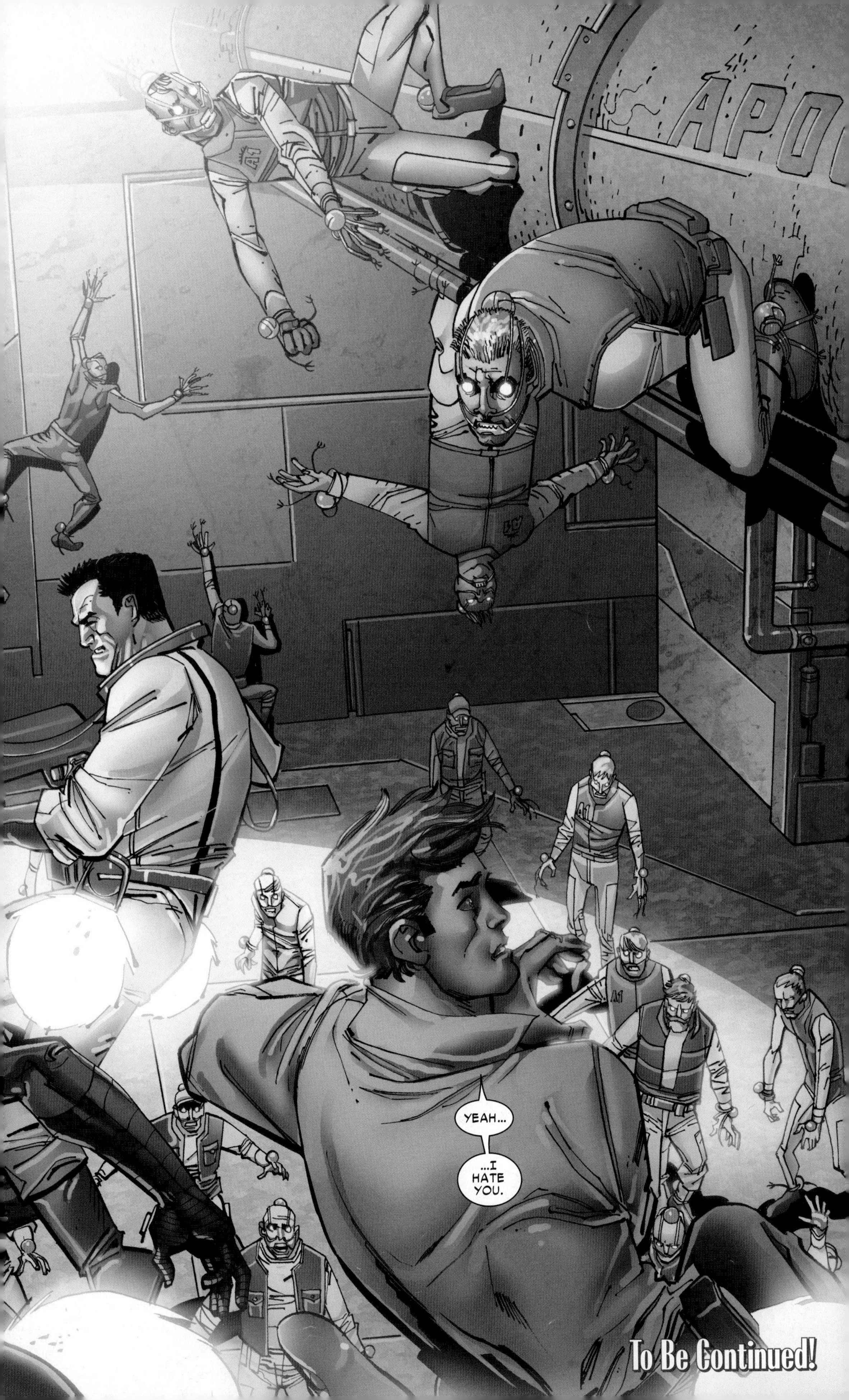
APOC
YEAH...
...I HATE YOU.
To Be Continued!

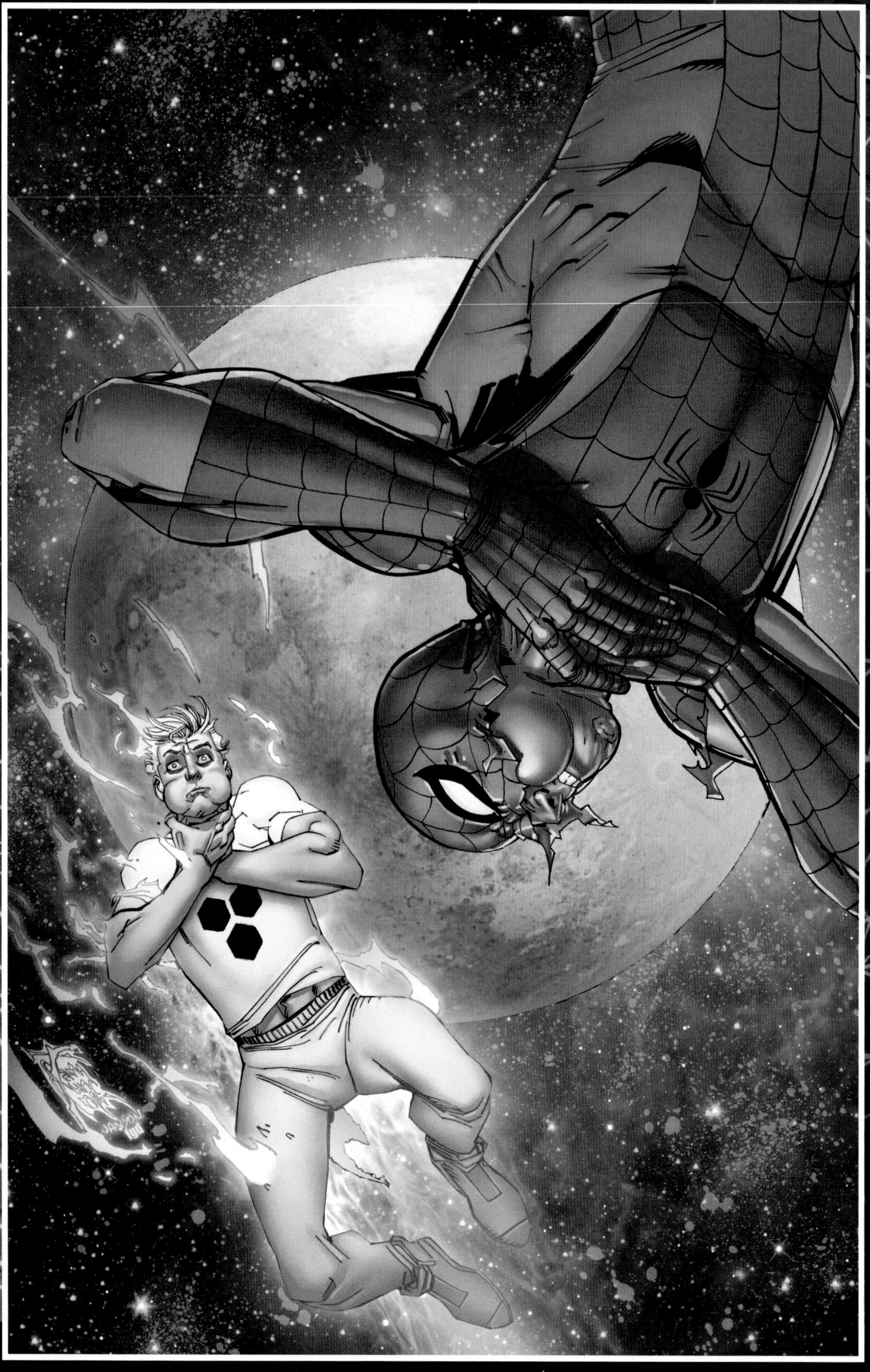
JANSON
'90

AMAZING SPIDER-MAN #681

COVER BY GIUSEPPE CAMUNCOLI, KLAUS JANSON & FRANK D'ARMATA

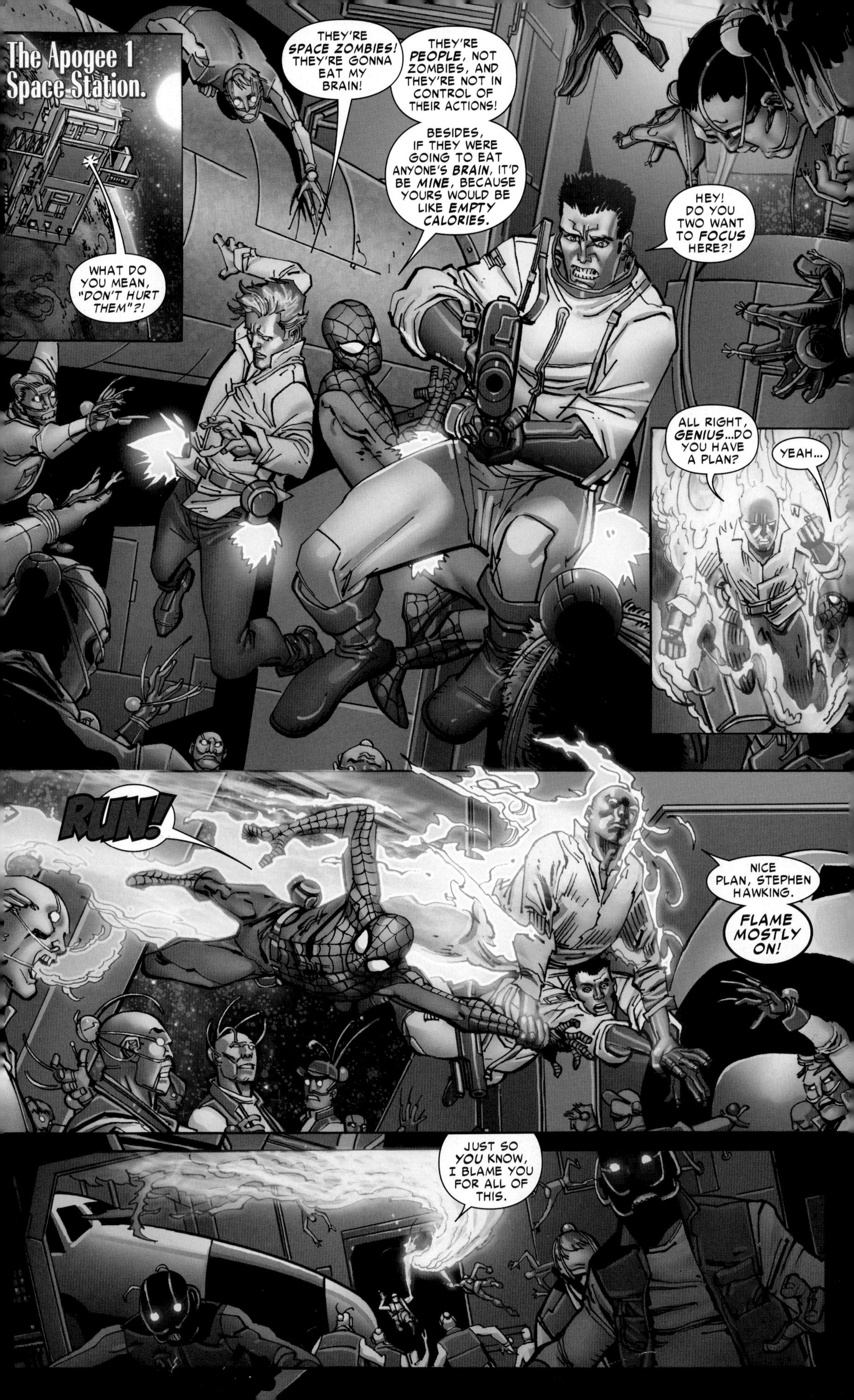
The Apogee 1 Space Station.
WHAT DO YOU MEAN, "DON'T HURT THEM"?!
THEY'RE SPACE ZOMBIES! THEY'RE GONNA EAT MY BRAIN!
THEY'RE PEOPLE, NOT ZOMBIES, AND THEY'RE NOT IN CONTROL OF THEIR ACTIONS!
BESIDES, IF THEY WERE GOING TO EAT ANYONE'S BRAIN, IT'D BE MINE, BECAUSE YOURS WOULD BE LIKE EMPTY CALORIES.
HEY! DO YOU TWO WANT TO FOCUS HERE?!
ALL RIGHT, GENIUS...DO YOU HAVE A PLAN?
YEAH...
RUN!
NICE PLAN, STEPHEN HAWKING.
FLAME MOSTLY ON!
JUST SO YOU KNOW, I BLAME YOU FOR ALL OF THIS.

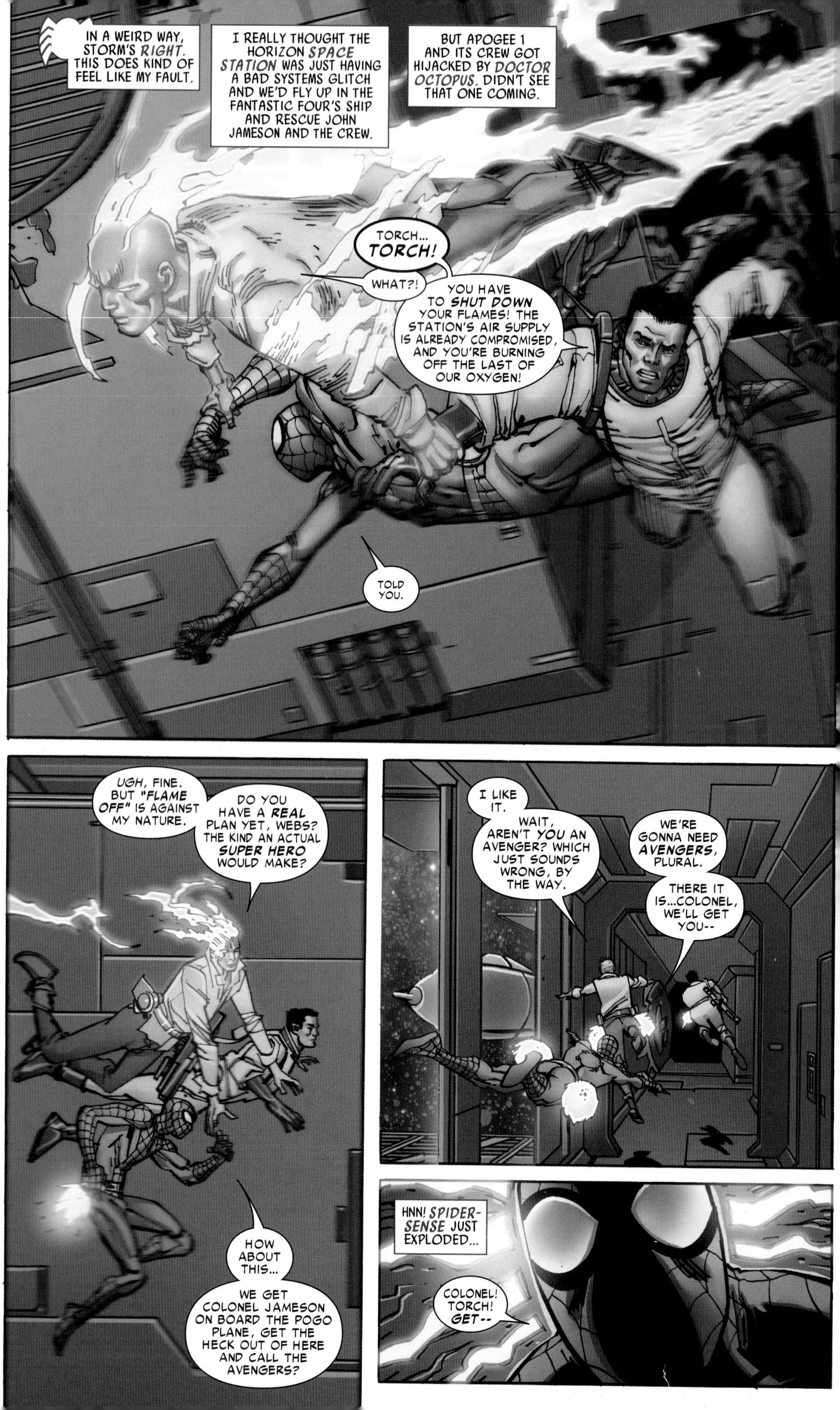
IN A WEIRD WAY, STORM'S RIGHT. THIS DOES KIND OF FEEL LIKE MY FAULT.
I REALLY THOUGHT THE HORIZON SPACE STATION WAS JUST HAVING A BAD SYSTEMS GLITCH AND WE'D FLY UP IN THE FANTASTIC FOUR'S SHIP AND RESCUE JOHN JAMESON AND THE CREW.
BUT APOGEE 1 AND ITS CREW GOT HIJACKED BY DOCTOR OCTOPUS. DIDN'T SEE THAT ONE COMING.
TORCH... TORCH!
WHAT?!
YOU HAVE TO SHUT DOWN YOUR FLAMES! THE STATION'S AIR SUPPLY IS ALREADY COMPROMISED, AND YOU'RE BURNING OFF THE LAST OF OUR OXYGEN!
TOLD YOU.
UGH, FINE. BUT "FLAME OFF" IS AGAINST MY NATURE.
DO YOU HAVE A REAL PLAN YET, WEBS? THE KIND AN ACTUAL SUPER HERO WOULD MAKE?
HOW ABOUT THIS...
WE GET COLONEL JAMESON ON BOARD THE POGO PLANE, GET THE HECK OUT OF HERE AND CALL THE AVENGERS?
I LIKE IT.
WAIT, AREN'T YOU AN AVENGER? WHICH JUST SOUNDS WRONG, BY THE WAY.
WE'RE GONNA NEED AVENGERS, PLURAL.
THERE IT IS...COLONEL, WE'LL GET YOU--
HNN! SPIDER-SENSE JUST EXPLODED...
COLONEL! TORCH! GET--

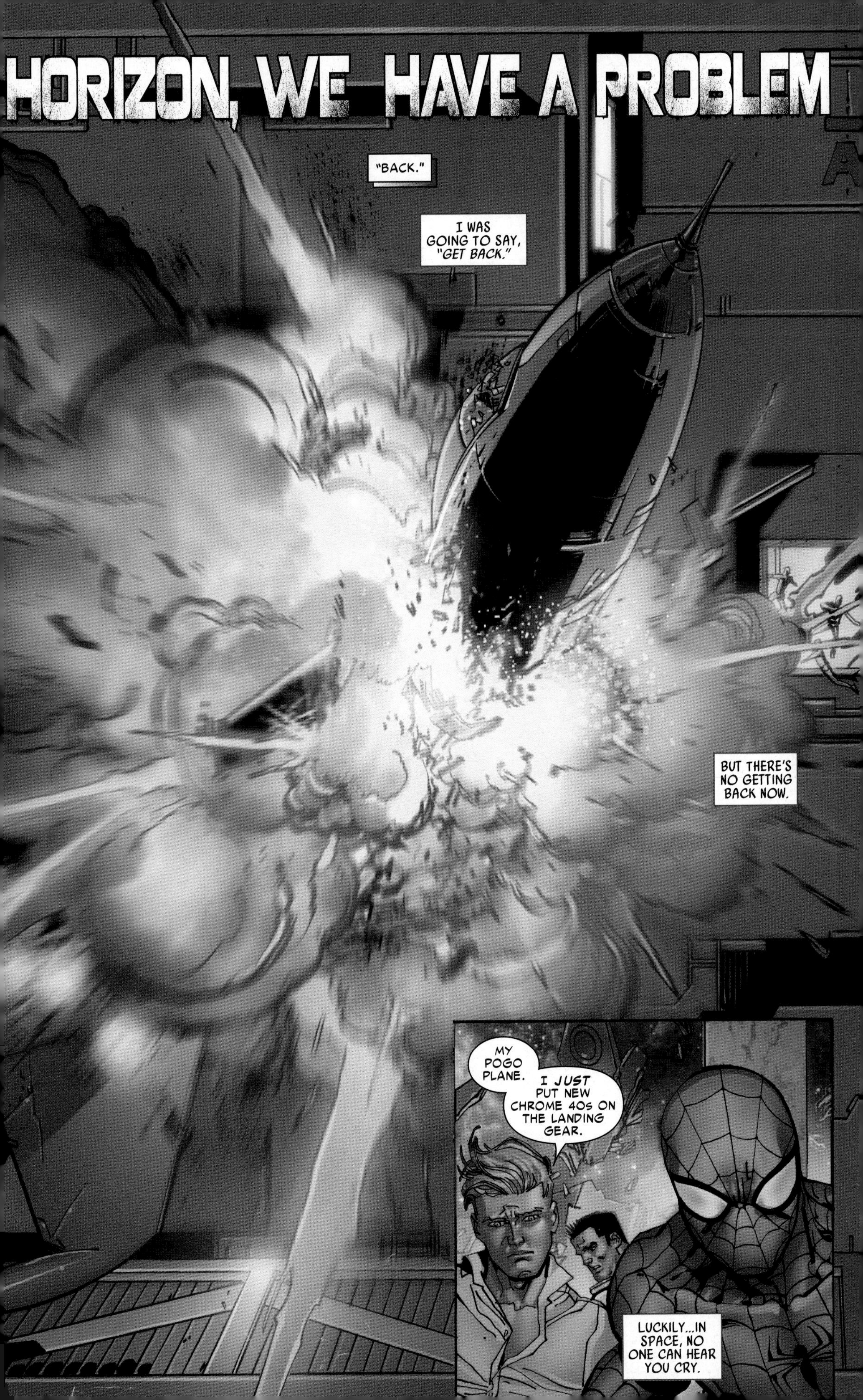
HORIZON, WE HAVE A PROBLEM
"BACK."
I WAS GOING TO SAY, "GET BACK."
BUT THERE'S NO GETTING BACK NOW.
MY POGO PLANE.
I JUST PUT NEW CHROME 40s ON THE LANDING GEAR.
LUCKILY...IN SPACE, NO ONE CAN HEAR YOU CRY.

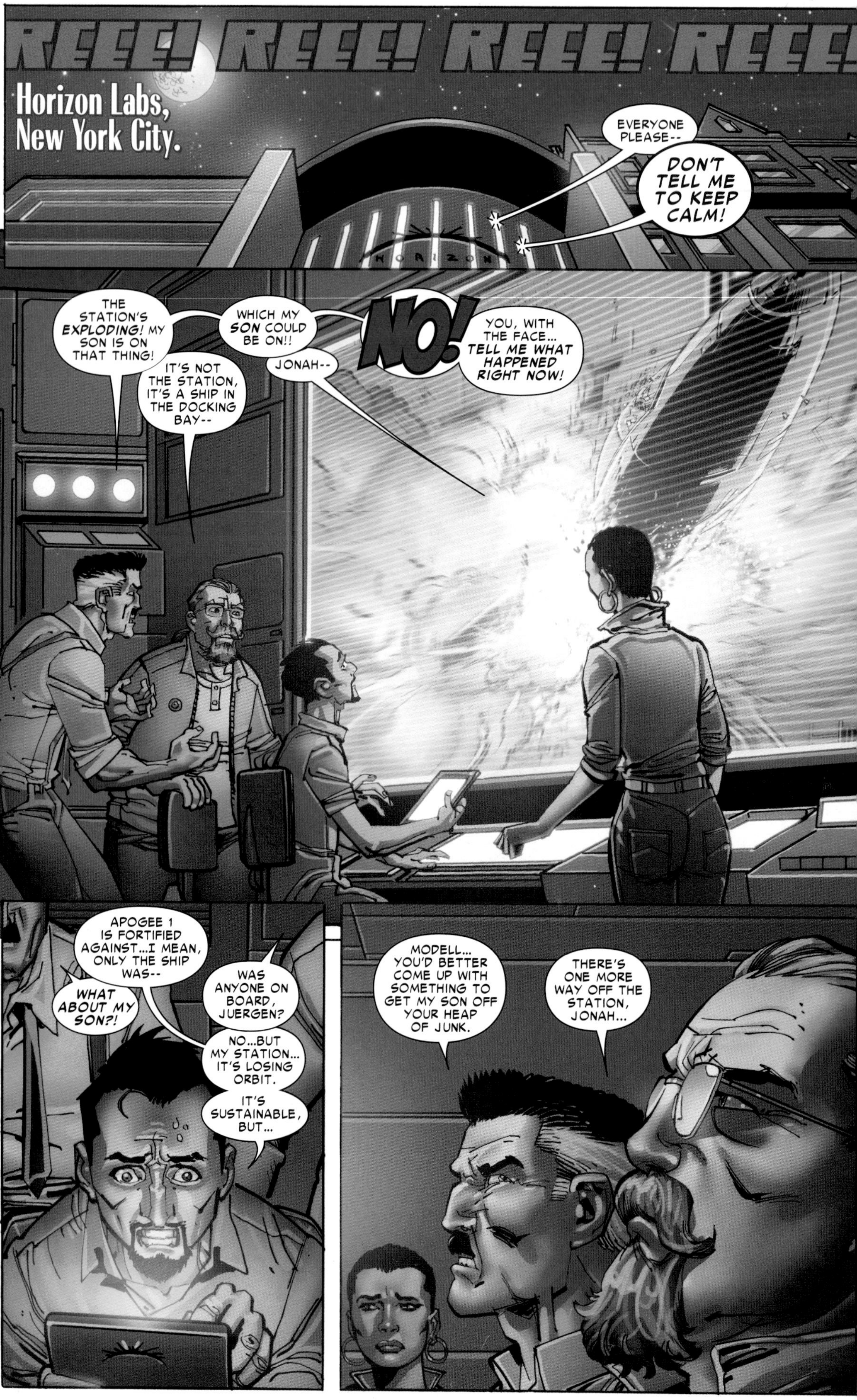
REEE! REEE! REEE! REEE!
Horizon Labs, New York City.
EVERYONE PLEASE--
DON'T TELL ME TO KEEP CALM!
THE STATION'S EXPLODING! MY SON IS ON THAT THING!
IT'S NOT THE STATION, IT'S A SHIP IN THE DOCKING BAY--
WHICH MY SON COULD BE ON!!
JONAH--
NO!
YOU, WITH THE FACE... TELL ME WHAT HAPPENED RIGHT NOW!
APOGEE 1 IS FORTIFIED AGAINST...I MEAN, ONLY THE SHIP WAS--
WHAT ABOUT MY SON?!
WAS ANYONE ON BOARD, JUERGEN?
NO...BUT MY STATION... IT'S LOSING ORBIT.
IT'S SUSTAINABLE, BUT...
MODELL... YOU'D BETTER COME UP WITH SOMETHING TO GET MY SON OFF YOUR HEAP OF JUNK.
THERE'S ONE MORE WAY OFF THE STATION, JONAH...

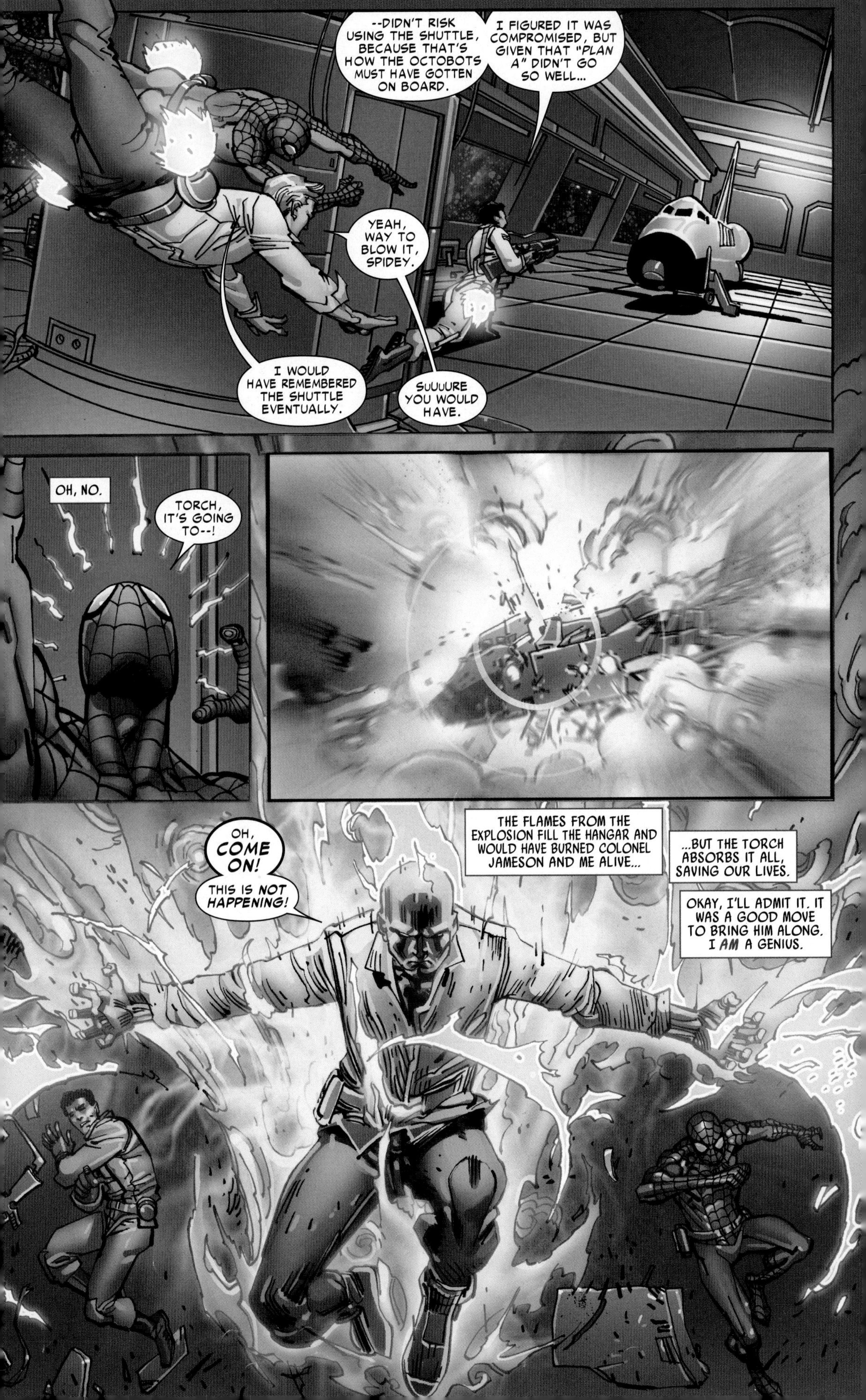
--DIDN'T RISK USING THE SHUTTLE, BECAUSE THAT'S HOW THE OCTOBOTS MUST HAVE GOTTEN ON BOARD.
I FIGURED IT WAS COMPROMISED, BUT GIVEN THAT "PLAN A" DIDN'T GO SO WELL...
YEAH, WAY TO BLOW IT, SPIDEY.
I WOULD HAVE REMEMBERED THE SHUTTLE EVENTUALLY.
SUUUURE YOU WOULD HAVE.
OH, NO.
TORCH, IT'S GOING TO--!
OH, COME ON!
THIS IS NOT HAPPENING!
THE FLAMES FROM THE EXPLOSION FILL THE HANGAR AND WOULD HAVE BURNED COLONEL JAMESON AND ME ALIVE...
...BUT THE TORCH ABSORBS IT ALL, SAVING OUR LIVES.
OKAY, I'LL ADMIT IT. IT WAS A GOOD MOVE TO BRING HIM ALONG. I AM A GENIUS.

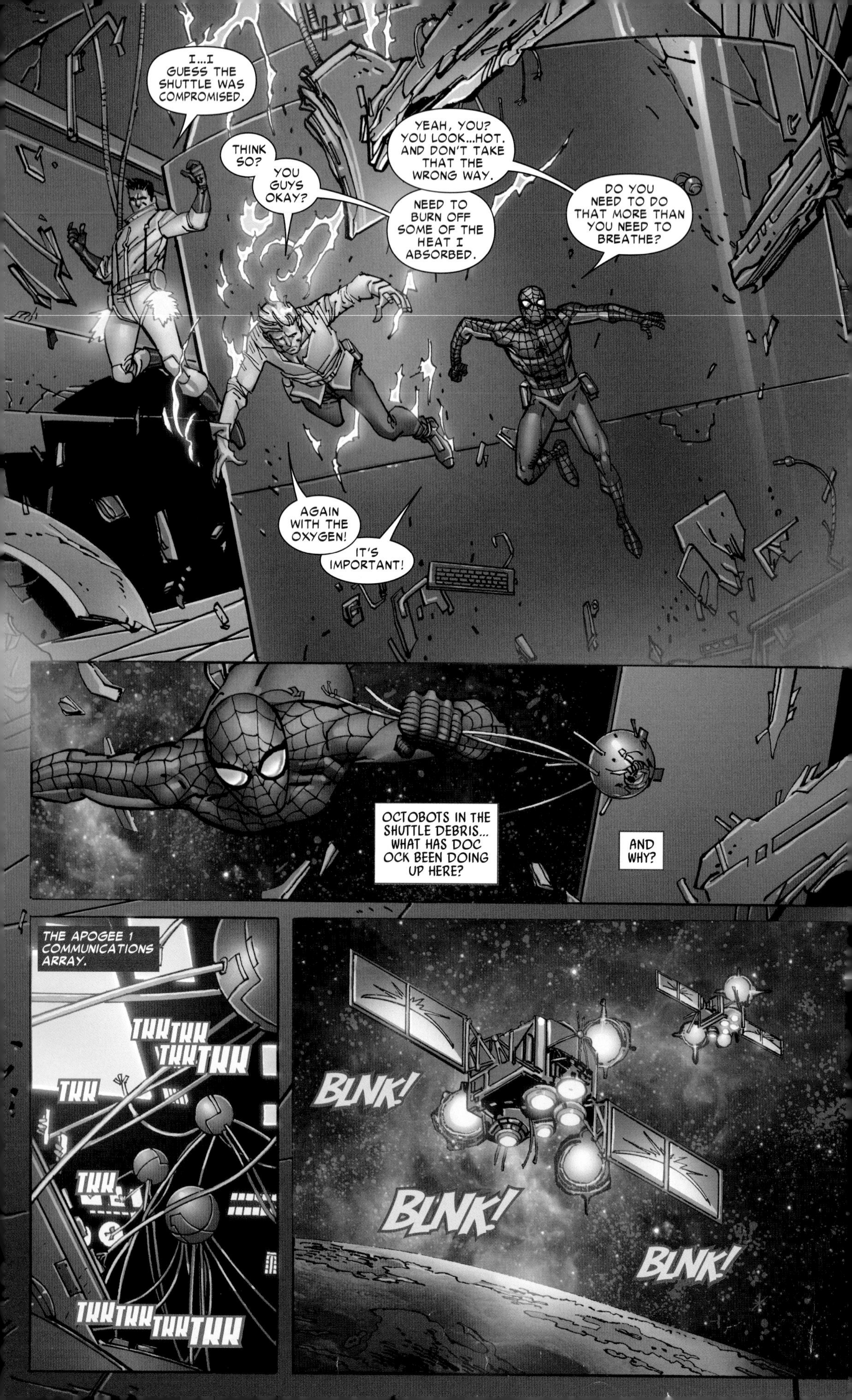
I...I GUESS THE SHUTTLE WAS COMPROMISED.
THINK SO?
YOU GUYS OKAY?
YEAH, YOU? YOU LOOK...HOT. AND DON'T TAKE THAT THE WRONG WAY.
NEED TO BURN OFF SOME OF THE HEAT I ABSORBED.
DO YOU NEED TO DO THAT MORE THAN YOU NEED TO BREATHE?
AGAIN WITH THE OXYGEN!
IT'S IMPORTANT!
OCTOBOTS IN THE SHUTTLE DEBRIS... WHAT HAS DOC OCK BEEN DOING UP HERE?
AND WHY?
THE APOGEE 1 COMMUNICATIONS ARRAY.
TKKTKK TKKTKK
TKK
TKK
TKKTKKTKKTKK
BLNK!
BLNK!
BLNK!

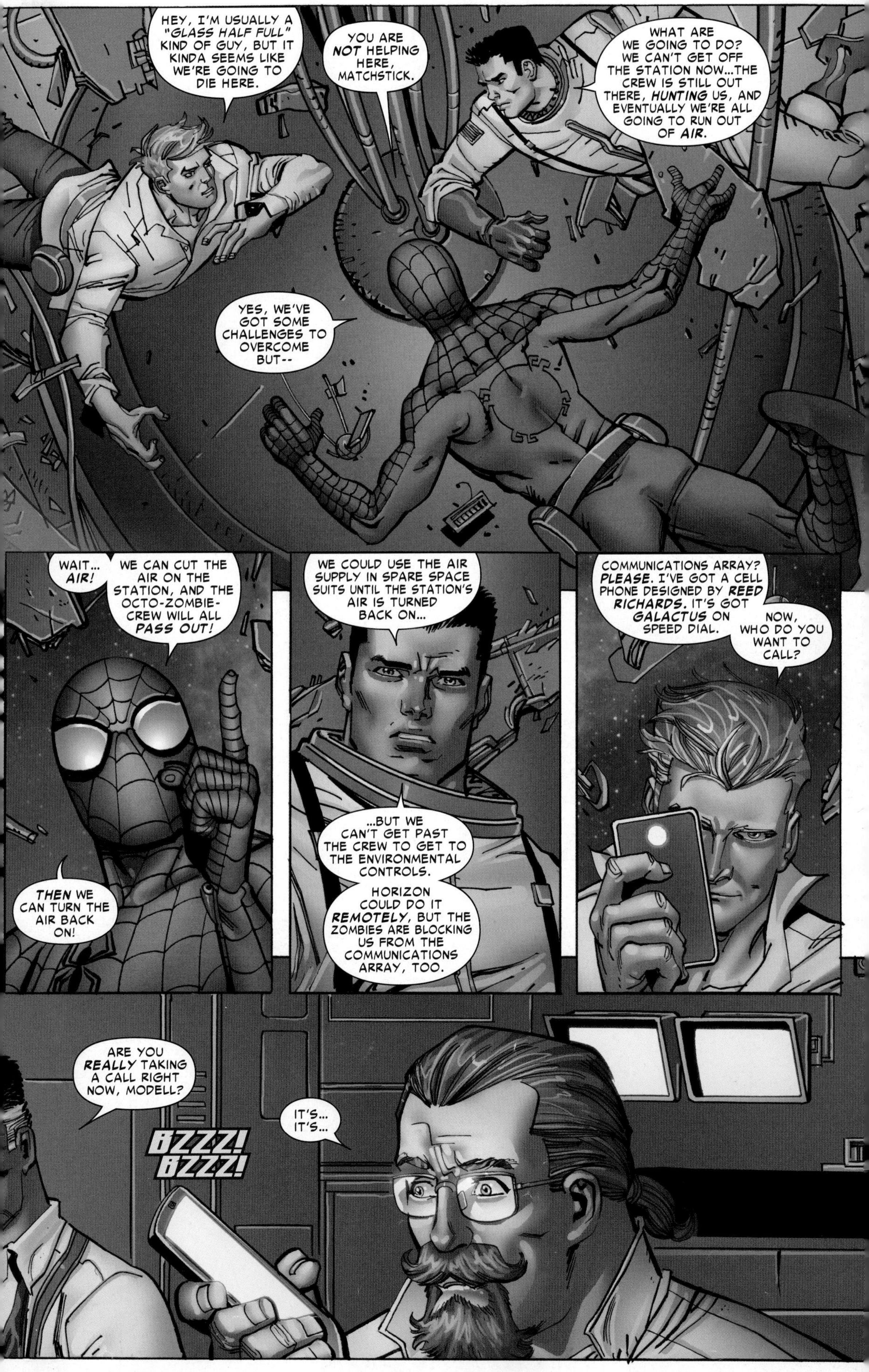
HEY, I'M USUALLY A "GLASS HALF FULL" KIND OF GUY, BUT IT KINDA SEEMS LIKE WE'RE GOING TO DIE HERE.
YOU ARE NOT HELPING HERE, MATCHSTICK.
WHAT ARE WE GOING TO DO? WE CAN'T GET OFF THE STATION NOW...THE CREW IS STILL OUT THERE, HUNTING US, AND EVENTUALLY WE'RE ALL GOING TO RUN OUT OF AIR.
YES, WE'VE GOT SOME CHALLENGES TO OVERCOME BUT--
WAIT... AIR!
WE CAN CUT THE AIR ON THE STATION, AND THE OCTO-ZOMBIE-CREW WILL ALL PASS OUT!
THEN WE CAN TURN THE AIR BACK ON!
WE COULD USE THE AIR SUPPLY IN SPARE SPACE SUITS UNTIL THE STATION'S AIR IS TURNED BACK ON...
...BUT WE CAN'T GET PAST THE CREW TO GET TO THE ENVIRONMENTAL CONTROLS.
HORIZON COULD DO IT REMOTELY, BUT THE ZOMBIES ARE BLOCKING US FROM THE COMMUNICATIONS ARRAY, TOO.
COMMUNICATIONS ARRAY? PLEASE. I'VE GOT A CELL PHONE DESIGNED BY REED RICHARDS. IT'S GOT GALACTUS ON SPEED DIAL.
NOW, WHO DO YOU WANT TO CALL?
ARE YOU REALLY TAKING A CALL RIGHT NOW, MODELL?
BZZZ! BZZZ!
IT'S... IT'S...

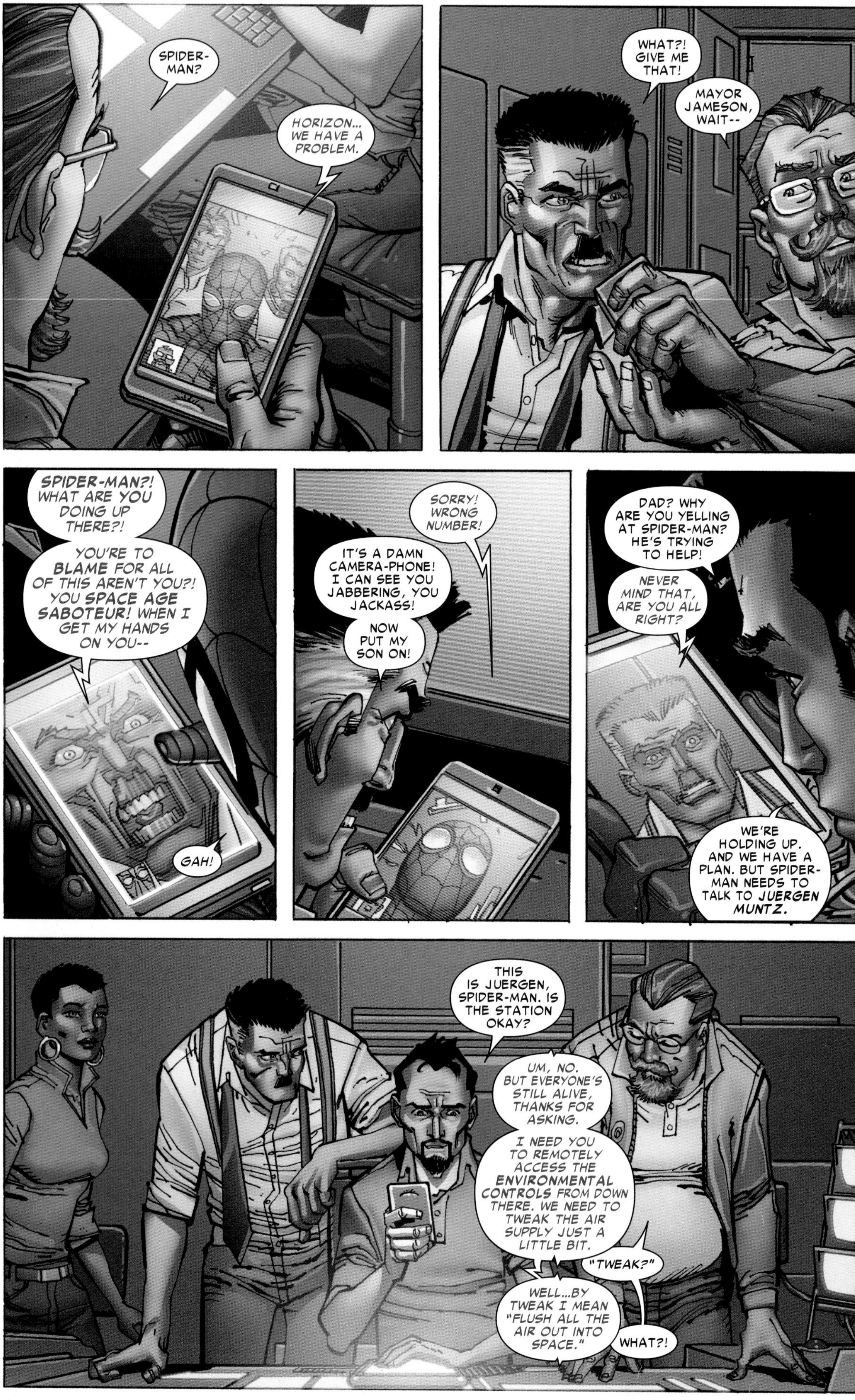
SPIDER-MAN?
HORIZON... WE HAVE A PROBLEM.
WHAT?! GIVE ME THAT!
MAYOR JAMESON, WAIT--
SPIDER-MAN?! WHAT ARE YOU DOING UP THERE?!
YOU'RE TO BLAME FOR ALL OF THIS AREN'T YOU?! YOU SPACE AGE SABOTEUR! WHEN I GET MY HANDS ON YOU--
GAH!
SORRY! WRONG NUMBER!
IT'S A DAMN CAMERA-PHONE! I CAN SEE YOU JABBERING, YOU JACKASS!
NOW PUT MY SON ON!
DAD? WHY ARE YOU YELLING AT SPIDER-MAN? HE'S TRYING TO HELP!
NEVER MIND THAT, ARE YOU ALL RIGHT?
WE'RE HOLDING UP. AND WE HAVE A PLAN. BUT SPIDER-MAN NEEDS TO TALK TO JUERGEN MUNTZ.
THIS IS JUERGEN, SPIDER-MAN. IS THE STATION OKAY?
UM, NO. BUT EVERYONE'S STILL ALIVE, THANKS FOR ASKING.
I NEED YOU TO REMOTELY ACCESS THE ENVIRONMENTAL CONTROLS FROM DOWN THERE. WE NEED TO TWEAK THE AIR SUPPLY JUST A LITTLE BIT.
"TWEAK?"
WELL...BY TWEAK I MEAN "FLUSH ALL THE AIR OUT INTO SPACE."
WHAT?!

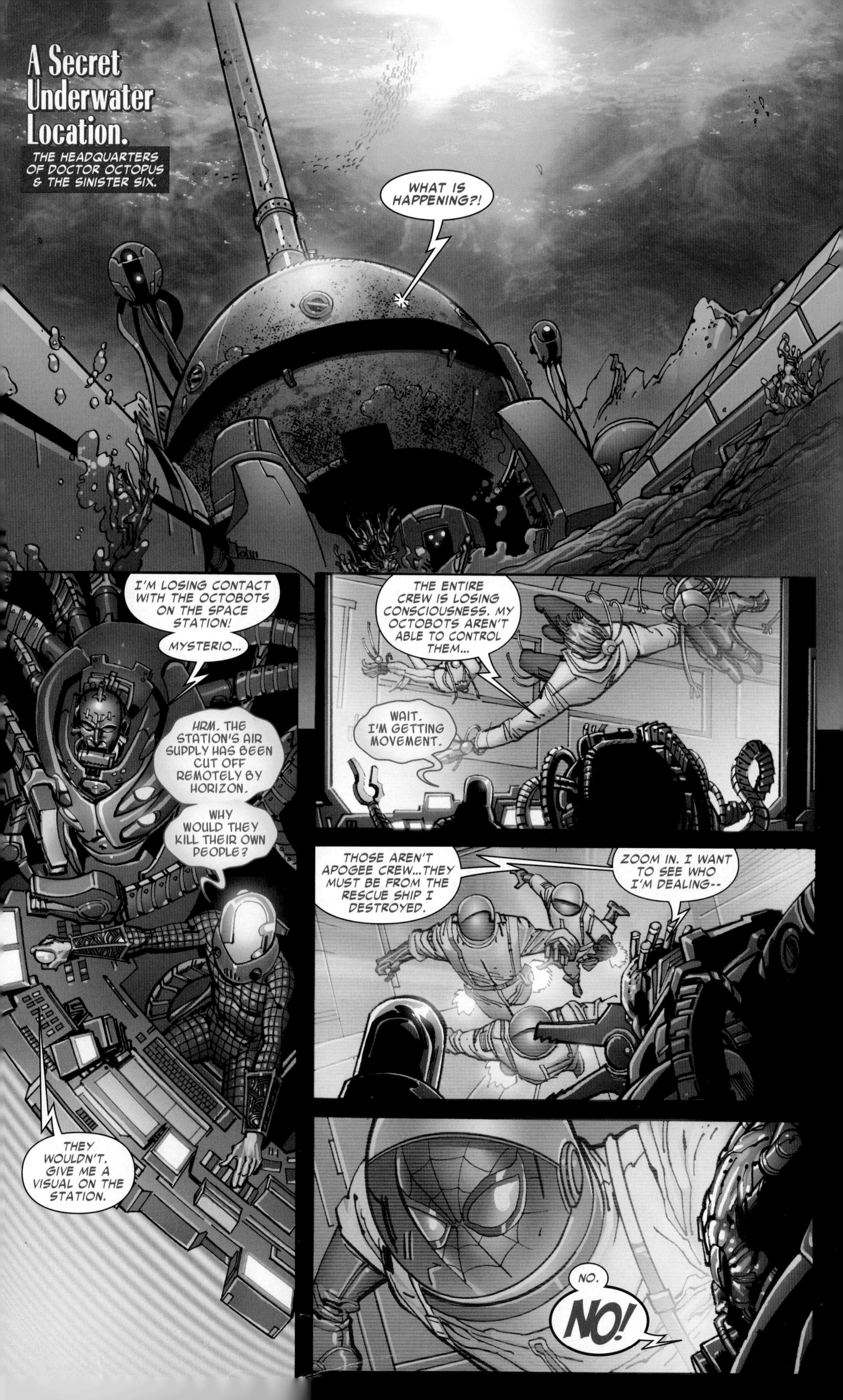
A Secret Underwater Location.
THE HEADQUARTERS OF DOCTOR OCTOPUS & THE SINISTER SIX.
WHAT IS HAPPENING?!
I'M LOSING CONTACT WITH THE OCTOBOTS ON THE SPACE STATION!
MYSTERIO...
HRM. THE STATION'S AIR SUPPLY HAS BEEN CUT OFF REMOTELY BY HORIZON.
WHY WOULD THEY KILL THEIR OWN PEOPLE?
THEY WOULDN'T. GIVE ME A VISUAL ON THE STATION.
THE ENTIRE CREW IS LOSING CONSCIOUSNESS. MY OCTOBOTS AREN'T ABLE TO CONTROL THEM...
WAIT. I'M GETTING MOVEMENT.
THOSE AREN'T APOGEE CREW...THEY MUST BE FROM THE RESCUE SHIP I DESTROYED.
ZOOM IN. I WANT TO SEE WHO I'M DEALING--
NO.
NO!

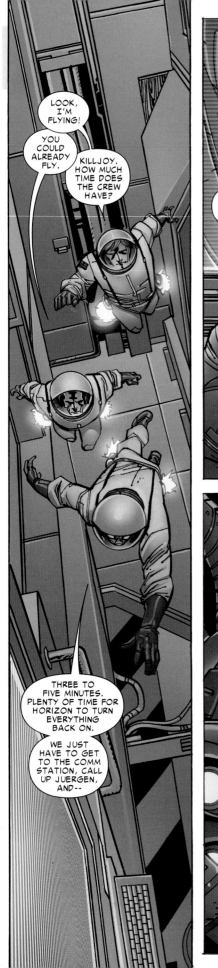

LOOK, I'M FLYING!

YOU COULD ALREADY FLY.

KILLJOY. HOW MUCH TIME DOES THE CREW HAVE?

THREE TO FIVE MINUTES. PLENTY OF TIME FOR HORIZON TO TURN EVERYTHING BACK ON.

WE JUST HAVE TO GET TO THE COMM STATION, CALL UP JUERGEN, AND--

SPIDER-MAN!

YOU... ARE NOT JUERGEN.

YOU'VE MEDDLED IN MY PLANS FOR THE LAST TIME!

DOC? OTTO?

YOU'RE NOT LOOKING SO GOOD, ARE YOU OKAY?

YES...AS YOU CAN SEE, SINCE LAST WE MET, MY CONDITION HAS...

...WORSENED

DOC...

SAVE YOUR PITY. SAVE IT FOR YOURSELF.

FOR WHILE I MAY ONLY HAVE WEEKS LEFT TO LIVE...

...YOU ONLY HAVE SECONDS.

CLICK!

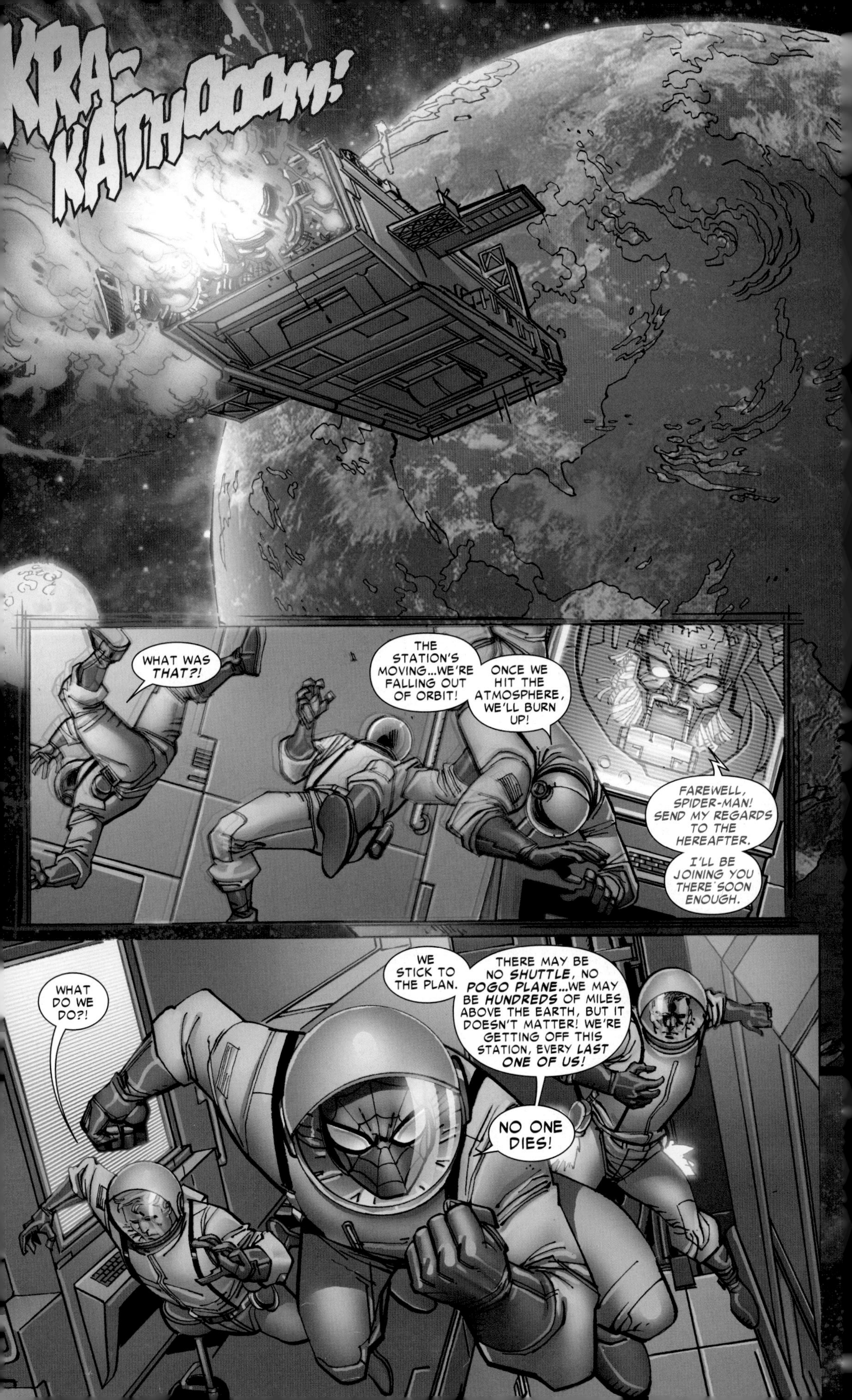
KRA-KATHOOOM!
WHAT WAS THAT?!
THE STATION'S MOVING...WE'RE FALLING OUT OF ORBIT!
ONCE WE HIT THE ATMOSPHERE, WE'LL BURN UP!
FAREWELL, SPIDER-MAN! SEND MY REGARDS TO THE HEREAFTER.
I'LL BE JOINING YOU THERE SOON ENOUGH.
WHAT DO WE DO?!
WE STICK TO THE PLAN.
THERE MAY BE NO SHUTTLE, NO POGO PLANE...WE MAY BE HUNDREDS OF MILES ABOVE THE EARTH, BUT IT DOESN'T MATTER! WE'RE GETTING OFF THIS STATION, EVERY LAST ONE OF US!
NO ONE DIES!

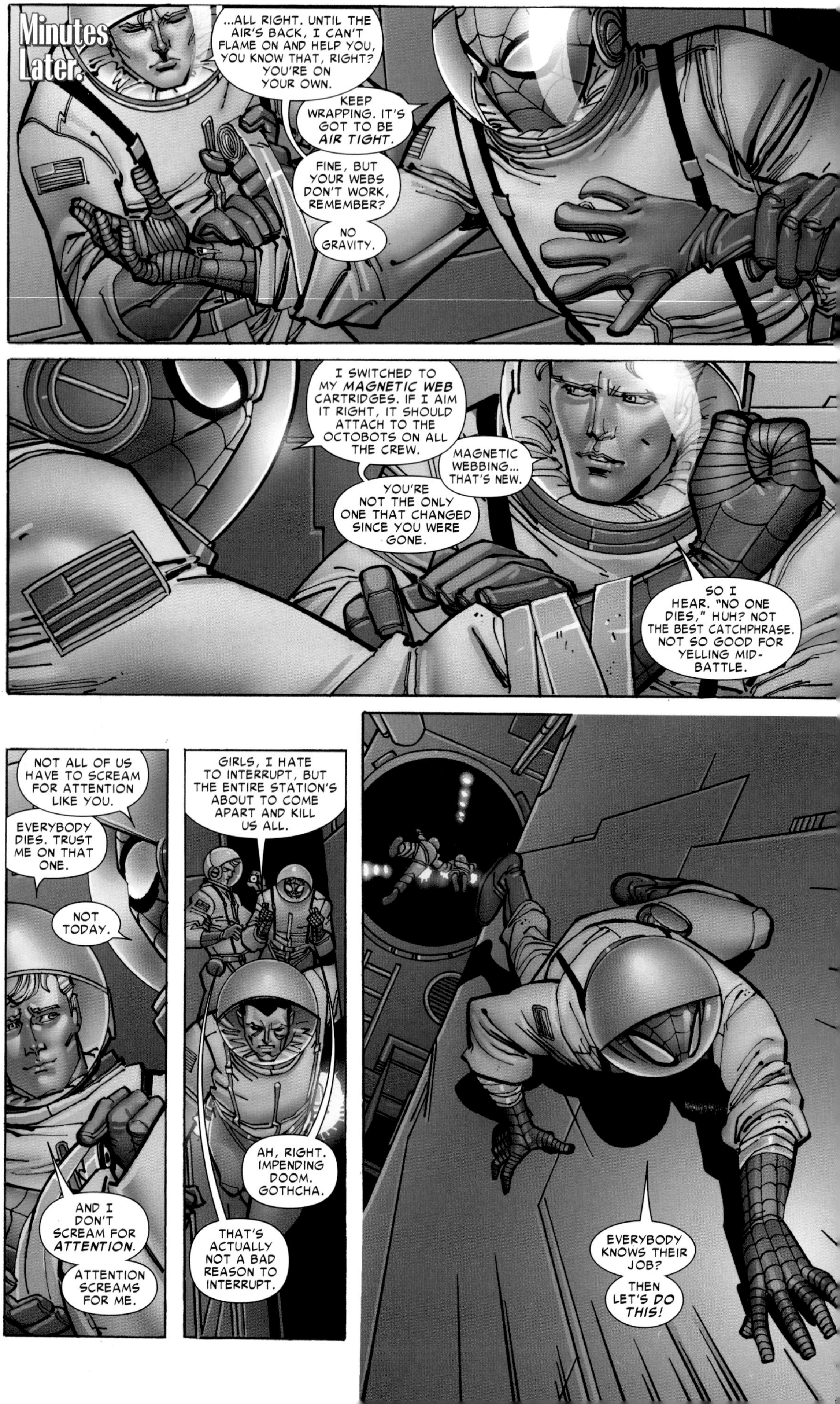
Minutes Later.
...ALL RIGHT. UNTIL THE AIR'S BACK, I CAN'T FLAME ON AND HELP YOU, YOU KNOW THAT, RIGHT? YOU'RE ON YOUR OWN.
KEEP WRAPPING. IT'S GOT TO BE AIR TIGHT.
FINE, BUT YOUR WEBS DON'T WORK, REMEMBER?
NO GRAVITY.
I SWITCHED TO MY MAGNETIC WEB CARTRIDGES. IF I AIM IT RIGHT, IT SHOULD ATTACH TO THE OCTOBOTS ON ALL THE CREW.
MAGNETIC WEBBING... THAT'S NEW.
YOU'RE NOT THE ONLY ONE THAT CHANGED SINCE YOU WERE GONE.
SO I HEAR. "NO ONE DIES," HUH? NOT THE BEST CATCHPHRASE. NOT SO GOOD FOR YELLING MID-BATTLE.
NOT ALL OF US HAVE TO SCREAM FOR ATTENTION LIKE YOU.
EVERYBODY DIES. TRUST ME ON THAT ONE.
NOT TODAY.
AND I DON'T SCREAM FOR ATTENTION.
ATTENTION SCREAMS FOR ME.
GIRLS, I HATE TO INTERRUPT, BUT THE ENTIRE STATION'S ABOUT TO COME APART AND KILL US ALL.
AH, RIGHT. IMPENDING DOOM. GOTCHA.
THAT'S ACTUALLY NOT A BAD REASON TO INTERRUPT.
EVERYBODY KNOWS THEIR JOB?
THEN LET'S DO THIS!

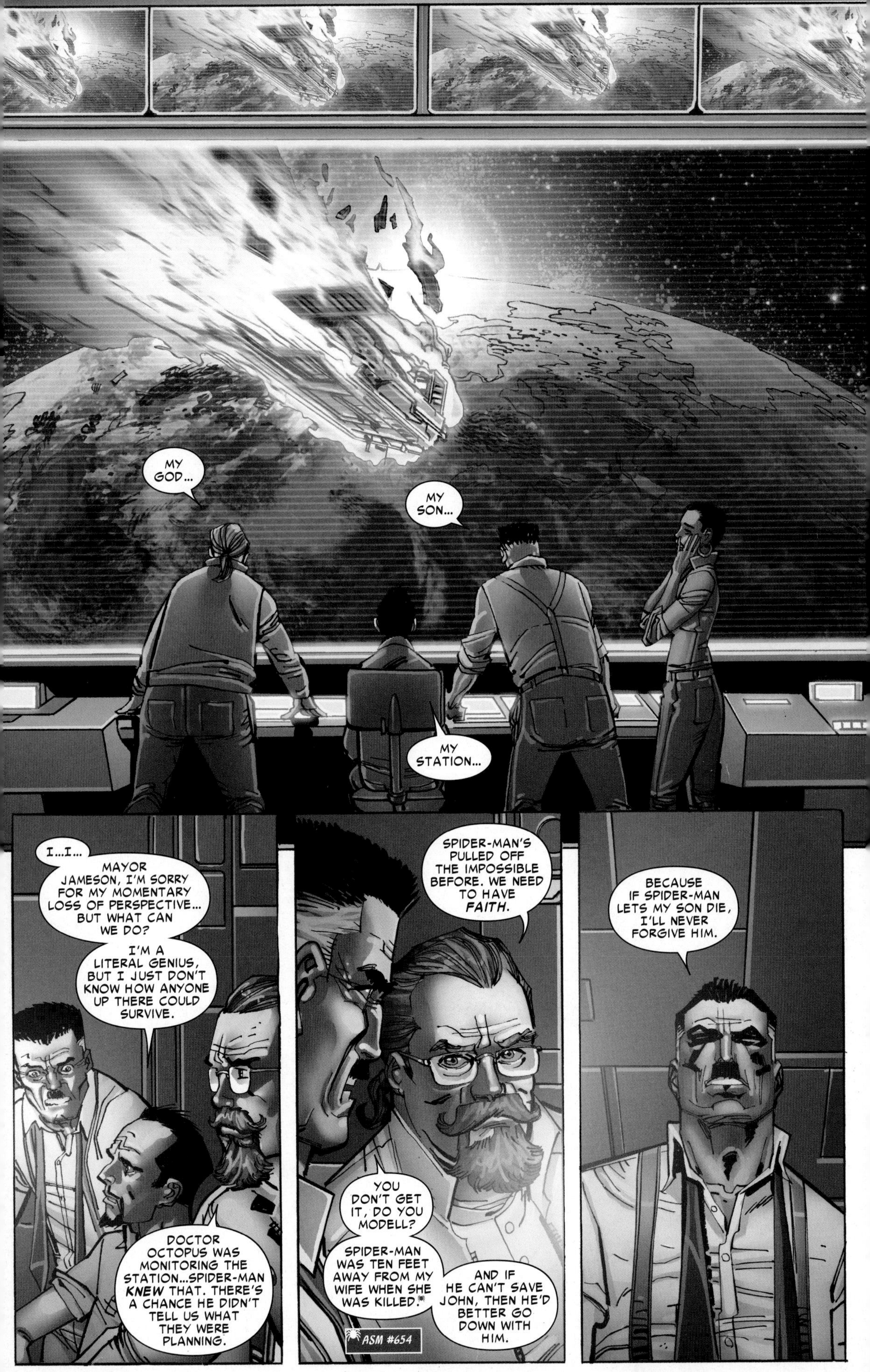
MY GOD...
MY SON...
MY STATION...
I...I...
MAYOR JAMESON, I'M SORRY FOR MY MOMENTARY LOSS OF PERSPECTIVE... BUT WHAT CAN WE DO?
I'M A LITERAL GENIUS, BUT I JUST DON'T KNOW HOW ANYONE UP THERE COULD SURVIVE.
DOCTOR OCTOPUS WAS MONITORING THE STATION...SPIDER-MAN KNEW THAT. THERE'S A CHANCE HE DIDN'T TELL US WHAT THEY WERE PLANNING.
SPIDER-MAN'S PULLED OFF THE IMPOSSIBLE BEFORE. WE NEED TO HAVE FAITH.
YOU DON'T GET IT, DO YOU MODELL?
SPIDER-MAN WAS TEN FEET AWAY FROM MY WIFE WHEN SHE WAS KILLED.*
ASM #654
AND IF HE CAN'T SAVE JOHN, THEN HE'D BETTER GO DOWN WITH HIM.
BECAUSE IF SPIDER-MAN LETS MY SON DIE, I'LL NEVER FORGIVE HIM.

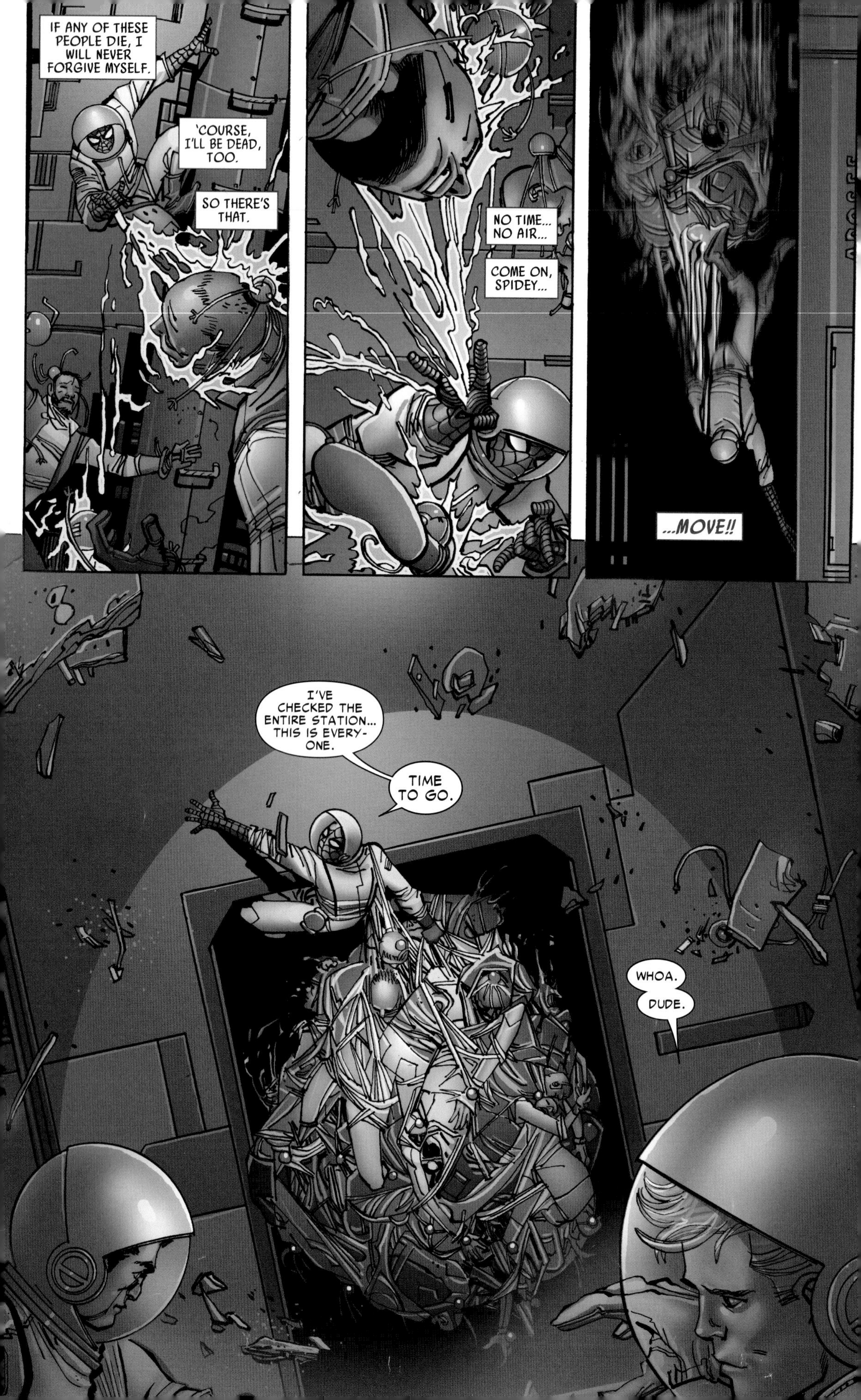
IF ANY OF THESE PEOPLE DIE, I WILL NEVER FORGIVE MYSELF.
'COURSE, I'LL BE DEAD, TOO.
SO THERE'S THAT.
NO TIME... NO AIR...
COME ON, SPIDEY...
...MOVE!!
I'VE CHECKED THE ENTIRE STATION... THIS IS EVERY-ONE.
TIME TO GO.
WHOA.
DUDE.

SHOULD WE PRY THE OCTOBOTS OFF THEM FIRST?

THEY'RE KIND OF CREEPY, AND YOU KNOW... THEY COULD *ZOMBIE-OUT* AGAIN.

THE MAGNETIC WEBBING SHOULD BLOCK ANY SIGNAL THAT DOC OCK COULD SEND. THEY SHOULD BE SAFE FOR NOW.

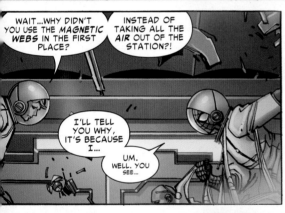

WAIT...WHY DIDN'T YOU USE THE *MAGNETIC WEBS* IN THE FIRST PLACE?

INSTEAD OF TAKING ALL THE *AIR* OUT OF THE STATION?!

I'LL TELL YOU WHY, IT'S BECAUSE I... UM. WELL, YOU SEE...

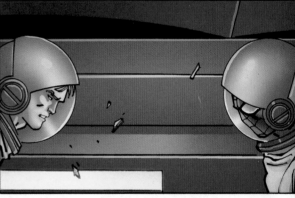

YOU ARE THE! BIGGEST! IDIOT! *EVER!*

MISTAKES WERE MADE, OKAY? AND I DON'T REMEMBER YOU COMING UP WITH ANY BRILLIANT PLANS!

MORON!

THAT'S RICH, *YOU* CALLING ME MORON! WHEN PEOPLE CALL YOU "*FLAME BRAIN*," YOU HAVE TO ASK WHAT THE SECOND PART MEANS!

YO! KNOCK IT OFF! THIS WHOLE STATION IS ABOUT TO BE DESTROYED, REMEMBER?!

OH, RIGHT. THAT.

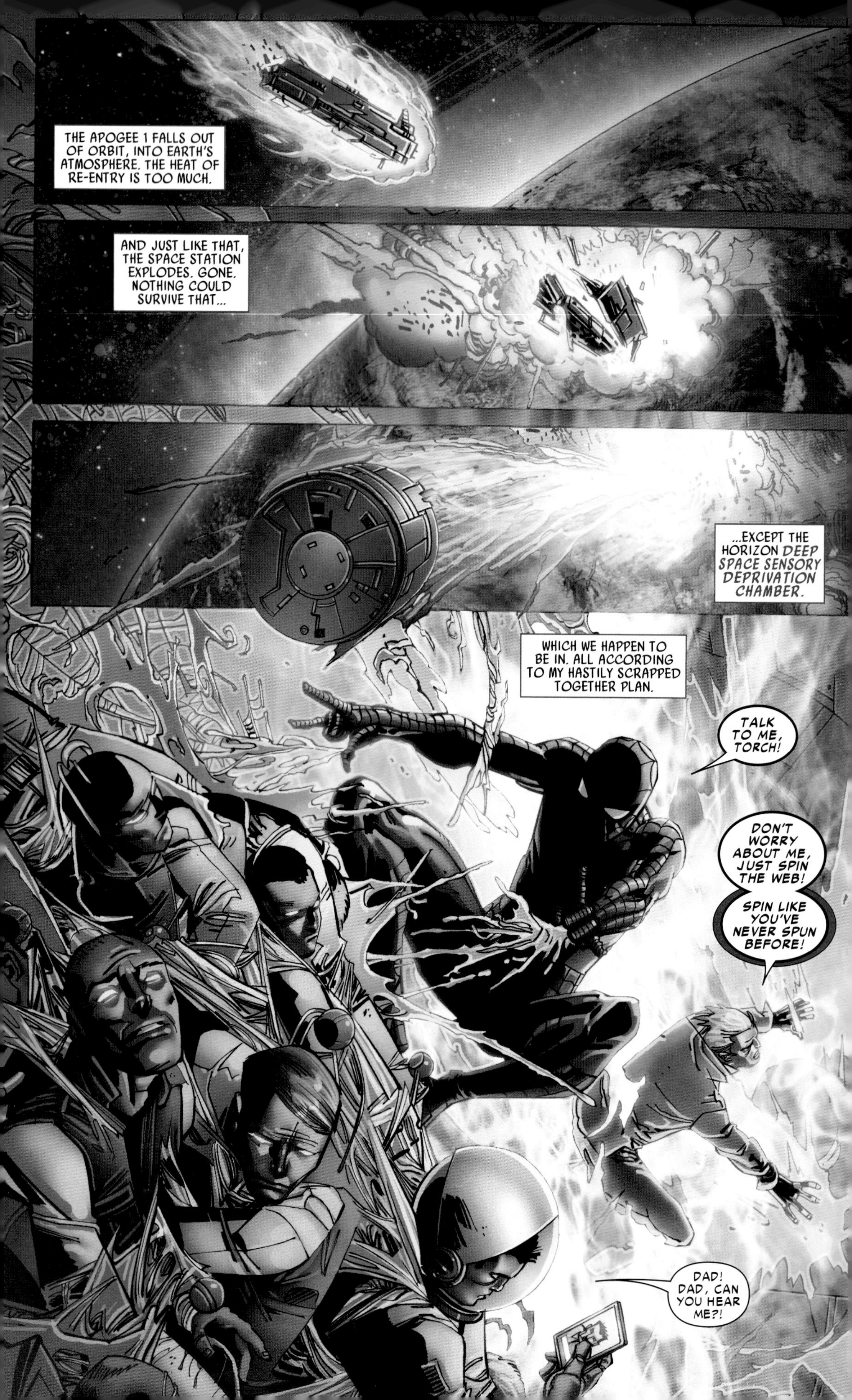
THE APOGEE 1 FALLS OUT OF ORBIT, INTO EARTH'S ATMOSPHERE. THE HEAT OF RE-ENTRY IS TOO MUCH.
AND JUST LIKE THAT, THE SPACE STATION EXPLODES. GONE. NOTHING COULD SURVIVE THAT...
...EXCEPT THE HORIZON DEEP SPACE SENSORY DEPRIVATION CHAMBER.
WHICH WE HAPPEN TO BE IN. ALL ACCORDING TO MY HASTILY SCRAPPED TOGETHER PLAN.
TALK TO ME, TORCH!
DON'T WORRY ABOUT ME, JUST SPIN THE WEB!
SPIN LIKE YOU'VE NEVER SPUN BEFORE!
DAD! DAD, CAN YOU HEAR ME?!

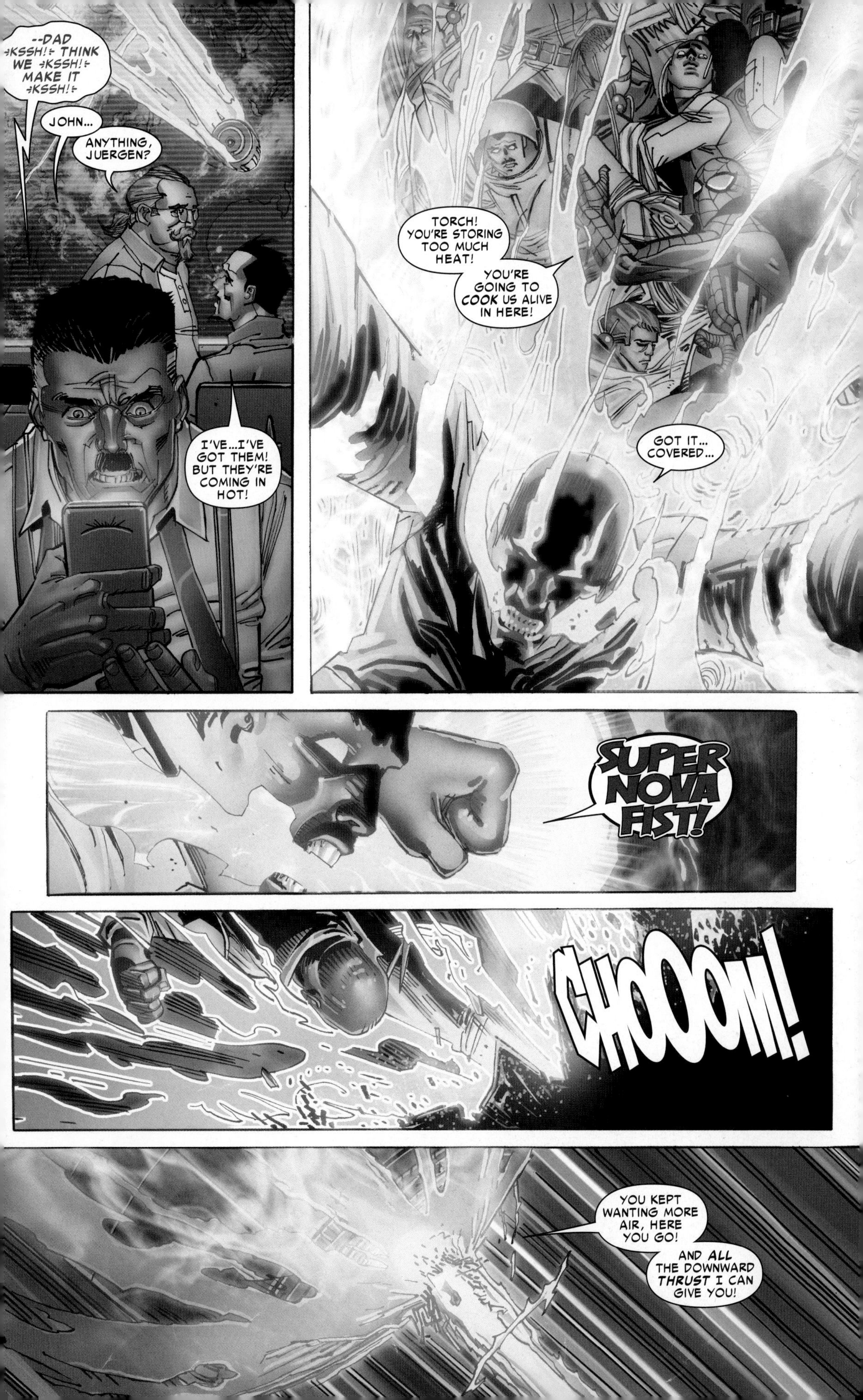
--DAD ⚡KSSH!⚡ THINK WE ⚡KSSH!⚡ MAKE IT ⚡KSSH!⚡
JOHN...
ANYTHING, JUERGEN?
I'VE...I'VE GOT THEM! BUT THEY'RE COMING IN HOT!
TORCH! YOU'RE STORING TOO MUCH HEAT!
YOU'RE GOING TO COOK US ALIVE IN HERE!
GOT IT... COVERED...
SUPER NOVA FIST!
CHOOOM!
YOU KEPT WANTING MORE AIR, HERE YOU GO!
AND ALL THE DOWNWARD THRUST I CAN GIVE YOU!

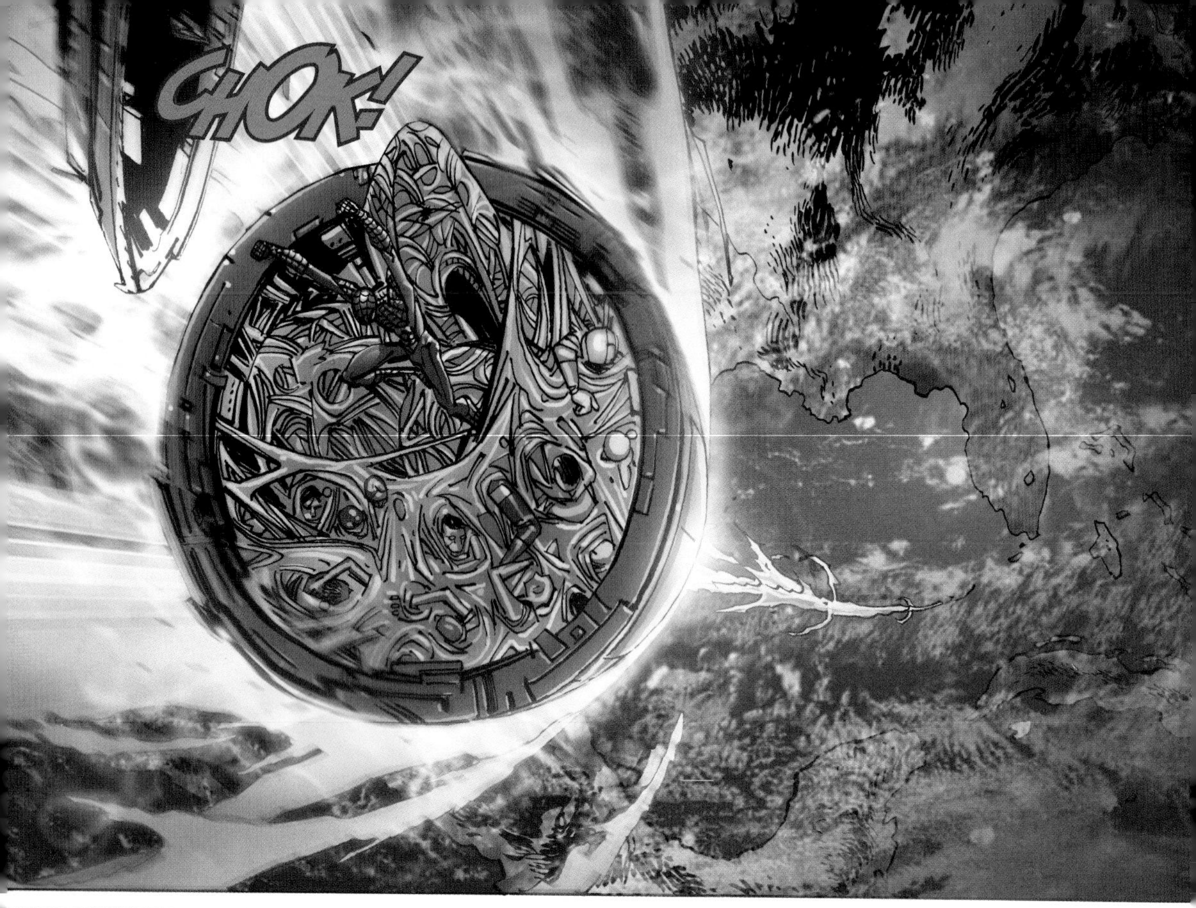
CHOK!
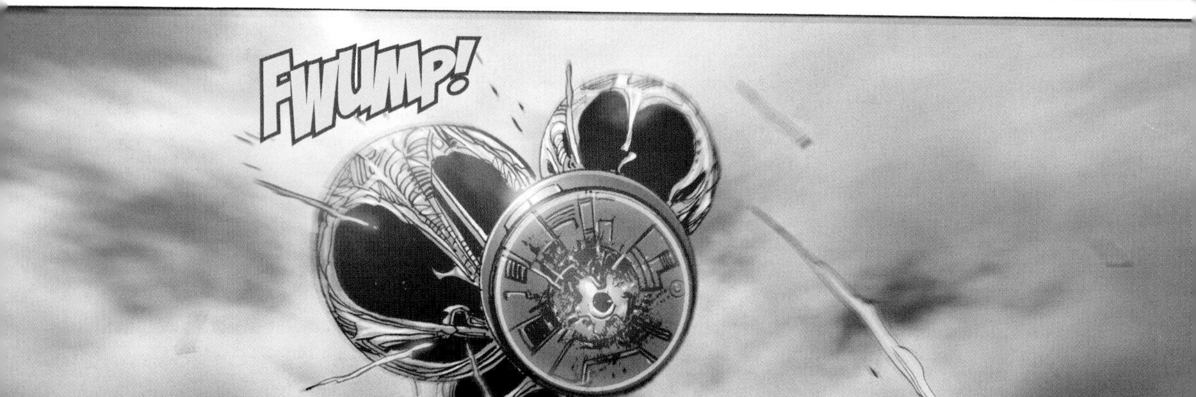
FWUMP!
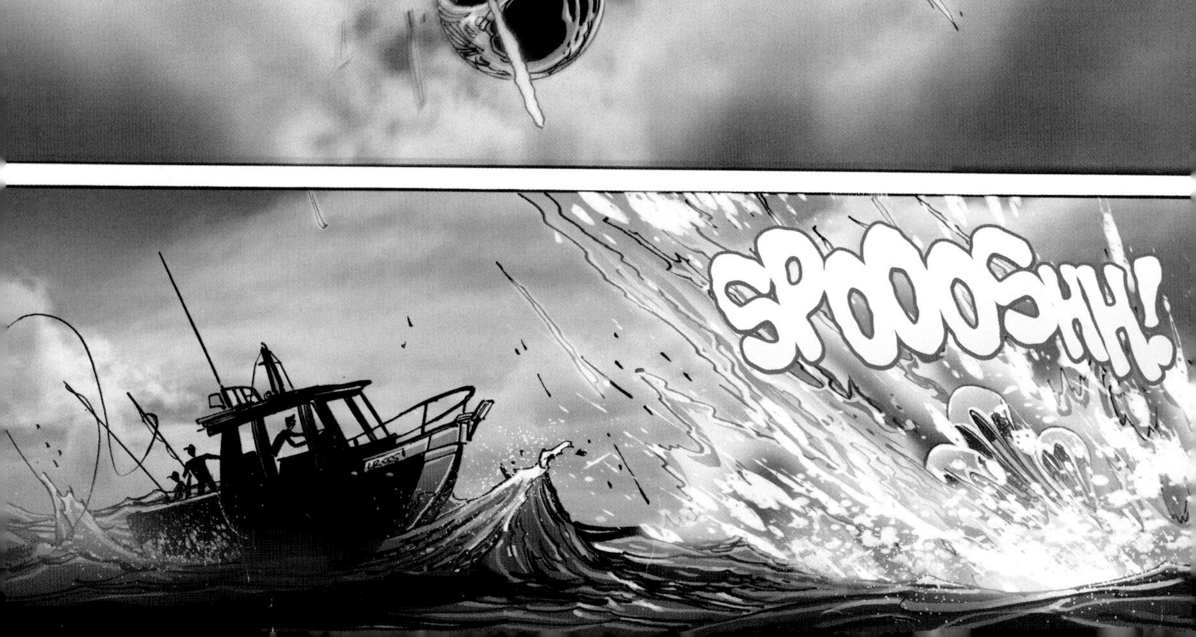
SPOOOSHH!

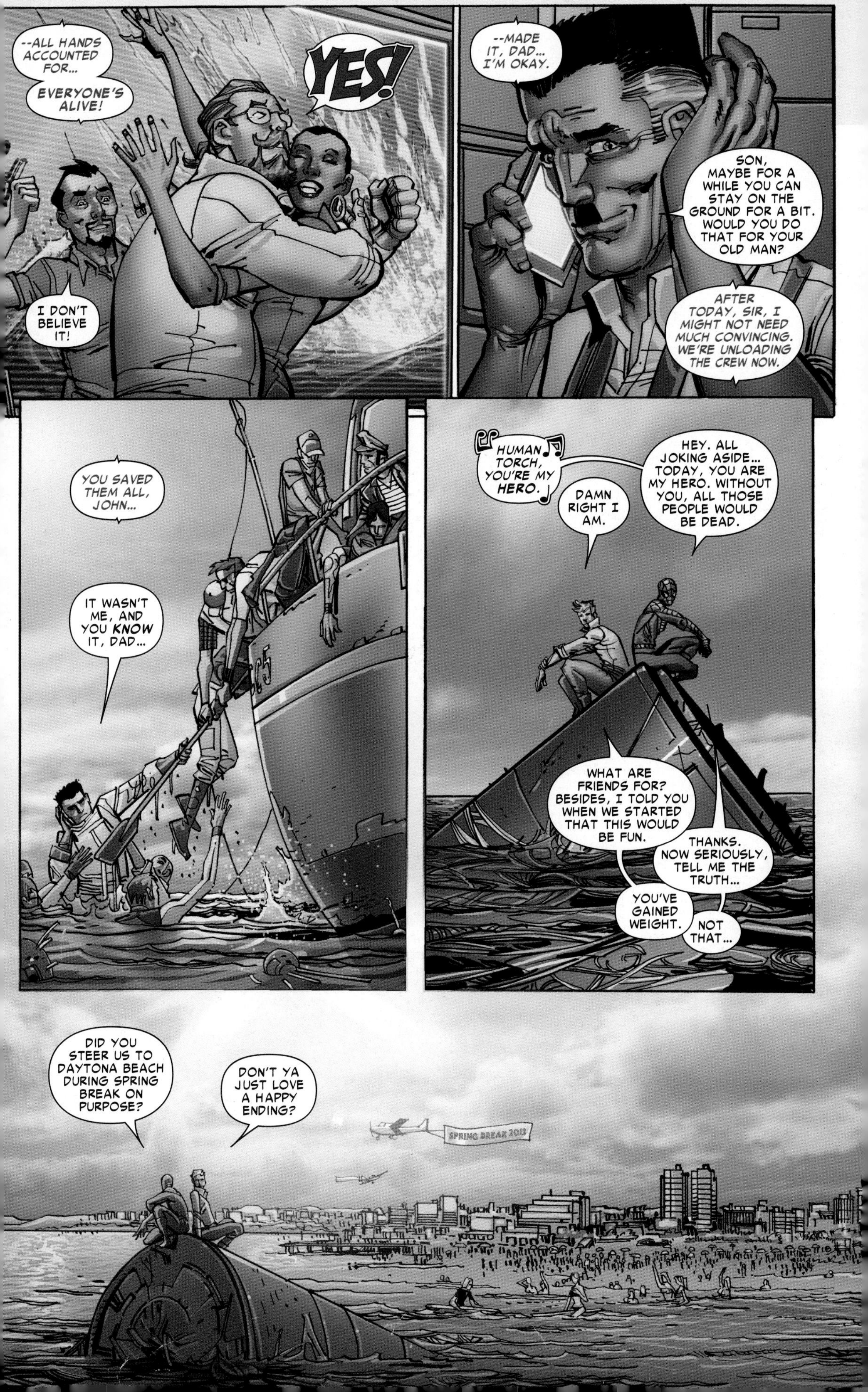
--ALL HANDS ACCOUNTED FOR...
EVERYONE'S ALIVE!
YES!
I DON'T BELIEVE IT!
--MADE IT, DAD... I'M OKAY.
SON, MAYBE FOR A WHILE YOU CAN STAY ON THE GROUND FOR A BIT. WOULD YOU DO THAT FOR YOUR OLD MAN?
AFTER TODAY, SIR, I MIGHT NOT NEED MUCH CONVINCING. WE'RE UNLOADING THE CREW NOW.
YOU SAVED THEM ALL, JOHN...
IT WASN'T ME, AND YOU KNOW IT, DAD...
HUMAN TORCH, YOU'RE MY HERO.
HEY. ALL JOKING ASIDE... TODAY, YOU ARE MY HERO. WITHOUT YOU, ALL THOSE PEOPLE WOULD BE DEAD.
DAMN RIGHT I AM.
WHAT ARE FRIENDS FOR? BESIDES, I TOLD YOU WHEN WE STARTED THAT THIS WOULD BE FUN.
THANKS. NOW SERIOUSLY, TELL ME THE TRUTH...
YOU'VE GAINED WEIGHT.
NOT THAT...
DID YOU STEER US TO DAYTONA BEACH DURING SPRING BREAK ON PURPOSE?
DON'T YA JUST LOVE A HAPPY ENDING?
SPRING BREAK 2012

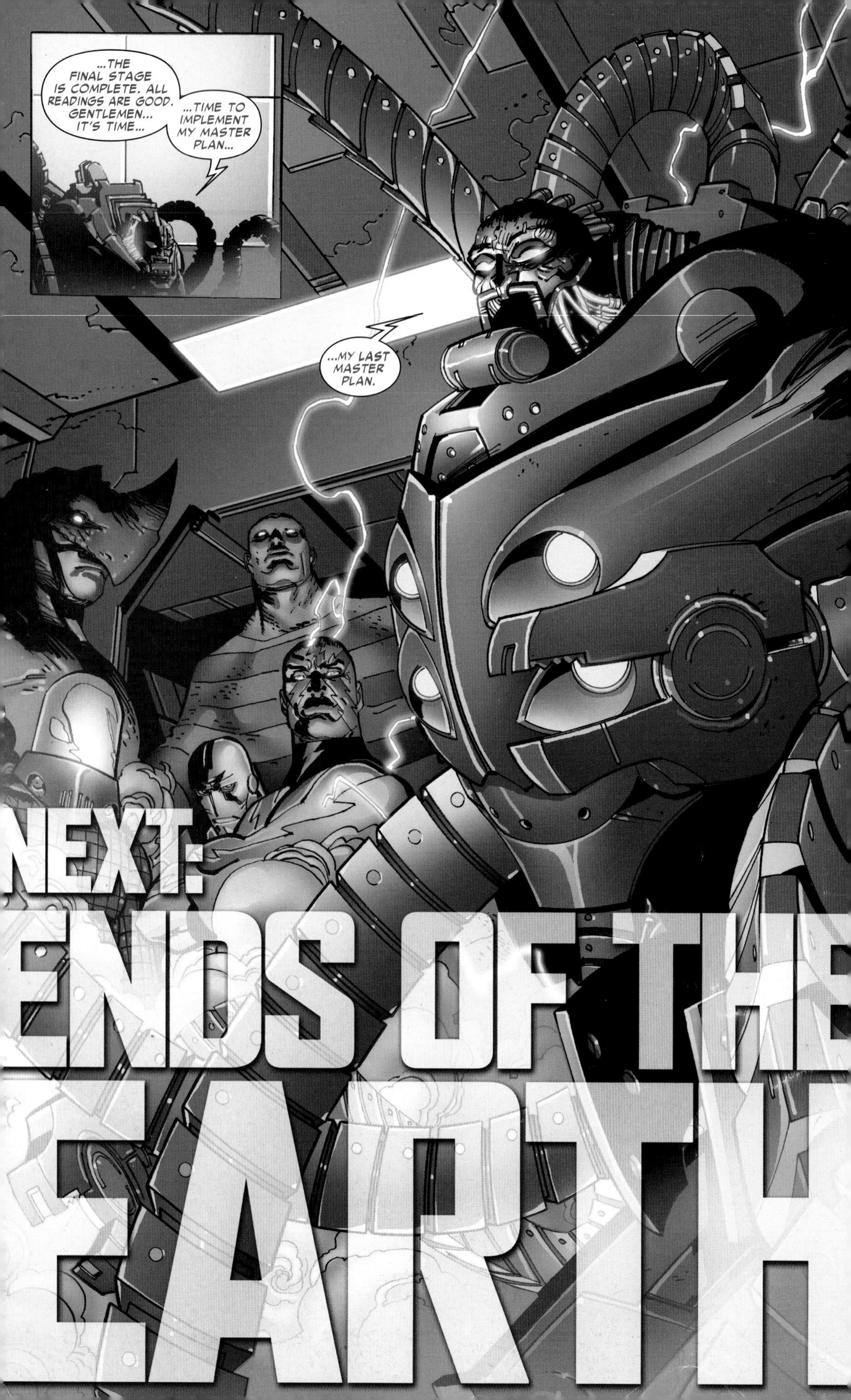
...THE FINAL STAGE IS COMPLETE. ALL READINGS ARE GOOD. GENTLEMEN... IT'S TIME...
...TIME TO IMPLEMENT MY MASTER PLAN...
...MY LAST MASTER PLAN.
NEXT:
ENDS OF THE EARTH

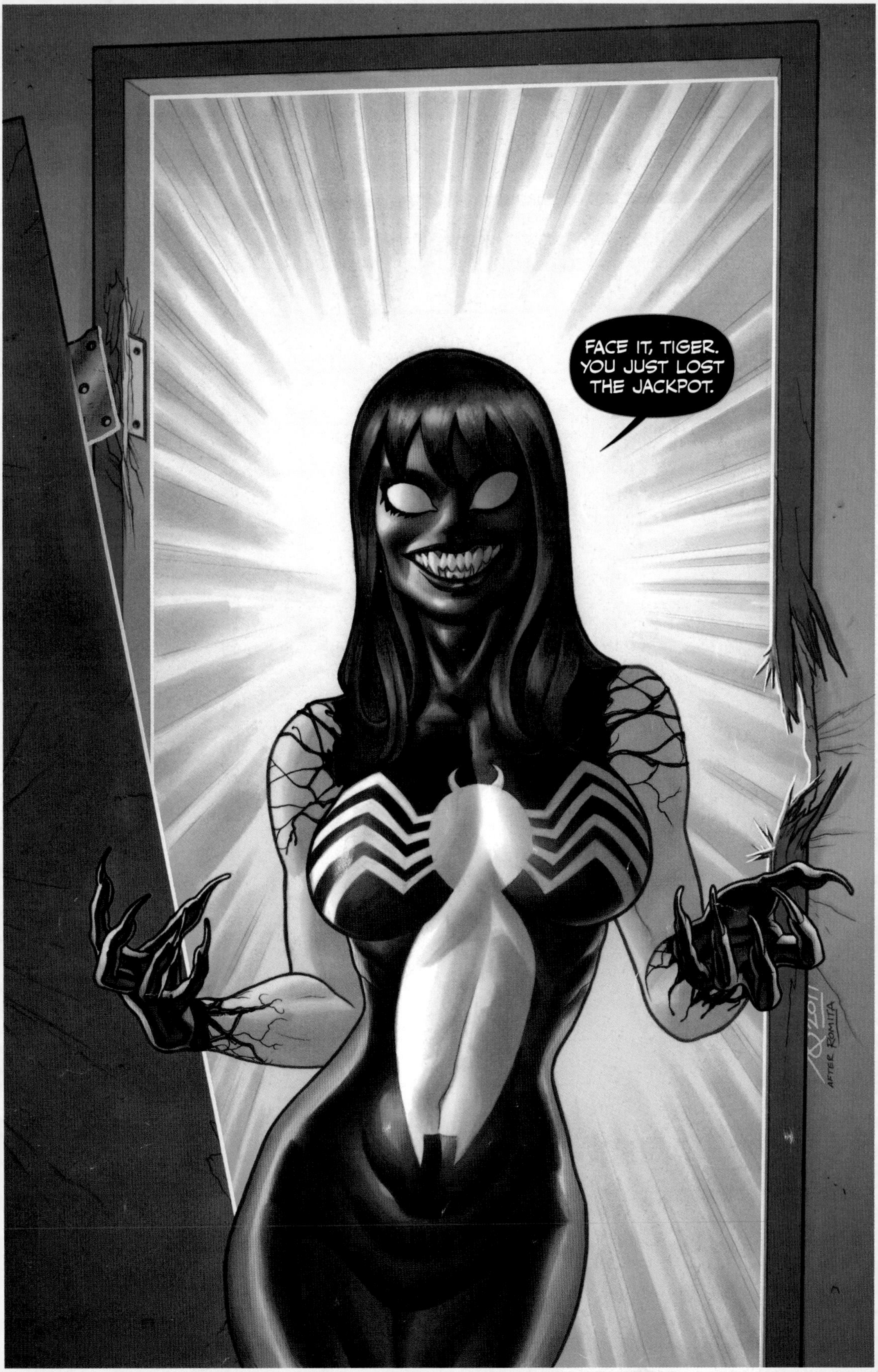
FACE IT, TIGER. YOU JUST LOST THE JACKPOT.
AFTER ROMITA

Read Spider-Man's Big Time Adventures In These Hardcovers

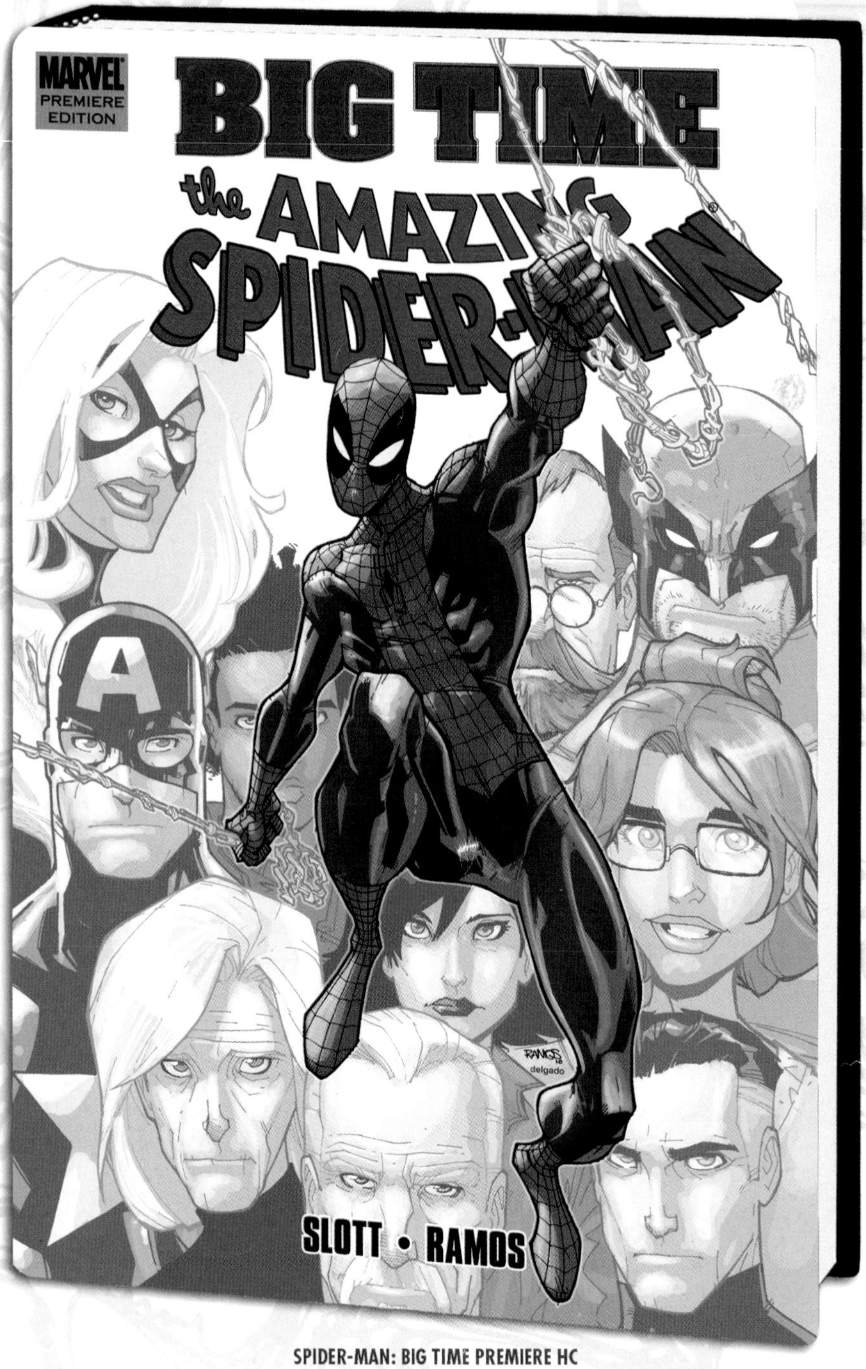
MARVEL PREMIERE EDITION
BIG TIME
the AMAZING SPIDER-MAN
SLOTT • RAMOS

SPIDER-MAN: BIG TIME PREMIERE HC
978-0-7851-4623-0

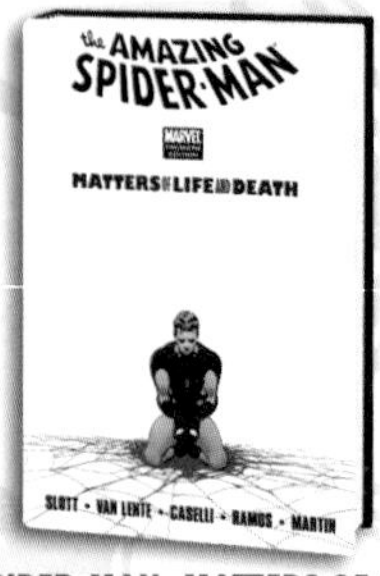
the AMAZING SPIDER-MAN
MATTERS OF LIFE AND DEATH
SLOTT • VAN LENTE • CASELLI • RAMOS • MARTIN

SPIDER-MAN: MATTERS OF LIFE AND DEATH PREMIERE HC
978-0-7851-5102-9

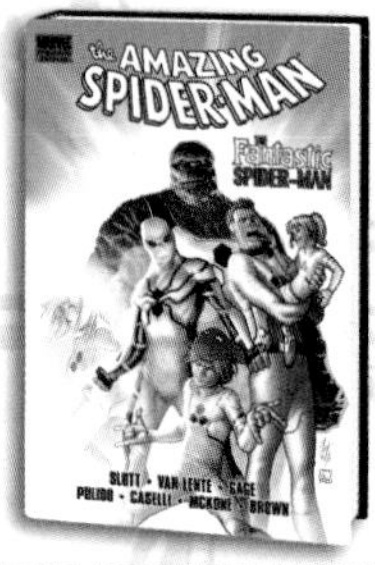
the AMAZING SPIDER-MAN
the Fantastic SPIDER-MAN

SPIDER-MAN: THE FANTASTIC SPIDER-MAN PREMIERE HC
978-0-7851-5106-7

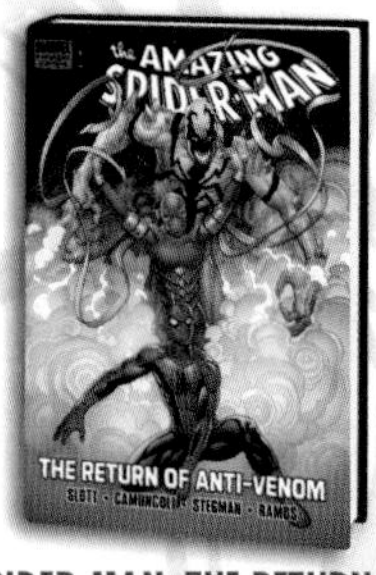
the AMAZING SPIDER-MAN
THE RETURN OF ANTI-VENOM

SPIDER-MAN: THE RETURN OF ANTI-VENOM PREMIERE HC
978-0-7851-5108-1

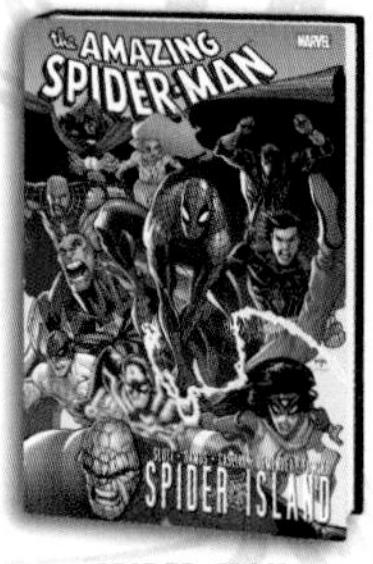
the AMAZING SPIDER-MAN
SPIDER ISLAND

SPIDER-MAN: SPIDER-ISLAND HC
978-0-7851-5104-3

On Sale Now

MARVEL
www.marvel.com